Moments
with
God

Daily Encouragement from
Our Daily Bread.

Discovery House is affiliated with Our Daily Bread Ministries, Grand Rapids, Michigan.

Requests for permission to quote from this book should be directed to: Permissions Department, Discovery House, PO Box 3566, Grand Rapids, MI 49501, or contact us by email at permissionsdept@dhp.org.

All Scripture quotations, unless otherwise indicated, are taken from the Holy Bible, New International Version®, NIV®. Copyright © 1973, 1978, 1984, 2011 by Biblica, Inc.™ Used by permission of Zondervan. All rights reserved worldwide. www.zondervan.com. The "NIV" and "New International Version" are trademarks registered in the United States Patent and Trademark office by Biblica, Inc.™

ISBN: 978-1-62707-910-5

Printed in the United States of America

First printing in 2018

Introduction

You've picked up a copy of *Moments with God*, a collection of devotions from the pages of *Our Daily Bread*. This book is designed to assist you in your time with God. Here are some suggestions for getting the most out of your devotional reading.

Set aside a regular time and place. Your time will be more meaningful if you can concentrate and establish a regular practice.

Read the Bible passage. Those words from God's Word are the most important statements you will read each day. As you read God's Word, seek to learn more about God, your relationship with Him, and how He wants you to live each day.

Note the key verse. It is printed to the right of each article. You may want to memorize this key Bible verse.

Read the article thoughtfully. Reflect on what the writer is saying.

Reflect on the questions or personalize the words

of the prayer. The prayer may be used as a prayer-starter that expresses how you feel.

Use the closing "thought" to help you remember the key idea. The last statement in bold type on each page is what we call the "thought of the day."

Write down your discoveries. For example: What is God saying to you through His Word?

Take time to pray. Talk to the Lord about what you've discovered in His Word and your response to Him.

Share the lessons with others. When you talk with others, share what the Lord is teaching you from His Word.

It is our prayer that in these devotional articles you will find encouragement, hope, and comfort as you draw closer to God and grow in your love for Him.

THE OUR DAILY BREAD STAFF

This Could Be the Year

My dad was a pastor, and on the first Sunday of each new year he preached about the return of Christ, often quoting from 1 Thessalonians 4. His point was always the same: "This could be the year that Jesus will return. Are you ready to meet Him?" I'll never forget hearing that sermon at age 6, thinking, *If that's true, I'm not sure I will be among those He's coming for.*

I felt certain that my parents would be going to heaven, and I wanted to go too. So, when my dad came home after church, I asked how I could be sure. He opened the Bible, read some verses to me, and talked to me about my need for a Savior. It didn't take much to convince me of my sins. That day, my dad led me to Christ. I will be forever grateful to him for planting these truths in my heart.

> **TODAY'S READING**
> **1 Thess. 4:13–18**
>
> **We who are still alive and are left will . . . meet the Lord in the air. And so we will be with the Lord forever.**
>
> 1 Thessalonians 4:17

In an increasingly chaotic world, what a hopeful thought that this could be the year Jesus returns. More comforting still is the anticipation that all who trust Him for salvation will be gathered together, relieved from this world's suffering, sorrow, and fear. Best of all, we'll be with the Lord forever! ✿

JOE STOWELL

Lord, keep me always mindful of Your inevitable return.
Thanks for the assurance that this world is not all we have
but that a blessed eternity awaits all who trust in You.

Perhaps today! DR. M. R. DEHAAN

He Will Reply

was elated when I came upon the Twitter page of my favorite Korean movie star, so I decided to drop her a note. I crafted the best message I could and waited for a reply. I knew it was unlikely I would receive a response. A celebrity like her would receive an enormous amount of fan mail every day. Still, I hoped she would reply. But I was disappointed.

Thankfully, we know God responds to us. He is the "Most High," the "Almighty" (PS. 91:1). His position is exalted and His power is limitless, yet He is accessible to us. God invites: "Call upon Me, and I will answer" (V. 15 NKJV).

> **TODAY'S READING**
> **Psalm 91**
>
> **He will call on me, and I will answer him.** Psalm 91:15

An ancient legend tells of a monarch who hired weavers to make tapestries and garments for him. The king gave the silk and the patterns to the weavers with the strict instructions to seek his aid immediately if they had any difficulties. One young weaver was happy and successful while the others were always experiencing trouble. When the boy was asked why he was so successful, he said, "Didn't you notice how often I called for the king?" They replied, "Yes, but he's very busy, and we thought you were wrong in disturbing him so frequently." The boy answered, "I just took him at his word, and he was always happy to help me!"

Our God is like that king—only so much greater. He is loving and kind enough to care about our smallest concern and faintest whisper. ✿

POH FANG CHIA

Lord, it's amazing to me that You—the God who created the universe—
care about me and want me to come to You in prayer.
Thank You for loving me so much.

We always have God's attention.

All His Benefits

A recurring difficulty on our journey of life is becoming so focused on what we need at the moment that we forget what we already have. I was reminded of that when our church choir sang a beautiful anthem based on Psalm 103. "Bless the LORD, O my soul, and forget not all His benefits" (V. 2 NKJV). The Lord is our forgiver, healer, redeemer, provider, satisfier, and renewer (VV. 4–5). How could we forget that? And yet we often do when the events of daily life shift our attention to pressing needs, recurring failures, and circumstances that seem out of control.

TODAY'S READING
Psalm 103

Praise the LORD, my soul, and forget not all his benefits. Psalm 103:2

The writer of this psalm calls us to remember, "The LORD is compassionate and gracious . . . . He does not treat us as our sins deserve or repay us according to our iniquities. For as high as the heavens are above the earth, so great is his love for those who fear him" (VV. 8, 10–11).

In our walk of faith, we come to Jesus Christ humbled by our unworthiness. There is no sense of entitlement as we receive His grace and are overwhelmed by the lavishness of His love. They remind us of all His benefits.

"Praise the LORD, my soul; all my inmost being, praise his holy name" (V. 1). 🌏

DAVID MCCASLAND

Heavenly Father, we pause to consider all we have in You.
Grant us eyes to see Your provision and help us to remember
every benefit You have given to us.

Love was when God became a man.

Is He Listening?

"**S**ometimes it feels** as if God isn't listening to me." Those words, from a woman who tried to stay strong in her walk with God while coping with an alcoholic husband, echo the heartcry of many believers. For many years, she asked God to change her husband. Yet it never happened.

What are we to think when we repeatedly ask God for something good—something that could easily glorify Him—but the answer doesn't come? Is He listening or not?

TODAY'S READING
Matt. 26:39–42; 27:45–46

My God, my God, why have you forsaken me? Matthew 27:46

Let's look at the life of the Savior. In the garden of Gethsemane, He agonized for hours in prayer, pouring out His heart and pleading, "Let this cup pass from Me" (MATT. 26:39 NKJV). But the Father's answer was clearly "No." To provide salvation, God had to send Jesus to die on the cross. Even though Jesus felt as if His Father had forsaken Him, He prayed intensely and passionately because He trusted that God was listening.

When we pray, we may not see how God is working or understand how He will bring good through it all. So we have to trust Him. We relinquish our rights and let God do what is best.

We must leave the unknowable to the all-knowing One. He is listening and working things out His way. 🕮   *DAVE BRANON*

Lord, we don't need to know the reason our prayers sometimes
go unanswered. Help us just to wait for Your time,
because You are good.

When we bend our knees to pray, God bends His ear to listen.

The Lonely Season

Amid the pile of post-Christmas mail I discovered a treasure—a handmade Christmas card painted on repurposed cardstock. Simple watercolor strokes evoked a scene of wintry hills livened with evergreens. Centered at the bottom, framed by red-berried holly, was this hand-printed message:

Peace be with you!

The artist was a prisoner and a friend of mine. As I admired his handiwork, I realized I hadn't written to him in 2 years!

Long ago, another prisoner was neglected as he waited in prison. "Only Luke is with me," wrote the apostle Paul to Timothy (2 TIM. 4:11). "No one came to my support, but everyone deserted me" (V. 16). Yet Paul found encouragement even in prison, and he wrote, "The Lord stood at my side and gave me strength" (V. 17). But surely Paul felt the lonely ache of abandonment.

> **TODAY'S READING**
> **2 Timothy 4:9–18**
>
> **I have not stopped giving thanks for you, remembering you in my prayers.**
> Ephesians 1:16

On the back of that wonderful Christmas card my friend wrote, "May the peace and joy and hope and love brought about through the birth of Jesus be with you and yours." He signed it, "Your brother in Christ." I put the card on my wall as a reminder to pray for him. Then I wrote to him.

Throughout this coming year let's reach out to the loneliest of our brothers and sisters. 🌱

TIM GUSTAFSON

What lonely people can I think of right now? Newcomers to town?
Prisoners? People in the hospital or in senior living centers?
What can I do, no matter how small, to reach out to them?

Reach out in friendship and encourage the lonely.

Ringing Reminders

Τ he clock tower at Westminster, which contains the bell known as Big Ben, is an iconic landmark in London, England. It is traditionally thought that the melody of the tower chimes was taken from the tune of "I Know That My Redeemer Liveth" from Handel's *Messiah*. Words were eventually added and put on display in the clock room:

TODAY'S READING
Psalm 37:21–31

Lord, through this hour be Thou our guide;
So by Thy power no foot shall slide.

These words allude to Psalm 37: "The LORD directs the steps of the godly. He delights in every detail of their lives. Though they stumble, they will never fall, for the LORD holds them by the hand" (VV. 23–24 NLT).

> **Though he may stumble, he will not fall, for the LORD upholds him with his hand.** Psalm 37:24

Notice how intimately involved God is in His children's experience: "He delights in every detail of their lives" (V. 23 NLT). Verse 31 adds, "The law of their God is in their hearts; their feet do not slip."

How extraordinary! The Creator of the universe not only upholds us and helps us but He also cares deeply about every moment we live. No wonder the apostle Peter was able to confidently invite us to "cast all your anxiety on him because he cares for you" (1 PETER 5:7). As the assurance of His care rings in our hearts, we find courage to face whatever comes our way. ✤

BILL CROWDER

Loving Father, thank You that every part of my life matters to You. Encourage me in my struggles so that I might walk in a way that reflects Your great love and honors Your great name.

No one is more secure than the one who is held in God's hand.

Walk Away from Worry

A few years ago, our Bible-study leader challenged us to memorize a chapter of the Bible and recite it to the group. Internally, I began to protest and groan. An entire chapter, in front of everyone? Memorization had never been my thing; I cringed as I imagined long silences while everyone watched me, waiting for the next words.

A few days later, I reluctantly leafed through my Bible, looking for a set of verses to learn by heart. Nothing seemed right until I landed in Philippians 4.

I read this verse in silence: "Be anxious for nothing, but in everything by prayer and supplication, with thanksgiving, let your requests be made known to God" (V. 6). That's when I knew which chapter to memorize, and how to walk away from my anxiety about the assignment.

> **TODAY'S READING**
> **Philippians 4:1–9**
>
> **Be anxious for nothing.** Philippians 4:6

God does not want us to agonize over future events, because worry paralyzes our prayer life. The apostle Paul reminds us that instead of fretting, we should ask God for help. When we continually take this approach to anxiety, God's peace will guard our hearts and minds (V. 7).

Someone once said tongue-in-cheek, "Why pray when you can worry?" The point is clear: Worry gets us nowhere, but prayer gets us in touch with the One who can handle all of our concerns. 🌿

JENNIFER BENSON SCHULDT

When you feel the tension mounting,
And across the busy day,
Only gloomy clouds are drifting
As you start to worry—pray!
ANON.

It's impossible to wring our hands when they are folded before God in prayer.

The Best Kind of Happiness

"**E**verybody's doing it**"** seemed like a winning argument when I was young. My parents never gave in to such pleas no matter how desperate I was to get permission to do something they believed was unsafe or unwise.

As we get older we add excuses and rationalizations to our repertoire of arguments for having our own way: "No one will get hurt." "It's not illegal." "He did it to me first." "She won't find out." Behind each argument is the belief that what we want is more important than anything else.

Eventually, this faulty way of thinking becomes the basis for our beliefs about God. One of the lies we sometimes choose to believe is that we, not God, are the center of the universe. We think we will be carefree and happy only when we reorder the world according to our desires. This lie is convincing because it promises an easier, speedier way to get what we want. It argues, "God is love, so He wants me to do whatever will make me happy." But this way of thinking leads to heartache, not happiness.

Jesus told those who believed in Him that the truth would make them truly free (JOHN 8:31–32). But He also warned, "Everyone who sins is a slave to sin" (V. 34). The best kind of happiness comes from the freedom we find when we accept the truth that Jesus is the way to a full and satisfying life. 🔷 *JULIE ACKERMAN LINK*

> **TODAY'S READING**
> **John 8:31–38**
>
> **If you hold to my teaching, you are really my disciples. Then you will know the truth, and the truth will set you free.** John 8:31–32

Lord, we confess our tendency to rationalize everything to get what we think we want. Guide us today so that we choose to obey Your commands instead of pursuing our own desires.

There are no shortcuts to true happiness.

Wells of Salvation

When people drill holes deep into the earth, it is normally for pulling up core samples of rock, accessing oil, or finding water.

In Isaiah 12, we learn that God wanted His people, who were living in a spiritual desert as well as a geographical desert, to discover His "wells of salvation." The prophet Isaiah compared God's salvation to a well from which the most refreshing of all waters can be drawn. After many years of turning their back on God, the nation of Judah was destined for exile as God allowed foreign invaders to conquer the nation, scattering the people. Yet, said the prophet Isaiah, a remnant would eventually return to their homeland as a sign that God was with them (ISA. 11:11–12).

> TODAY'S READING
> **Isaiah 12**
>
> **With joy you will draw water from the wells of salvation.** Isaiah 12:3

Isaiah 12 is a hymn, praising God for His faithfulness in keeping His promises, especially the promise of salvation. Isaiah encouraged the people that deep in God's "wells of salvation" they would experience the cool water of God's grace, strength, and joy (VV. 1–3). This would refresh and strengthen their hearts and cause praise and gratitude to God (VV. 4–6).

God wants each of us to discover through confession and repentance the deep, cool waters of joy found in the everlasting well of His salvation. 🌿

MARVIN WILLIAMS

What will you do to draw deeply from God's well to find His joy, refreshment, and strength?

The wells of God's salvation never run dry.

True Shelter

I n March 2014 a tribal conflict broke out in my hometown area, forcing my father's household, along with other refugees, to take cover in the region's capital city. Throughout history, people who have felt unsafe in their homelands have traveled to other places searching for safety and something better.

As I visited and talked with people from my hometown, I thought of the cities of refuge in Joshua 20:1–9. These were cities designated as places of safety for those fleeing from "relatives seeking revenge" in the case of an accidental killing (V. 3 NLT). They offered peace and protection.

> TODAY'S READING
> **Joshua 20:1–9**
>
> **The name of the LORD is a fortified tower; the righteous run to it and are safe.**
>
> Proverbs 18:10

People today still seek places of refuge, although for a variety of reasons. But as needed as these sanctuaries are, supplying shelter and food, they cannot completely meet the needs of refugees and fugitives. That rest is found only in God. Those who walk with God find true shelter and the safest protection in Him. When ancient Israel was sent into exile, the Lord said, "I have been a sanctuary [safe haven] for them in the countries where they have gone" (EZEK. 11:16).

With the psalmist, we can say confidently to the Lord, "You are my hiding place; you will protect me from trouble and surround me with songs of deliverance" (32:7). 🌼   *LAWRENCE DARMANI*

Father, thank You for being a rock to which we can flee and that
no matter where we are or in what circumstances we find ourselves,
You are there with us. Help us to remember that even in the
darkest of nights, You are our strong tower.

Nothing can shake those who are secure in God's hands.

You Have Value

After my mother-in-law died, my wife and I discovered a cache of US Indian Head pennies in a dresser drawer in her apartment. She wasn't a coin collector, as such, but she lived in the era when these pennies were in circulation and she had accumulated a few.

Some of these coins are in excellent condition; others are not. They are so worn and tarnished you can hardly see the imprint. All bear the stamp "One Cent" on the opposite side. Although a penny these days has little value and many consider them useless, this one-cent coin would have bought a newspaper in its day. And collectors still find value in them, even those that have been battered and abused.

> TODAY'S READING
> **Romans 5:6–11**
>
> **You were bought at a price.**
>
> 1 Corinthians 6:20

Perhaps you feel tarnished, worn, old, or out of circulation. Even so, God finds value in you. The Creator of the universe wants you—not for your mind, your body, your clothes, your achievements, your intellect, or your personality, but because you are you! He would go any distance and pay any price to possess you (1 COR. 6:20).

In fact He did. He came down to earth from heaven and purchased you with His own blood (ROM. 5:6, 8–9). That's how much He wants you. You are valuable in His eyes, and He loves you. 🌿

DAVID ROPER

As I think about Your love for me, Father, I wonder with amazement how You could love someone like me—and I praise You.

Christ's death is the measure of God's love for you.

Hold On!

A cowboy friend of mine who grew up on a ranch in Texas has a number of colorful sayings. One of my favorites is "It don't take much water to make good coffee." And when someone ropes a steer too big to handle or is in some kind of trouble, my friend will shout, "Hold everything you've got!" meaning "Help is on the way! Don't let go!"

TODAY'S READING
Revelation 3:7–13

I am coming soon. Hold on to what you have. Revelation 3:11

In the book of Revelation we find letters to "the seven churches in the province of Asia" (CHS. 2-3). These messages from God are filled with encouragement, rebuke, and challenge, and they speak to us today just as they did to the first-century recipients.

Twice in these letters we find the phrase, "Hold on to what you have." The Lord told the church at Thyatira, "Hold on to what you have until I come" (2:25). And to the church in Philadelphia He said, "I am coming soon. Hold on to what you have, so that no one will take your crown" (3:11). In the midst of great trials and opposition, these believers clung to God's promises and persevered in faith.

When our circumstances are harsh and sorrows outnumber joys, Jesus shouts to us, "Hold everything you've got! Help is on the way!" And with that promise, we can hold on in faith and rejoice. 🌿

DAVID MCCASLAND

Lord, we cling to Your promise, expect Your return, and hold on
with confidence as we say, "Even so, come, Lord Jesus!"

The promise of Christ's return calls us to persevere in faith.

Gates of Paradise

talian artist Lorenzo Ghiberti (1378–1455) spent years skillfully crafting images of Jesus's life into the bronze doors of Italy's Florence Baptistery. These bronze reliefs were so moving that Michelangelo called them the Gates of Paradise.

As an artistic treasure, the doors greet visitors with echoes of the gospel story. It was Jesus who said, "I am the gate; whoever enters through me will be saved" (JOHN 10:9). On the night before His crucifixion, He told His disciples, "I am the way and the truth and the life. No one comes to the Father except through me" (14:6). Within a few hours Jesus would say to one of the criminals being crucified at His side, "Today you will be with me in paradise" (LUKE 23:43).

TODAY'S READING
John 10:1–9

I am the gate; whoever enters through me will be saved. John 10:9

The apostle Peter a few weeks later boldly proclaimed to those who had called for Jesus's death that "there is no other name under heaven . . . by which we must be saved" (ACTS 4:12). Years later, the apostle Paul wrote that there is only one mediator between God and humanity—the man Christ Jesus (1 TIM. 2:5).

The gates of paradise are found in the Savior who offers everlasting life to all who believe and come to Him. Enter into the joy of His salvation. ❧   *DENNIS FISHER*

I needed a mediator because of my sin. Thank You, Jesus, for being the way to the Father by Your death and resurrection. I will be forever grateful.

Jesus died in our place to give us His peace.

Saying Goodbye

Saying goodbye is hard—to family and friends, to a favorite and familiar place, to an occupation or livelihood.

In Luke 9:57–62 our Lord describes the cost of being His disciple. A would-be follower says to Jesus, "I will follow you, Lord; but first let me go back and say goodbye to my family." Jesus responds, "No one who puts a hand to the plow and looks back is fit for service in the kingdom of God" (VV. 61–62). Is He asking His followers to say goodbye to everything and every relationship considered precious?

In the Chinese language there is no direct equivalent of the English word *goodbye*. The two Chinese characters used to translate this word really mean "see you again." Becoming a disciple of Christ may sometimes mean others will reject us, but it does not mean we say goodbye to people in the sense that we are to forget all our past relationships. Saying goodbye means that God wants us to follow Him on His terms—wholeheartedly. Then we will see people again from the right perspective.

God wants the best for us, but we must allow Him to take priority over everything else. ✿

C. P. HIA

> **TODAY'S READING**
> **Luke 9:57–62**
>
> **No one who puts a hand to the plow and looks back is fit for service in the kingdom of God.** Luke 9:62

Dear Lord, I want to follow You wholeheartedly.
Help me not to place anything or anyone before You.

When we follow Jesus we get a new perspective.

Minister of Reconciliation

As Dr. Martin Luther King Jr. preached on a Sunday morning in 1957, he fought the temptation to retaliate against a society steeped in racism.

"How do you go about loving your enemies?" he asked the Dexter Avenue Baptist congregation in Montgomery, Alabama. "Begin with yourself. . . . When the opportunity presents itself for you to defeat your enemy, that is the time which you must not do it."

Quoting from the words of Jesus, King said: "Love your enemies, bless them that curse you, do good to them that hate you, and pray for them which despitefully use you . . . ; that ye may be the children of your Father which is in heaven" (MATT. 5:44–45 KJV).

> **TODAY'S READING**
> **2 Cor. 5:16–21**
>
> While we were God's enemies, we were reconciled to him through the death of his Son.
> Romans 5:10

As we consider those who harm us, we are wise to remember our former status as enemies of God (SEE ROM. 5:10). But "[God] reconciled us to himself through Christ and gave us the ministry of reconciliation," wrote Paul (2 COR. 5:18). Now we have a holy obligation. "He has committed to us the message of reconciliation" (V. 19). We are to take that message to the world.

Racial and political tensions are nothing new. But the business of the church is never to feed divisiveness. We should not attack those unlike us or those who hold different opinions or even those who seek our destruction. Ours is a "ministry of reconciliation" that imitates the selfless servant-heart of Jesus. ✦

TIM GUSTAFSON

In Christ there is no east or west, in Him no south or north, but one great fellowship of love throughout the whole wide earth. *JOHN OXENHAM*

Hate destroys the hater as well as the hated. MARTIN LUTHER KING JR.

Desiring Growth

The axolotl (pronounced ACK-suh-LAH-tuhl) is a biological enigma. Instead of maturing into adult form, this endangered Mexican salamander retains tadpole-like characteristics throughout its life. Writers and philosophers have used the axolotl as a symbol of someone who fears growth.

TODAY'S READING
Hebrews 5:11–14

In Hebrews 5 we learn about Christians who were avoiding healthy growth, remaining content with spiritual "milk" intended for new believers. Perhaps because of fear of persecution, they weren't growing in the kind of faithfulness to Christ that would enable them to be strong enough to suffer with Him for the sake of others (VV. 7–10). Instead they

Anyone who lives on milk . . . is not acquainted with the teaching about righteousness.

Hebrews 5:13

were in danger of sliding backward from the Christlike attitudes they had already shown (6:9–11). They weren't ready for a solid diet of self-sacrifice (5:14). So the author wrote, "We have much to say about this, but it is hard to make it clear to you because you no longer try to understand" (V. 11).

Axolotls follow the natural pattern set for them by their Creator. But followers of Christ are designed to grow into spiritual maturity. As we do, we discover that growing up in Him involves more than our own peace and joy. Growth in His likeness honors God as we unselfishly encourage others. 🍂 *KEILA OCHOA*

Lord, I want to grow, so help me to go deeper into Your Word.
Teach me more each day, so that I am better equipped to serve
and worship You.

The more we live on a diet of God's Word, the more we grow.

A Hint of Heaven

The world-class botanical garden across the street from our church was the setting for an all-church community gathering. As I walked around the gardens greeting people I have known for years, catching up with those I hadn't seen recently, and enjoying the beautiful surroundings cared for by people who know and love plants, I realized that the evening was rich with symbols of how the church is supposed to function—a little hint of heaven on earth.

A garden is a place where each plant is placed in an environment in which it will thrive. Gardeners prepare the soil, protect the plants from pests, and make sure each one receives the food, water, and sunlight it needs. The result is a beautiful, colorful, and fragrant place for people to enjoy.

> **TODAY'S READING**
> **1 Cor. 14:6–12,26**
>
> **Since you are eager for gifts of the Spirit, try to excel in those that build up the church.**
>
> 1 Corinthians 14:12

Like a garden, church is meant to be a place where everyone works together for the glory of God and the good of all; a place where everyone flourishes because we are living in a safe environment; a place where people are cared for according to their needs; where each of us does work we love—work that benefits others (1 COR. 14:26).

Like well-cared-for plants, people growing in a healthy environment have a sweet fragrance that draws people to God by displaying the beauty of His love. The church is not perfect, but it really is a hint of heaven. ❧   *JULIE ACKERMAN LINK*

How can you promote the health of your church? Ask God to help you serve others as Christ serves us. Serve in a role that matches your skills and interests. Listen well to others and pray for them.

Hearts fragrant with the love of Christ display His beauty.

What's in the Bank?

In the winter of 2009, a large passenger plane made an emergency landing in New York's Hudson River. The pilot, Captain Chesley Sullenberger, who landed the plane safely with no casualties, was later asked about those moments in the air when he was faced with a life-or-death decision. "One way of looking at this," he said, "might be that for 42 years I've been making small, regular deposits in this bank of experience, education, and training. And on [that day] the balance was sufficient so that I could make a very large withdrawal."

Most of us will at some time face a crisis. Perhaps it will be a job termination or the results of a medical test, or the loss of a precious family member or friend. It is in those times that we must dig down deep into the reserves of our spiritual bank account.

> **TODAY'S READING**
> **Ephesians 2:4–7**
>
> Let us then approach God's throne of grace with confidence, so that we may receive mercy and find grace to help us in our time of need. Hebrews 4:16

And what might we find there? If we have enjoyed a deepening relationship with God, we've been making regular "deposits" of faith. We have experienced His grace (2 COR. 8:9; EPH. 2:4–7). We trust the promise of Scripture that God is just and faithful (DEUT. 32:4; 2 THESS. 3:3).

God's love and grace are available when His children need to make a "withdrawal" (PS. 9:10; HEB. 4:16). ✹   *CINDY HESS KASPER*

Great is Your faithfulness, O Lord God! Each day I see You provide
for me and show me mercy. Thank You.

Remembering God's faithfulness in the past strengthens us for the future.

You First!

Tibetan-born Sherpa Nawang Gombu and American Jim Whittaker reached the top of Mount Everest on May 1, 1963. As they approached the peak, each considered the honor of being the first of the two to step to the summit. Whittaker motioned for Gombu to move ahead, but Gombu declined with a smile, saying, "You first, Big Jim!" Finally, they decided to step to the summit at the same time.

TODAY'S READING
Philippians 2:1–11

[Jesus] humbled himself. Philippians 2:8

Paul encouraged the Philippian believers to demonstrate this kind of humility. He said, "Let each of you look out not only for his own interests, but also for the interests of others" (PHIL. 2:4 NKJV). Selfishness and superiority can divide people, but humility unites us, since it is the quality of "being one in spirit and of one mind" (V. 2).

When quarrels and disagreements occur, we can often diffuse them by giving up our right to be right. Humility calls us to show grace and gentleness when we would rather insist on our own way. "In humility value others above yourselves" (V. 3).

Practicing humility helps us to become more like Jesus who, for our sake, "humbled himself by becoming obedient to death" (VV. 7–8). Following in Jesus's footsteps means backing away from what is best for us and doing what is best for others. ✏

JENNIFER BENSON SCHULDT

Jesus, You gave up Your life for me.
Help me to see each sacrifice I make as a reflection of Your humility.
In putting others first, let me honor You.

Humility promotes unity.

Real People, Real God

Several years ago I received a letter from an *Our Daily Bread* reader after I had written about a family tragedy. "When you told about your tragedy," this person wrote, "I realized that the writers were real people with real problems." How true that is! I look across the list of men and women who pen these articles, and I see cancer and wayward children and unful-filled dreams and many other kinds of loss. We are indeed just regular, real peo-ple writing about a real God who under-stands our real problems.

TODAY'S READING
Philippians 3:17–21

**Join together
in following my
example.** Philippians 3:17

The apostle Paul stands out in the Real People Hall of Fame. He had physical problems. He had legal issues. He had interpersonal relationship struggles to deal with. And in all of this messy reality, he was setting an example for us. In Philippians 3:17, he said, "Join together in following my example, brothers and sisters, and just as you have us as a model, keep your eyes on those who live as we do."

Those around us who need the gospel—who need Jesus—are looking for believable people who can point them to our perfect Savior. And that means we must be real. ✸ *DAVE BRANON*

You, Lord, are perfection. Yet You welcome us imperfect people
to come to You for salvation. You sent Your perfect Son to earth
to die for us. Help us to be real and genuine as we seek to
point people to You.

If we are true to God, we will not be false to people.

Welcome Home!

When we were going through a particularly challenging time with our son, a friend pulled me aside after a church meeting. "I want you to know that I pray for you and your son every day," he said. Then he added: "I feel so guilty."

"Why?" I asked.

"Because I've never had to deal with prodigal children," he said. "My kids pretty much played by the rules. But it wasn't because of anything I did or didn't do. Kids," he shrugged, "make their own choices."

> **TODAY'S READING**
> **Luke 15:11–24**
>
> **While he was still a long way off, his father saw him and was filled with compassion for him.** Luke 15:20

I wanted to hug him. His compassion was a reminder, a gift from God, communicating to me the Father's understanding for my struggle with my son.

No one understands the struggle with prodigals better than our heavenly Father. The story of the prodigal son in Luke 15 is our story and God's. Jesus told it on behalf of all sinners who so desperately need to come home to their Creator and discover the warmth of a loving relationship with Him.

Jesus is God in the flesh seeing us in the distance and looking on us with compassion. He is God running to us and throwing His arms around us. He is heaven's kiss welcoming the repentant sinner home (V. 20).

God hasn't just left the porch light on for us. He's out on the front porch watching, waiting, calling us home. ✒ *JAMES BANKS*

We ask again today, Lord, that our prodigals would come home.

Our loved ones may spurn our appeals, reject our message, oppose our arguments, despise our persons—but they are helpless against our prayers.
J. SIDLOW BAXTER

A Prisoner No More

A middle-aged man approached me after I led a workshop at his place of employment and asked this question: "I've been a Christian nearly my whole life, but I'm constantly disappointed in myself. Why is it that I always seem to keep doing the things I wish I didn't do and never seem to do the things I know I should? Isn't God getting tired of me?" Two men standing next to me also seemed eager to hear the response.

> **TODAY'S READING**
> **Romans 7:15–25**
>
> I do not understand what I do. For what I want to do I do not do, but what I hate I do. Romans 7:15

That's a common struggle that even the apostle Paul experienced. "I do not understand what I do," he said, "For what I want to do I do not do, but what I hate I do" (ROM. 7:15). But here's some good news: We don't have to stay in that trap of discouragement. To paraphrase Paul as he writes in Romans 8, the key is to stop focusing on the law and start focusing on Jesus. We can't do anything about our sinfulness in our own strength. The answer is not "try harder to be good at keeping the rules." Instead, we must focus on the One who shows us mercy and cooperate with the Spirit who changes us.

When we focus on the law, we are constantly reminded that we'll never be good enough to deserve God's grace. But when we focus on Jesus, we become more like Him. ✪ *RANDY KILGORE*

I sometimes get caught in the cycle of trying harder to be good,
failing, getting discouraged, and giving up.
Help me, Lord, to depend on Your grace and to draw near to You
so that You can change my heart.

Focus on Jesus.

Lessons for Little Ones

When my daughter described a problem she was having in the school lunchroom, I immediately wondered how I could fix the issue for her. But then another thought occurred. Maybe God had allowed the problem so she could see Him at work and get to know Him better. Instead of running to the rescue, I decided to pray with her. The trouble cleared up without any help from me!

> TODAY'S READING
> **Proverbs 22:1–16**
>
> **Start children off on the way they should go.** Proverbs 22:6

This situation showed my little one that God cares for her, that He listens when she prays, and that He answers prayers. The Bible says there's something significant about learning these lessons early in life. If we "start children off on the way they should go, . . . when they are old they will not turn from it" (PROV. 22:6). When we start kids off with an awareness of Jesus and His power, we are giving them a place to return to if they wander and a foundation for spiritual growth throughout their lives.

Consider how you might foster faith in a child. Point out God's design in nature, tell a story about how He has helped you, or invite a little one to thank God with you when things go right. God can work through you to tell of His goodness throughout all generations. ❧

JENNIFER BENSON SCHULDT

Dear God, I pray that You will raise up believers in the next generation. Show me how I can encourage young people to trust in You.

We influence future generations by living for Christ today.

Honoring God

The church service was still in progress, and we had some visitors there that morning. The speaker was only halfway through his sermon when I noticed one of our visitors walking out. I was curious and concerned, so I walked out to talk with her.

"You're leaving so soon," I said, approaching her. "Is there a problem I can help with?" She was frank and forthright. "Yes," she said, "my problem is that sermon! I don't accept what the preacher is saying." He had said that no matter what we accomplish in life, the credit and praise belong to God. "At least," the woman moaned, "I deserve *some* credit for my achievements!"

> TODAY'S READING
> **John 15:1–5**
>
> **[Jesus said,] "If you remain in me and I in you, you will bear much fruit."**
> John 15:5

I explained to her what the pastor meant. People do deserve recognition and appreciation for what they do. Yet even our gifts and talents are from God, so He gets the glory. Even Jesus, the Son of God, said, "The Son can do nothing by himself; he can do only what he sees his Father doing" (JOHN 5:19). He told His followers, "Apart from me you can do nothing" (15:5).

We acknowledge the Lord as the one who helps us to accomplish everything. ❧ 　　　　　　　　　*LAWRENCE DARMANI*

Lord, let me not forget to acknowledge You
for all that You do for me and enable me to do.

God's children do His will for His glory.

Careless Words

My daughter has had a lot of ill health recently, and her husband has been wonderfully caring and supportive. "You have a real treasure there!" I said.

"You didn't think that when I first knew him," she said with a grin.

She was quite right. When Icilda and Philip got engaged, I was concerned. They were such different personalities. We have a large and noisy family, and Philip is more reserved. And I had shared my misgivings with my daughter quite bluntly.

> TODAY'S READING
> **James 3:1–12**
>
> **The tongue is a small part of the body, but it makes great boasts.** James 3:5

I was horrified to realize that the critical things I said so casually 15 years ago had stayed in her memory and could possibly have destroyed a relationship that has proved to be so right and happy. It reminded me how much we need to guard what we say to others. So many of us are quick to point out what we consider to be weaknesses in family, friends, or work colleagues, or to focus on their mistakes rather than their successes. "The tongue is a small part of the body," says James (3:5), yet the words it shapes can either destroy relationships or bring peace and harmony to a situation in the workplace, the church, or the family.

Perhaps we should make David's prayer our own as we start each day: "Set a guard over my mouth, LORD; keep watch over the door of my lips" (PS. 141:3). ✒   *MARION STROUD*

Father, please curb my careless speech
and put a guard on my tongue today and every day.

A word fitly spoken is like apples of gold in settings of silver.
PROVERBS 25:11 NKJV

When Questions Remain

On October 31, 2014, an experimental spacecraft broke apart during a test flight and crashed into the Mojave Desert. The copilot died while the pilot miraculously survived. Investigators soon determined what had happened, but not why. The title of a newspaper article about the crash began with the words "Questions remain."

TODAY'S READING
Job 23:1–12

He knows the way that I take. Job 23:10

Throughout life we may experience sorrows for which there are no adequate explanation. Some are catastrophic events with far-reaching effects while others are personal, private tragedies that alter our individual lives and families. We want to know why, but we seem to find more questions than answers. Yet even as we struggle with "Why?" God extends His unfailing love to us.

When Job lost his children and his wealth in a single day (JOB 1:13–19), he sank into an angry depression and resisted any attempted explanations by his friends. Yet he held out hope that someday there would be an answer from God. Even in the darkness Job could say, "[God] knows the way that I take; when he has tested me, I will come forth as gold" (23:10).

Oswald Chambers said, "There will come one day a personal and direct touch from God when every tear and perplexity, every oppression and distress, every suffering and pain, and wrong and injustice will have a complete and ample and overwhelming explanation."

Today, as we face life's unanswered questions, we can find help and hope in God's love and promises. ✪   *DAVID MCCASLAND*

When we face unanswered questions, we find help and hope in God's love.

What Is It?

My mother taught Sunday school for decades. One week she wanted to explain how God supplied food for the Israelites in the wilderness. To make the story come alive, she created something to represent "manna" for the kids in her class. She cut bread into small pieces and topped them with honey. Her recipe was inspired by the Bible's description of manna that says it "tasted like wafers made with honey" (EX. 16:31).

> **TODAY'S READING**
> **Exodus 16:11–31**
>
> **When the Israelites saw it, they said to each other, "What is it?"** Exodus 16:15

When the Israelites first encountered God's bread from heaven, it appeared on the ground outside their tents like frost. "When [they] saw it, they said to each other, 'What is it?' " (V. 15). The Hebrew word *man* means "what," so they called it *manna*. They discovered they could grind it and form it into loaves or cook it in a pot (NUM. 11:7–8). Whatever it was, it had a baffling arrival (EX. 16:4,14), a unique consistency (V. 14), and a short expiration date (VV. 19–20).

Sometimes God provides for us in surprising ways. This reminds us that He is not bound by our expectations, and we can't predict what He will choose to do. While we wait, focusing on who He is rather than what we think He should do will help us find joy and satisfaction in our relationship with Him. 🌢

JENNIFER BENSON SCHULDT

Dear God, please help me to freely accept Your provision and the way You choose to deliver it. Thank You for caring for me and meeting my needs.

Those who let God provide will always be satisfied.

Before the Phone

As a mom of young children I'm sometimes susceptible to panic. My first reaction is to call my mom on the phone and ask her what to do with my son's allergy or my daughter's sudden cough.

Mom is a great resource, but when I read the Psalms, I'm reminded of how often we need the kind of help that no mortal can give. In Psalm 18 David was in great danger. Afraid, close to death, and in anguish, he called on the Lord.

> TODAY'S READING
> **Psalm 18:1–6**
>
> **In my distress I called to the LORD.**
> Pslam 18:6

David could say, "I love you, LORD" because he understood God was a fortress, a rock, and a deliverer (VV. 1–2). God was his shield, his salvation, and his stronghold. Maybe we cannot understand David's praise because we have not experienced God's help. It may be that we reach for the phone before going to God for advice and help.

Surely God puts people in our lives to give us help and comfort. But let's also remember to pray. God will hear us. As David sang, "From his temple he heard my voice; my cry came before him, into his ears" (V. 6). When we go to God, we join David's song and enjoy Him as our rock, our fortress, and our deliverer.

Next time you reach for the phone, remember also to pray. ❤

KEILA OCHOA

Dear Lord, help me to remember You are my deliverer,
and You always hear my cry.

Prayer is the bridge between panic and peace.

Her Father's Zoo

June Williams was only 4 when her father bought 7 acres of land to build a zoo without bars or cages. Growing up she remembers how creative her father was in trying to help wild animals feel free in confinement. Today Chester Zoo is one of England's most popular wildlife attractions. Home to 11,000 animals on 110 acres of land, the zoo reflects her father's concern for animal welfare, education, and conservation.

TODAY'S READING
1 Kings 4:29–34

The righteous care for the needs of their animals, but the kindest acts of the wicked are cruel. Proverbs 12:10

Solomon had a similar interest in all creatures great and small. In addition to studying the wildlife of the Middle East, he imported exotic animals like apes and monkeys from far-off lands (1 KINGS 10:22). But one of his proverbs shows us that Solomon's knowledge of nature went beyond intellectual curiosity. When he expressed the spiritual implications of how we treat our animals, he mirrored something of the heart of our Creator: "The righteous care for the needs of their animals, but the kindest acts of the wicked are cruel" (PROV. 12:10).

With God-given wisdom, Solomon saw that our relationship to our Creator affects not only how we treat people but also how much thoughtful consideration we give to the creatures in our care. 🌱 *MART DEHAAN*

Father in heaven, when we think about the wonder and diversity of Your animal kingdom, please help us not only to worship You, but to care for what You've entrusted to us.

God is the real Owner of all of us.

The Mention of His Name

When the soloist began to sing during our Sunday service, the congregation gave him full, hushed attention. His mellow bass-baritone voice brought them the soul-touching words of an old song by Gordon Jensen. The song's title expresses a truth that grows more precious the older we become: "He's as Close as the Mention of His Name."

> **TODAY'S READING**
> **John 16:17–24**
>
> I will see you again and you will rejoice, and no one will take away your joy.
> John 16:22

We've all experienced times of separation from our loved ones. A child marries and moves far away. Parents are separated from us because of career or health. A child goes off to school in another state or country. True, we have texting and Skype. But we are *here* and they are *there*. And then there is the separation of death.

But as believers in Christ, we have His promise that we are never alone. Though we may feel alone, He hasn't gone anywhere. He's right here, right now, always and forever. When He left this earth, He told His followers, "Surely I am with you always, to the very end of the age" (MATT. 28:20). He also promised us, "Never will I leave you; never will I forsake you" (HEB. 13:5).

The silent plea, the whispered mention of His name, even the very thought of Him brings us solace and reassurance. "He's as close as the mention of his name." ❧

DAVE EGNER

Jesus, thank You that You are near.
I need You.

Jesus never abandons or forgets His own.

He Came for You

I n his novels *The Trial* and *The Castle,* Franz Kafka (1883–1924) portrays life as a dehumanizing existence that turns people into a sea of empty faces without identity or worth. Kafka said, "The conveyer belt of life carries you on, no one knows where. One is more of an object, a thing, than a living creature."

Early in His ministry, Jesus went to a synagogue in Nazareth, stood up in front of the crowd, and read from Isaiah: "The Spirit of the Lord is on me because he has anointed me to proclaim good news to the poor. He has sent me to proclaim freedom for the prisoners and recovery of sight for the blind, to set the oppressed free, to proclaim the year of the Lord's favor" (LUKE 4:18–19).

> **TODAY'S READING**
> **Luke 4:14–21**
>
> **The Spirit of the Lord is on me, because he has anointed me to proclaim good news to the poor.** Luke 4:18

Then Christ sat down and declared, "Today this scripture is fulfilled in your hearing" (V. 21). Centuries earlier, the prophet Isaiah had proclaimed these words (ISA. 61:1–2). Now Jesus announced that He was the fulfillment of that promise.

Notice who Jesus came to rescue—the poor, broken-hearted, captive, blind, and oppressed. He came for people dehumanized by sin and suffering, by brokenness and sorrow. He came for us! 🍃 *BILL CROWDER*

For those who sin and those who suffer. For those who suffer because of sin. For those who sin to alleviate suffering.
Lord, have mercy on us.
ROBERT GELINAS, THE MERCY PRAYER

No matter how impersonal the world may seem, Jesus loves each of us as if we were His only child.

Always Pray and Don't Give Up

Are you going through one of those times when it seems every attempt to resolve a problem is met with a new difficulty? You thank the Lord at night that it's taken care of but awake to find that something else has gone wrong and the problem remains.

During an experience like that, I was reading the gospel of Luke and was astounded by the opening words of chapter 18: "Then Jesus told his disciples a parable to show them that they should always pray and not give up" (V. 1). I had read the story of the persistent widow many times but never grasped why Jesus told it (VV. 2–8). Now I connected those opening words with the story. The lesson to His followers was very clear: "Always pray and never give up."

Prayer is not a means of coercing God to do what we want. It is a process of recognizing His power and plan for our lives. In prayer we yield our lives and circumstances to the Lord and trust Him to act in His time and in His way.

As we rely on God's grace not only for the outcome of our requests but for the process as well, we can keep coming to the Lord in prayer, trusting His wisdom and care for us.

Our Lord's encouragement to us is clear: Always pray and don't give up! 🌿

DAVID MCCASLAND

> **TODAY'S READING**
> **Luke 18:1–8**
>
> **Jesus told his disciples a parable to show them that they should always pray and not give up.** Luke 18:1

Lord, in the difficulty I face today, guard my heart, guide my words, and show Your grace. May I always turn to You in prayer.

Prayer changes everything.

Leave a Legacy

When a road-construction foreman was killed in an accident, the love of this man for his family, co-workers, and community resulted in an overwhelming sense of loss. His country church couldn't accommodate all the mourners, so planners moved the service to a much larger building. Friends and family packed the auditorium! The message was clear: Tim touched many lives in a way uniquely his. So many would miss his kindness, sense of humor, and enthusiasm for life.

> TODAY'S READING
> **2 Chronicles 21:4–20**
>
> **Even the Son of Man did not come to be served, but to serve.** Mark 10:45

As I returned from the funeral, I thought about the life of King Jehoram. What a contrast! His brief reign of terror is traced in 2 Chronicles 21. To solidify his power, Jehoram killed his own brothers and other leaders (V. 4). Then he led Judah into idol worship. The record tells us, "He passed away, to no one's regret" (V. 20). Jehoram thought that brute force would ensure his legacy. It did. He is forever commemorated in Scripture as an evil man and a self-centered leader.

Although Jesus also was a king, He came to Earth to be a servant. As He went about doing good, He endured the hatred of those who grasped for power. In the process, this Servant-King gave His life away.

Today, Jesus lives along with His legacy. That legacy includes those who understand that life isn't just about themselves. It's about Jesus—the One who longs to wrap His strong, forgiving arms around anyone who turns to Him. 🟡 *TIM GUSTAFSON*

Lord, in Your death as well as in Your life, You served others.
In some small way, help us to serve others with our lives today.

A life lived for God leaves a lasting legacy.

Training for Life

I recently met a woman who has pushed her body and mind to the limit. She climbed mountains, faced death, and even broke a Guinness world record. Now she's engaged in a different challenge—that of raising her special-needs child. The courage and faith she employed while ascending the mountains she now pours into motherhood.

In 1 Corinthians, the apostle Paul speaks of a runner competing in a race. After urging a church enamored with their rights to give consideration to one another (CH. 8), he explains how he sees the challenges of love and self-sacrifice to be like a marathon of endurance (CH. 9). As followers of Jesus, they are to relinquish their rights in obedience to Him.

> **TODAY'S READING**
> **1 Cor. 9:24–27**
>
> I discipline my body and bring it into subjection, lest... I myself should become disqualified.
>
> 1 Corinthians 9:27 NKJV

As athletes train their bodies that they might win the crown, we too train our bodies and minds for our souls to flourish. As we ask the Holy Spirit to transform us, moment by moment, we leave our old selves behind. Empowered by God, we stop ourselves from uttering that cruel word. We put away our electronic device and remain present with our friends. We don't have to speak the last word in a disagreement.

As we train to run in the Spirit of Christ, how might God want to mold us today? ❧

AMY BOUCHER PYE

Lord, let me not demand my rights,
but train to win the prize that lasts forever.

Training leads to transformation.

Hidden Treasure

My husband and I read in different ways. Since English is a second language for Tom, he has a tendency to read slowly, word-for-word. I often speed-read by skimming. But Tom retains more than I do. He can easily quote something he read a week ago, while my retention can evaporate seconds after I turn away from the screen or book.

Skimming is also a problem when I'm reading the Bible—and not just the genealogies. I'm tempted to skim familiar passages, stories I've heard since I was a child, or a psalm that is part of a familiar chorus.

> TODAY'S READING
> **Proverbs 2:1–5**
>
> **Search for [insight and understanding] as for hidden treasure.** Proverbs 2:4

Proverbs 2 encourages us to make the effort to know God better by carefully seeking a heart of understanding. When we read the Bible carefully and invest time memorizing Scripture, we absorb its truths more deeply (VV. 1–2). Sometimes reading the Word aloud helps us to hear and understand the wisdom of God more fully. And when we pray the words of Scripture back to God and ask Him for "insight and understanding" (V. 3), we enjoy a conversation with the Author.

We come to know God and His wisdom when we search for it with our whole heart. We find understanding when we seek it like silver and search for it like hidden treasure. 🕊 *CINDY HESS KASPER*

Dear Lord, help me to slow down and listen to what You want to teach me through Your Word so I can be the person You want me to be.

Read the Bible carefully and study it prayerfully.

A Serving Leader

n traditional African societies, leadership succession is a serious decision. After a king's demise, great care is taken selecting the next ruler. Besides being from a royal family, the successor must be strong, fearless, and sensible. Candidates are questioned to determine if they will serve the people or rule with a heavy hand. The king's successor needs to be someone who leads but also serves.

TODAY'S READING
1 Kings 12:1–15

> **Whoever wants to become great among you must be your servant.**
> Matthew 20:26

Even though Solomon made his own bad choices, he worried over his successor. "Who knows whether that person will be wise or foolish? Yet they will have control over all the fruit of my toil into which I have poured my effort and skill" (ECCL. 2:19). His son Rehoboam was that successor. He demonstrated a lack of sound judgment and ended up fulfilling his father's worst fear.

When the people requested more humane working conditions, it was an opportunity for Rehoboam to show servant leadership. "If today you will be a servant to these people and serve them . . . ," the elders advised, "they will always be your servants" (1 KINGS 12:7). But he rejected their counsel. Rehoboam failed to seek God. His harsh response to the people divided the kingdom and accelerated the spiritual decline of God's people (12:14–19).

In the family, the workplace, at church, or in our neighborhood—we need His wisdom for the humility to serve rather than be served. ❧

LAWRENCE DARMANI

Dear Lord, please give me a humble servant's heart.
Help me to lead and follow with humility and compassion.

A good leader is a good servant.

What Will Be

You and I have something in common. We live in a mixed-up, tarnished world and we have never known anything different. Adam and Eve, however, could remember what life was like before the curse. They could recall the world as God intended it to be—free of death, hardship, and pain (GEN. 3:16–19). In pre-fall Eden, hunger, unemployment, and illness did not exist. No one questioned God's creative power or His plan for human relationships.

<blockquote>
TODAY'S READING
Revelation 22:1–5

No longer will there be any curse.

Revelation 22:3
</blockquote>

The world we have inherited resembles God's perfect garden only slightly. To quote C. S. Lewis, "This is a good world gone wrong, but [it] still retains the memory of what ought to have been." Fortunately, the cloudy memory of what the earth should have been is also a prophetic glimpse into eternity. There, just as Adam and Eve walked and talked with God, believers will see His face and serve Him directly. There will be nothing between God and us. "No longer will there be any curse" (REV. 22:3). There will be no sin, no fear, and no shame.

The past and its consequences may cast a shadow on today, but a believer's destiny carries the promise of something better—life in a place as perfect as Eden. 🌱 *JENNIFER BENSON SCHULDT*

Dear God, help me to remember that even though this world does not measure up to Your original design there is much to enjoy and much to do for You and others. Thank You for the promise of life with You in a perfect setting.

One day God will put everything right.

The Factory of Sadness

As a lifelong Cleveland Browns football fan, I grew up knowing my share of disappointment. Despite being one of only four teams to have never appeared in a Super Bowl championship game, the Browns have a loyal fan base that sticks with the team year in and year out. But because the fans usually end up disappointed, many of them now refer to the home stadium as the "Factory of Sadness."

> TODAY'S READING
> **John 16:28–33**
>
> **[God] will wipe every tear from their eyes.**
> Revelation 21:4

The broken world we live in can be a "factory of sadness" too. There seems to be an endless supply of heartache and disappointment, whether from our own choices or things beyond our control.

Yet the follower of Christ has hope—not only in the life to come but for this very day. Jesus said, "I have told you these things, so that in me you may have peace. In this world you will have trouble. But take heart! I have overcome the world" (JOHN 16:33). Notice that without minimizing the struggles or sadness we may experience, Christ counters them with His promises of peace, joy, and ultimate victory.

Great peace is available in Christ, and it's more than enough to help us navigate whatever life throws at us. 🌐 *BILL CROWDER*

When peace, like a river, attendeth my way,
when sorrows like sea billows roll; whatever my lot,
Thou hast taught me to say, It is well, it is well, with my soul.
HORATIO G. SPAFFORD

Our hope and peace are found in Jesus.

Can't Take It Back

I couldn't take my actions back. A woman had parked her car and blocked my way of getting to the gas pump. She hopped out to drop off some recycling items, and I didn't feel like waiting, so I honked my horn at her. Irritated, I put my car in reverse and drove around another way. I immediately felt bad about being impatient and unwilling to wait 30 seconds (at the most) for her to move. I apologized to God. Yes, she should have parked in the designated area, but I could have spread kindness and patience instead of harshness. Unfortunately it was too late to apologize to her—she was gone.

> **TODAY'S READING**
> **Galatians 5:13–26**
>
> **The fruit of the Spirit is . . . gentleness and self-control.**
>
> Galatians 5:22–23

Many of the Proverbs challenge us to think about how to respond when people get in the way of our plans. There's the one that says, "Fools show their annoyance at once" (PROV. 12:16). And "It is to one's honor to avoid strife, but every fool is quick to quarrel" (20:3). Then there's this one that goes straight to the heart: "Fools give full vent to their rage, but the wise bring calm in the end" (29:11).

Growing in patience and kindness seems pretty difficult sometimes. But the apostle Paul says it is the work of God, the "fruit of the Spirit" (GAL. 5:22-23). As we cooperate with Him and depend on Him, He produces that fruit in us. Please change us, Lord. ✹

ANNE CETAS

Make me a gentle person, Lord. One who doesn't quickly react in frustration to every annoyance that comes my way. Give me a spirit of self-control and patience.

God tests our patience to enlarge our hearts.

Secret Menu

Meat Mountain is a super-sandwich layered with six kinds of meat. Stacked with chicken tenders, three strips of bacon, two cheeses, and much more, it looks like it should be a restaurant's featured item.

But Meat Mountain isn't on any restaurant's published menu. The sandwich represents a trend in off-menu items known only by social media or word of mouth. It seems that competition is driving fast-food restaurants to offer a secret menu to in-the-know customers.

> **TODAY'S READING**
> **John 4:31–34**
>
> **I have food to eat that you know nothing about.**
> John 4:32

When Jesus told His disciples that He had "food" they knew nothing about, it must have seemed like a secret menu to them (JOHN 4:32). He sensed their confusion and explained that His food was to do the will of His Father and to finish the work given to Him (V. 34).

Jesus had just spoken to a Samaritan woman at Jacob's well about living water she had never heard of. As they talked, He revealed a supernatural understanding of her unquenched thirst for life. When He disclosed who He was, she left her water pot behind and ran to ask her neighbors, "Could this be the Messiah?" (V. 29).

What was once a secret can now be offered to everyone. Jesus invites all of us to trust His ability to satisfy the deepest needs of our hearts. As we do, we discover how to live not just by our physical appetites but by the soul-satisfying Spirit of our God. ❧ *MART DEHAAN*

Father, we praise You for revealing Your truth to us.
Help us live each day in the power of Your Spirit.

Only Christ the Living Bread can satisfy the world's spiritual hunger.

Jesus Over Everything

My friend's son decided to wear a sports jersey over his school clothing one day. He wanted to show support for his favorite team that would be playing an important game later that night. Before leaving home, he put something on over his sports jersey—it was a chain with a pendant that read, "Jesus." His simple action illustrated a deeper truth: Jesus deserves first place over everything in our lives.

> TODAY'S READING
> **Colossians 1:15–20**
>
> **He is before all things.** Colossians 1:17

Jesus is above and over all. "He is before all things, and in him all things hold together" (COL. 1:17). Jesus is supreme over all creation (VV. 15–16). He is "the head of the body, the church" (V. 18). Because of this, He should have first place in all things.

When we give Jesus the highest place of honor in each area of our lives, this truth becomes visible to those around us. At work, are we laboring first for God or only to please our employer? (3:23). How do God's standards show up in the way we treat others? (VV. 12–14). Do we put Him first as we live our lives and pursue our favorite pastimes?

When Jesus is our greatest influence in all of life, He will have His rightful place in our hearts. 🕮 *JENNIFER BENSON SCHULDT*

Dear Jesus, You deserve the best of my time, energy, and affection.
I crown You King of my heart and Lord over everything I do.

Put Jesus first.

Turn Off the Scoreboard

At his son's wedding reception, my friend Bob offered advice and encouragement to the newlyweds. In his speech he told of a football coach in a nearby town who, when his team lost a game, kept the losing score on the scoreboard all week to remind the team of their failure. While that may be a good football strategy, Bob wisely advised, it's a terrible strategy in marriage. When your spouse upsets you or fails you in some way, don't keep drawing attention to the failure. Turn off the scoreboard.

TODAY'S READING
Ephesians 4:25-32

Forgiving each other, just as in Christ God forgave you. Ephesians 4:32

What great advice! Scripture is full of commands for us to love each other and overlook faults. We are reminded that love "keeps no record of wrongs" (1 COR. 13:5) and that we should be ready to forgive one another "just as in Christ God forgave you" (EPH. 4:32).

I am deeply grateful that God turns off the scoreboard when I fail. He doesn't simply forgive when we repent; He removes our sin as far as the east is from the west (PS. 103:12). With God, forgiveness means that our sin is out of sight *and* out of mind. May He give us grace to extend forgiveness to those around us. ❧

JOE STOWELL

Lord, thank You for not holding my sins against me and for granting me a second chance. Help me today to forgive others just as You have so freely forgiven me.

Forgive as God forgives you—don't keep score.

Undigested Knowledge

I n his book on language, British diplomat Lancelot Oliphant (1881–1965) observed that many students give correct answers on tests but fail to put those lessons into practice. "Such undigested knowledge is of little use," declared Oliphant.

Author Barnabas Piper noticed a parallel in his own life: "I thought I was close to God because I knew all the answers," he said, "but I had fooled myself into thinking that was the same as *relationship* with Jesus."

TODAY'S READING
John 8:39–47

If you hold to my teaching, you are really my disciples.
John 8:31

At the temple one day, Jesus encountered people who thought they had all the right answers. They were proudly proclaiming their status as Abraham's descendants yet refused to believe in God's Son.

"If you were Abraham's children," said Jesus, "then you would do what Abraham did" (JOHN 8:39). And what was that? Abraham "believed the LORD, and he credited it to him as righteousness" (GEN. 15:6). Still, Jesus's hearers refused to believe. "The only Father we have is God himself," they said (JOHN 8:41). Jesus replied, "Whoever belongs to God hears what God says. The reason you do not hear is that you do not belong to God" (V. 47).

Piper recalls how things "fell apart" for him before he "encountered God's grace and the person of Jesus in a profound way." When we allow God's truth to transform our lives, we gain much more than the right answer. We introduce the world to Jesus. ❧

TIM GUSTAFSON

Father, thank You that You receive anyone who turns to You in faith.

Faith is not accepting the fact of God but of receiving the life of God.

Ice Flowers

Fifteen-year-old **Wilson Bentley** was captivated by the intricate beauty of snowflakes. He looked with fascination through an old microscope his mother had given him and made hundreds of sketches of their remarkable designs, but they melted too quickly to adequately capture their detail. Several years later, in 1885, he had an idea. He attached a bellows camera to the microscope and, after much trial and error, took his first picture of a snowflake. During his lifetime Bentley would capture 5,000 snowflake images and each one was a unique design. He described them as "tiny miracles of beauty" and "ice flowers."

> TODAY'S READING
> **1 Cor. 12:4–14**
>
> **There are different kinds of gifts, but the same Spirit distributes them.** 1 Corinthians 12:4

No two snowflakes are alike, yet all come from the same source. So it is with followers of Christ. We all come from the same Creator and Redeemer, yet we are all different. In God's glorious plan He has chosen to bring a variety of people together into a unified whole, and He has gifted us in various ways. In describing the diversity of gifts to believers, Paul writes: "There are different kinds of gifts, but the same Spirit distributes them. There are different kinds of service, but the same Lord. There are different kinds of working, but in all of them and in everyone it is the same God at work" (1 COR. 12:4–6).

Thank God for the unique contribution you can offer as you help and serve others. 🌿 *DENNIS FISHER*

Dear Lord, thank You for the unique way that You have gifted me.
Help me to use my gifts faithfully to serve You and others.

Each person is a unique expression of God's loving design.

The Ease of Ingratitude

Thwip, thwap. Thwip, thwap.

The windshield wipers slamming back and forth trying to keep up with the pelting rain only added to my irritation as I adjusted to driving the used car I had just purchased—an old station wagon with 80,000+ miles and no side-impact airbag protection for the kids.

To get this station wagon, and some badly needed cash for groceries, I had sold the last "treasure" we owned: a 1992 Volvo station wagon *with* side-impact airbag protection for the kids. By then, everything else was gone. Our house and our savings had all disappeared under the weight of uncovered medical expenses from life-threatening illnesses.

> **TODAY'S READING**
> **Hebrews 12:18–29**
>
> **Since we are receiving a kingdom that cannot be shaken, let us be thankful.** Hebrews 12:28

"Okay, God," I actually said out loud, "now I can't even protect my kids from side-impact crashes. If anything happens to them, let me tell You what I'm going to do . . ."

Thwip, thwap. Thwip, thwap. (Gulp.)

I was instantly ashamed. In the previous 2 years God had spared both my wife and my son from almost certain death, and yet here I was whining about "things" I had lost. Just like that I'd learned how quickly I could grow ungrateful to God. The loving Father, who did not spare *His* own Son so I could be saved, had actually spared *my* son in a miraculous fashion.

"Forgive me, Father," I prayed. *Already done, My child.* ❂

RANDY KILGORE

How easy it is, Lord, to let the trials of the moment strip us of the memory of Your protection and provision. Praise You, Father, for Your patience and Your unending, unconditional love.

Thankfulness is the soil in which joy thrives.

A Widow's Choice

When a good friend suddenly lost her husband to a heart attack, we grieved with her. As a counselor, she had comforted many others. Now, after 40 years of marriage, she faced the unwelcome prospect of returning to an empty house at the end of each day.

In the midst of her grief, our friend leaned on the One who "is close to the brokenhearted." As God walked with her through her pain, she told us she would choose to "wear the label *widow* proudly," because she felt it was the label God had given her.

> **TODAY'S READING**
> **Psalm 34:15–22**
>
> **The LORD is close to the brokenhearted.**
> Psalm 34:18

All grief is personal, and others may grieve differently than she does. Her response doesn't diminish her grief or make her home less empty. Yet it reminds us that even in the midst of our worst sorrows, our sovereign and loving God can be trusted.

Our heavenly Father suffered a profound separation of His own. As Jesus hung on the cross He cried out, "My God, my God, why have you forsaken me?" (MATT. 27:46). Yet He endured the pain and separation of crucifixion for our sins out of love for us!

He understands! And because "the LORD is close to the brokenhearted" (PS. 34:18), we find the comfort we need. He is near. ❧

DAVE BRANON

Dear heavenly Father, as we think about the sadness that comes
from the death of a loved one, help us to cling to You
and trust Your love and goodness.
Thank You for being close to our broken hearts.

God shares in our sorrow.

Grandma's Recipe

Many families have a secret recipe, a special way of cooking a dish that makes it especially savory. For us Hakkas (my Chinese ethnic group), we have a traditional dish called abacus beads, named for its beadlike appearance. Really, you have to try it!

Of course Grandma had the best recipe. Each Chinese New Year at the family reunion dinner we would tell ourselves, "We should really learn how to cook this." But we never got around to asking Grandma. Now she is no longer with us, and her secret recipe is gone with her.

We miss Grandma, and it's sad to lose her recipe. It would be far more tragic if we were to fail to preserve the legacy of faith entrusted to us. God intends that every generation share with the next generation about the mighty acts of God. "One generation commends [God's] works to another," said the psalmist (PS. 145:4), echoing Moses's earlier instructions to "remember the days of old.... Ask your father and he will tell you, your elders, and they will explain to you" (DEUT. 32:7).

As we share our stories of how we received salvation and the ways the Lord has helped us face challenges, we encourage each other and honor Him. He designed us to enjoy family and community and to benefit from each other. 🌱 *POH FANG CHIA*

> **TODAY'S READING**
> **Psalm 145:1–13**
>
> **Remember the days of old; consider the generations long past. Ask your father and he will tell you, your elders, and they will explain to you.**
>
> Deuteronomy 32:7

Is there someone from a different age group with whom you can share your own faith journey? How about asking someone from an older generation to share their story with you. What might you learn?

What we teach our children today will influence tomorrow's world.

Opening Doors

Charlie Sifford is an important name in American sports. He became the first African-American playing member of the Professional Golfers Association (PGA) Tour, joining a sport that, until 1961, had a "whites only" clause in its bylaws. Enduring racial injustice and harassment, Sifford earned his place at the game's highest level, won two tournaments, and in 2004 was the first African American inducted into the World Golf Hall of Fame. Charlie Sifford opened the doors of professional golf for players of all ethnicities.

> TODAY'S READING
> **Matthew 28:16–20**
>
> **Therefore go and make disciples of all nations.**
>
> Matthew 28:19

Opening doors is also a theme at the heart of the gospel mission. Jesus said, "Therefore go and make disciples of all nations, baptizing them in the name of the Father and of the Son and of the Holy Spirit, and teaching them to obey everything I have commanded you. And surely I am with you always, to the very end of the age" (MATT. 28:19–20).

The word *nations* (V. 19) is from the Greek word *ethnos*, which is also the source of the word *ethnic*. In other words, "Go and make disciples of all ethnicities." Jesus's work on the cross opened the way to the Father for everyone.

Now we have the privilege of caring for others as God has cared for us. We can open the door for someone who never dreamed they'd be welcomed personally into the house and family of God. ✿   *BILL CROWDER*

Lord, help me to be sensitive to others I meet today.
Give me the words to tell others about You.

Jesus opened the doors of salvation to all who will believe.

Solitude and Service

Comedian **Fred Allen** said, "A celebrity is a person who works hard all his life to become well-known, then wears dark glasses to avoid being recognized." Fame often brings loss of privacy along with a relentless frenzy of attention.

When Jesus began His public ministry of teaching and healing, He was catapulted into the public eye and thronged by people seeking help. Crowds followed Him wherever He went. But Jesus knew that having regular time alone with God was essential to maintaining strength and perspective.

> TODAY'S READING
> **Luke 9:1–2,10–17**
>
> **He welcomed them and spoke to them about the kingdom of God, and healed those who needed healing.** Luke 9:11

After Jesus's twelve disciples returned from their successful mission "to proclaim the kingdom of God and to heal the sick," He took them to a quiet place to rest (LUKE 9:2,10). Soon, however, crowds of people found them and Jesus welcomed them. He "spoke to them about the kingdom of God, and healed those who needed healing" (V. 11). Instead of sending them away to find food, the Lord provided an outdoor picnic for 5,000! (VV. 12–17).

Jesus was not immune to the pressure of curious and hurting people, but He maintained the balance of public service and private solitude by taking time for rest and for prayer alone with His Father (LUKE 5:16).

May we follow our Lord's example as we serve others in His name. ❧

DAVID MCCASLAND

Dear Father, as Jesus Your Son and our Savior honored You in solitude and service to others, may we follow His example in our lives.

Turning down the volume of life allows you to listen to God.

The Voice of Faith

The news was numbing. The tears came so quickly that she couldn't fight them. Her mind raced with questions, and fear threatened to overwhelm her. Life had been going along so well, when it was abruptly interrupted and forever changed without warning.

Tragedy can come in many forms—the loss of a loved one, an illness, the loss of wealth or our livelihood. And it can happen to anyone at any time.

Although the prophet Habakkuk knew that tragedy was coming, it still struck fear in his heart. As he waited for the day when Babylon would invade the kingdom of Judah, his heart pounded, his lips quivered, and his legs trembled (HAB. 3:16).

> **TODAY'S READING**
> **Habakkuk 3:16–19**
>
> **Though the fig tree does not bud... yet I will rejoice in the LORD.**
>
> Habakkuk 3:17–18

Fear is a legitimate emotion in the face of tragedy, but it doesn't have to immobilize us. When we don't understand the trials we are going through, we can recount how God has worked in history (VV. 3-15). That's what Habakkuk did. It didn't dispel his fear, but it gave him the courage to move on by choosing to praise the Lord (V. 18).

Our God who has proven Himself faithful throughout the years is always with us. Because His character doesn't change, in our fear we can say with a confident voice of faith, "The Sovereign LORD is my strength!" (V. 19). 🖤

POH FANG CHIA

Dear Lord, when my world is turned upside down,
help me to trust You. You have always been faithful to me.

We can learn the lesson of trust in the school of trial.

Four Ways to Look

Joan was struggling with some difficult issues with her children when she sat down for a worship service. Exhausted, she wanted to "resign" from motherhood. Then the speaker began to share encouragement for those who feel like quitting. These four thoughts that Joan heard that morning helped her to keep going:

Look up and pray. Asaph prayed all night long and even expressed feelings that God had forgotten and rejected him (PS. 77:9–10). We can tell God everything and be honest about our feelings. We can ask Him anything. His answer may not come right away or in the form we want or expect, but He won't criticize us for asking.

> TODAY'S READING
> **Psalm 77:1–15**
>
> **I will consider all your works and meditate on all your mighty deeds.**
>
> Psalm 77:12

Look back and remember what God has done in the past for you and others. Asaph didn't talk to God only about the pain; he also recalled God's power and mighty works for him and God's people. He wrote, "I will remember the deeds of the LORD; yes, I will remember your miracles of long ago" (V. 11).

Look forward. Think about the good that might come out of the situation. What might you learn? What might God want to do? What do you know He will do because His ways are perfect? (V.13).

Look again. This time look at your circumstances with eyes of faith. Remind yourself that He is the God of great wonders and can be trusted (V. 14).

May these ideas help us gain perspective and keep moving in our faith journey with Jesus. ☙

ANNE CETAS

Lord, I can't help but see my problems. Help me not to be discouraged and weary, but to see You in the midst of them.

Our problems are opportunities to discover God's solutions.

The View from the Mountain

Our valley in Idaho can be very cold in the winter. Clouds and fog roll in and blanket the ground, trapping frigid air under warmer layers above. But you can get above the valley. There's a road nearby that winds up the flank of Shafer Butte, a 7,500-foot mountain that rises out of our valley. A few minutes of driving and you break out of the fog and emerge into the warmth and brilliance of a sunlit day. You can look down on the clouds that shroud the valley below and see it from a different point of view.

TODAY'S READING
Philippians 4:8–13

> **Since, then, you have been raised with Christ, set your hearts on things above.**
> Colossians 3:1

Life is like that at times. Circumstances seem to surround us with a fog that sunlight cannot penetrate. Yet *faith* is the way we get above the valley—the means by which we "set [our] hearts on things above" (COL. 3:1). As we do, the Lord enables us to rise above our circumstances and find courage and calmness for the day. As the apostle Paul wrote, "I have learned to be content whatever the circumstances" (PHIL. 4:11).

We can climb out of our misery and gloom. We can sit for a time on the mountainside and through Christ who gives us strength (V. 13) we can gain a different perspective. 🌱 *DAVID ROPER*

Although I can't always see You or what You're doing, Lord,
I rest in Your love for me.

Faith can lift you above your fears.

Unanswered

One of my biggest struggles is unanswered prayer. Maybe you can relate. You ask God to rescue a friend from addiction, to grant salvation to a loved one, to heal a sick child, to mend a relationship. All these things you think must be God's will. For years you pray. But you hear nothing back from Him and you see no results.

You remind the Lord that He's powerful. That your request is a good thing. You plead. You wait. You doubt—maybe He doesn't hear you, or maybe He isn't so powerful after all. You quit asking—for days or months. You feel guilty about doubting. You remember that God wants you to take your needs to Him, and you tell Him your requests again.

> **TODAY'S READING**
> **Luke 18:1–8**
>
> [Jesus] spoke a parable to them, that men always ought to pray and not lose heart.
> Luke 18:1

We may sometimes feel we're like the persistent widow in Jesus's parable recorded in Luke 18. She keeps coming to the judge, badgering him and trying to wear him down so he'll give in. But we know that God is kinder and more powerful than the judge in the parable. We trust Him, for He is good and wise and sovereign. We remember that Jesus said we "always ought to pray and not lose heart" (V. 1).

So we ask Him, "Summon Your power, O God; show us Your strength, O God, as You have done before" (PS. 68:28 NIV). And then we trust Him . . . and wait. *ANNE CETAS*

Pray on, then, child of God, pray on;
This is your duty and your task.
To God the answering belongs;
Yours is the simpler part—to ask. —*CHISHOLM*

Delay is not denial, so keep praying.

A Better View

As a child, I loved to climb trees. The higher I climbed, the more I could see. Occasionally, in search of a better view, I might inch out along a branch until I felt it bend under my weight. Not surprisingly, my tree-climbing days are over. I suppose it isn't very safe—or dignified.

Zacchaeus, a wealthy man, set aside his dignity (and perhaps ignored his safety) when he climbed a tree one day in Jericho. Jesus was traveling through the city, and Zacchaeus wanted to get a look at Him. However, "because he was short he could not see over the crowd" (LUKE 19:3). Fortunately, those things did not stop him from seeing and even talking with Christ. Zacchaeus's plan worked! And when he met Jesus, his life was changed forever. "Salvation has come to this house," Jesus said (V. 9).

> TODAY'S READING
> **Luke 19:1–10**
>
> **Because he was short he could not see over the crowd.**
> Luke 19:3

We too can be prevented from seeing Jesus. Pride can blind us from seeing Him as the Wonderful Counselor. Anxiety keeps us from knowing Him as the Prince of Peace (ISA. 9:6). Hunger for status and stuff can prevent us from seeing Him as the true source of satisfaction—the Bread of Life (JOHN 6:48).

What are you willing to do to get a better view of Jesus? Any sincere effort to get closer to Him will have a good result. God rewards people who earnestly seek Him (HEB. 11:6). 🕊

JENNIFER BENSON SCHULDT

Thank You Jesus for all that You are.
Show me more of Yourself as I read the Bible and pray.
Help me to pursue You with all of my heart and mind.

To strengthen your faith in God, seek the face of God.

The Forward Look

When the great Dutch painter Rembrandt died unexpectedly at age 63, an unfinished painting was found on his easel. It focuses on Simeon's emotion in holding the baby Jesus when He was brought to the temple in Jerusalem, 40 days after His birth. Yet the background and normal detail remain unfinished. Some art experts believe that Rembrandt knew the end of his life was near and—like Simeon—was ready to "be dismissed" (LUKE 2:29).

TODAY'S READING
Luke 2:21–35

Simeon . . . was righteous and devout . . . and the Holy Spirit was on him. Luke 2:25

The Holy Spirit was upon Simeon (V. 25), so it was no coincidence that he was in the temple when Mary and Joseph presented their firstborn son to God. Simeon, who had been looking for the promised Messiah, took the baby in his arms and praised God, saying: "Sovereign Lord, as you have promised, you may now dismiss your servant in peace. For my eyes have seen your salvation, which you have prepared in the sight of all nations: a light for revelation to the Gentiles, and the glory of your people Israel" (VV. 29–32).

Simeon was not longing for the glory days of Israel's history, but was looking ahead for the promised Messiah, who would come to redeem all nations.

Like Simeon, we can have an expectant, forward look in life because we know that one day we will see the Lord. ✪

DAVID MCCASLAND

Father, may we, like Simeon, be always looking ahead
for the appearing of Jesus our Lord.

Even so, come, Lord Jesus! REVELATION 22:20

Go Fever

On January 28, 1986, after five weather-related delays, the space shuttle *Challenger* lumbered heavenward amid a thunderous overture of noise and flame. A mere 73 seconds later, system failure tore the shuttle apart, and all seven crewmembers perished.

The disaster was attributed to an O-ring seal known to have vulnerabilities. Insiders referred to the fatal mistake as "go fever"—the tendency to ignore vital precautions in the rush to a grand goal.

Our ambitious human nature relentlessly tempts us to make ill-advised

> TODAY'S READING
> **Numbers 14:39–45**
>
> **Be still before the LORD and wait patiently for him.**
> Psalm 37:7

choices. Yet we are also prone to a fear that can make us overly cautious. The ancient Israelites demonstrated both traits. When the 12 scouts returned from spying out the Promised Land, 10 of the 12 saw only the obstacles (NUM. 13:26–33). "We can't attack those people; they are stronger than we are," they said (V. 31). After a fearful rebellion against the Lord that led to the death of the 10 spies, the people suddenly developed a case of "go fever." They said, "Now we are ready to go up to the land the LORD promised" (14:40). Without God, the ill-timed invasion failed miserably (VV. 41–45).

When we take our eyes off the Lord, we'll slide into one of two extremes. We'll impatiently rush ahead without Him, or we'll cower and complain in fear. Focusing on Him brings courage tempered with His wisdom. ✿   *TIM GUSTAFSON*

Before making a quick decision, consider why you want to make it quickly. Consider if it will honor God and what it might cost others. If you are afraid to make a decision, think about why that might be. Most of all, pray!

A moment of patience can prevent a great disaster.

How to Grow Old

"**How are you today,** Mama?" I asked casually. My 84-year-old friend, pointing to aches and pains in her joints, whispered, "Old age is tough!" Then she added earnestly, "But God has been good to me."

"Growing old has been the greatest surprise of my life," says Billy Graham in his book *Nearing Home.* "I am an old man now, and believe me, it's not easy." However, Graham notes, "While the Bible doesn't gloss over the problems we face as we grow older, neither does it paint old age as a time to be despised or a burden to be

> **TODAY'S READING**
> **Isaiah 46:4–13**
>
> I will sustain you and I will rescue you. Isaiah 46:4

endured with gritted teeth." He then mentions some of the questions he has been forced to deal with as he has aged, such as, "How can we not only learn to cope with the fears and struggles and growing limitations we face but also actually grow stronger inwardly in the midst of these difficulties?"

In Isaiah 46 we have God's assurance: "Even to your old age and gray hairs . . . I am he who will sustain you. I have made you and I will carry you; I will sustain you and I will rescue you" (V. 4).

We don't know how many years we will live on this earth or what we might face as we age. But one thing is certain: God will care for us throughout our life. 🌿

LAWRENCE DARMANI

Lord, please teach us to number our days so that we may
gain a heart of wisdom.
(SEE PSALM 90:12)

Don't be afraid to grow old; God goes with you!

Taking Notice

When I clean my house for a special event, I become discouraged because I think that guests won't notice what I clean, only what I don't clean. This brings to mind a larger philosophical and spiritual question: Why do humans more quickly see what's wrong than what's right? We are more likely to remember rudeness than kindness. Crimes seem to receive more attention than acts of generosity. And disasters grab our attention more quickly than the profound beauty all around us.

TODAY'S READING
Job 40:1–14

"Where were you when I laid the earth's foundation?"

Job 38:4

But then I realize I am the same way with God. I tend to focus on what He hasn't done rather than on what He has, on what I don't have rather than on what I have, on the situations that He has not yet resolved rather than on the many He has.

When I read the book of Job, I am reminded that the Lord doesn't like this any more than I do. After years of experiencing prosperity, Job suffered a series of disasters. Suddenly those became the focus of his life and conversations. Finally, God intervened and asked Job some hard questions, reminding him of His sovereignty and of everything Job didn't know and hadn't seen (JOB 38–40).

Whenever I start focusing on the negative, I hope I remember to stop, consider the life of Job, and take notice of all the wonders God has done and continues to do. ❧ *JULIE ACKERMAN LINK*

Consider keeping a "thanks" journal.
Write down each day one thing God has done for you.

When you think of all that's good, give thanks to God.

Growing Up

Watching my young grandson and his friends play T-Ball is entertaining. In this version of baseball, young players often run to the wrong base or don't know what to do with the ball if they happen to catch it. If we were watching a professional baseball game, these mistakes would not be so funny.

It's all a matter of maturity.

It's okay for young athletes to strug-gle—not knowing what to do or not get-ting everything exactly right. They are trying and learning. So we coach them and patiently guide them toward matu-rity. Then we celebrate their success as later they play with skill as a team.

TODAY'S READING
Ephesians 4:1–16

From him the whole body . . . grows and builds itself up in love.

Ephesians 4:16

Something similar happens in the life of those who follow Jesus. Paul pointed out that the church needs people who will "be patient, bearing with one another in love" (EPH. 4:2). And we need a variety of "coaches" (pastors, teachers, spiritual men-tors) to help us all move toward "unity in the faith" as we strive to "become mature" (V. 13).

The goal as we listen to preaching and teaching and enjoy life together in the church is to grow up to maturity in Christ (V. 15). Each of us is on this journey, and we can encourage each other on the road to maturity in Jesus. ❧

DAVE BRANON

Lord, help me to strive for maturity. Thank You for equipping the church
with men and women who can help me grow in my faith.
Show me who I can encourage today.

There's joy in the journey as we walk alongside each other.

Leaning into the Light

One day I received a bouquet of pink tulips. Their heads bobbed on thick stems as I settled them into a vase, which I placed at the center of our kitchen table. The next day, I noticed that the flowers were facing a different direction. The blossoms that once faced upward were now leaning to the side, opening and reaching toward sunlight that streamed in through a nearby window.

In one sense, we all were made to be like those flowers. God has called us to turn to the light of His love. Peter writes of the wonder of being called "out of darkness into [God's] wonderful light" (1 PETER 2:9). Before we come to know God, we live in the shadows of sin and death, which keep us separated from Him (EPH. 2:1–7). However, because of God's mercy and love, He made a way for us to escape spiritual darkness through the death and resurrection of His Son (COL. 1:13–14).

Jesus is the Light of the world, and everyone who trusts Him for the forgiveness of sin will receive eternal life. Only as we turn to Him will we increasingly reflect His goodness and truth (EPH. 5:8–9).

May we never forget to lean into the Light. ❂

JENNIFER BENSON SCHULDT

Joyful, joyful we adore You, God of glory, Lord of love;
hearts unfold like flowers before You, opening to the sun above.
HENRY VAN DYKE

Salvation from sin means moving from spiritual darkness to God's light.

Lurking Lions

When I was young, my dad would "scare" us by hiding in the bush and growling like a lion. Even though we lived in rural Ghana in the 1960s, it was almost impossible that a lion lurked nearby. My brother and I would laugh and seek out the source of the noise, thrilled that playtime with Dad had arrived.

One day a young friend came for a visit. As we played, we heard the familiar growl. Our friend screamed and ran. My brother and I knew the sound of my father's voice—any "danger" was merely a phantom lion—but a funny thing happened. We ran with her. My dad felt terrible that our friend had been frightened, and my brother and I learned not to be influenced by the panicked reaction of others.

TODAY'S READING
Numbers 14:1–9

The LORD is with us. Do not be afraid of them.

Numbers 14:9

Caleb and Joshua stand out as men unfazed by the panic of others. As Israel was poised to enter the Promised Land, Moses commissioned 12 scouts to spy out the region. They all saw a beautiful territory, but 10 focused on the obstacles and discouraged the entire nation (NUM. 13:27–33). In the process, they started a panic (14:1–4). Only Caleb and Joshua accurately assessed the situation (VV. 6–9). They knew the history of their Father and trusted Him to bring them success.

Some "lions" pose a genuine threat. Others are phantoms. Regardless, as followers of Jesus our confidence is in the One whose voice and deeds we know and trust. ❂   TIM GUSTAFSON

Lord, we face many fears today. Help us distinguish between real danger and empty threats, and help us trust You with all of it. May we live not in fear, but in faith.

The wicked flee though no one pursues,
but the righteous are as bold as a lion. PROVERBS 28:1

Written on Our Hearts

I n my neighborhood, religious inscriptions abound—on plaques, walls, doorposts, commercial vehicles, and even as registered names of businesses. *By the Grace of God* reads an inscription on a mini-bus; *God's Divine Favor Bookshop* adorns a business signboard. The other day I couldn't help smiling at this one on a Mercedes Benz: *Keep Off—Angels on Guard!*

But religious inscriptions, whether on wall plaques, jewelry, or T-shirts, are not a reliable indicator of a person's love for God. It's not the words on the outside that count but the truth we carry on the inside that reveals our desire to be changed by God.

TODAY'S READING
Deuteronomy 6:1–12

These commandments that I give you today are to be on your hearts.

Deuteronomy 6:6

I recall a program sponsored by a local ministry that distributed cards with Bible verses written on both sides that helped people memorize God's Word. Such a practice is in keeping with the instructions Moses gave the Israelites when he told them to write the commandments of God "on the doorframes of your houses and on your gates" (DEUT. 6:9). We are to treasure God's Word in our hearts (V. 6), to impress it on our children, and to talk about it "when [we] walk along the road, when [we] lie down and when [we] get up" (V. 7).

May our faith be real and our commitment true, so we can love the Lord our God with all our heart, soul, and strength (V. 5). 🌱

LAWRENCE DARMANI

Father, may Your words be more than nice sayings to us.
May they be written on our hearts so that we will love You and others.

When God's Word is hidden in our heart, His ways will become our ways.

For His Time

When South African pastor Andrew Murray was visiting England in 1895, he began to suffer pain from a previous back injury. While he was recuperating, his hostess told him of a woman who was in great trouble and wanted to know if he had any counsel for her. Murray said, "Give her this paper which I have been writing for my own [encouragement]. It may be that she will find it helpful." This is what Murray wrote:

TODAY'S READING
James 1:2–4

My times are in your hands.
Psalm 31:15

"In time of trouble say:

First—God brought me here. It is by His will I am in this strait place. In that I will rest.
Next—He will keep me in His love and give me grace in this trial to behave as His child.
Then—He will make the trial a blessing, teaching me lessons He intends me to learn, and working in me the grace He means to bestow.
Last—In His good time He can bring me out again—how and when He knows.
I am here—by God's appointment, in His keeping, under His training, for His time."

We want the instant solution, the quick fix, but some things cannot be disposed of so readily; they can only be accepted. God will keep us by His love. By His grace, we can rest in Him. ❧

DAVID ROPER

Dear Lord, it's hard to endure times of illness and suffering.
Comfort me and help me to trust You.

When God permits suffering, He also provides comfort.

Forward to God

n the days before telephones, email, and mobile phones, the telegram was usually the fastest means of communication. But only important news was sent by telegram, and such news was usually bad. Hence the saying, "The telegram boy always brings bad news."

It was wartime in ancient Israel when Hezekiah was king of Judah. Sennacherib, king of Assyria, had invaded and captured the cities of Judah. He then sent a letter to Hezekiah, a bad-news "telegram" urging his surrender. Hezekiah described the moment as "a day of distress and rebuke and disgrace" (2 KINGS 19:3).

> **TODAY'S READING**
> **2 Kings 19:9–20**
>
> **Give ear, LORD, and hear; open your eyes, LORD, and see.** 2 Kings 19:16

With taunts and scoffs, Sennacherib boasted of his past military campaigns, belittling the God of Israel and threatening mayhem (VV. 11–13). In that dreadful moment, King Hezekiah did an unusual thing with the bad-news letter: "He went up to the temple of the LORD and spread it out before the LORD" (V. 14). Then he prayed earnestly, acknowledging the power of God over their gloomy situation (VV. 15–19). God intervened in a powerful way (VV. 35–36).

Bad news can reach us at any time. In those moments, Hezekiah's action is a good example to follow. Spread out the news before the Lord in prayer and hear His reassurance: "I have heard your prayer" (V. 20). 🌱

LAWRENCE DARMANI

Heavenly Father, when people attack us, we tend to react defensively.
Teach us to turn to You instead of taking matters into our own hands.
We trust You and love You. Defend us today.

Prayer is the child's helpless cry to the Father's attentive ear.

The Power of God's Music

The Sound of Music, one of the most successful musical films ever produced, was released as a motion picture in 1965. It won many accolades, including five Academy Awards, as it captured the hearts and voices of people around the world. More than half a century later, people still attend special showings of the film where viewers come dressed as their favorite character and sing along during the performance.

TODAY'S READING
Colossians 3:12–17

Let the message of Christ dwell among you richly . . . with all wisdom through psalms, hymns, and songs from the Spirit. Colossians 3:16

Music is deeply rooted in our souls. And for followers of Jesus, it is a powerful means of encouraging each other along the journey of faith. Paul urged the believers in Colosse, "Let Christ's teaching live in your hearts, making you rich in the true wisdom. Teach and help one another along the right road with your psalms and hymns and Christian songs, singing God's praises with joyful hearts" (COL. 3:16 PHILLIPS).

Singing together to the Lord embeds the message of His love in our minds and souls. It is a powerful ministry of teaching and encouragement that we share together. Whether our hearts cry out, "Create in me a pure heart, O God" (PS. 51:10), or joyfully shout, "And he will reign forever and ever" (REV. 11:15), the power of music that exalts God lifts our spirits and grants us peace.

Let us sing to the Lord today. 🌱   *DAVID MCCASLAND*

Thank You, Lord, for Your gift of music.
We sing Your praise together and learn more of Your love and power.
What is your favorite hymn or worship song?

Music washes from the soul the dust of everyday life.

With Respect

The citizens of Israel were having some trouble with the government. It was the late 500s BC, and the Jewish people were eager to complete their temple that had been destroyed in 586 BC by Babylon. However, the governor of their region was not sure they should be doing that, so he sent a note to King Darius (EZRA 5:6–17).

In the letter, the governor says he found the Jews working on the temple and asks the king if they had permission to do so. The letter also records the Jews' respectful response that they had indeed been given permission by an earlier king (Cyrus) to rebuild. When the king checked out their story, he found it to be true: King Cyrus had said they could build the temple. So Darius not only gave them permission to rebuild, but he also paid for it! (SEE 6:1–12). After the Jews finished building the temple, they "celebrated with joy" because they knew God had "[changed] the attitude of the king" (6:22).

> **TODAY'S READING**
> **Ezra 5:6–17**
>
> **If it pleases the king, let a search be made in the royal archives of Babylon to see if King Cyrus . . . issue[d] a decree.**
>
> Ezra 5:17

When we see a situation that needs to be addressed, we honor God when we plead our case in a respectful way, trust that He is in control of every situation, and express gratitude for the outcome. 🌱

DAVE BRANON

Lord, help us to respond respectfully to situations around us.
We need Your wisdom for this.
May we always honor, trust, and praise You.

Respect for authority brings glory to God.

Abundant Supply

We have a hummingbird feeder in the garden, and we love to see the little birds come and drink from its sugary water. Recently, however, we went on a short trip and forgot to replenish its contents. When we came back, it was completely dry. *Poor birds!* I thought. *Because of my forgetfulness, they haven't had any nourishment.* Then I was reminded that I am not the one who feeds them: God is.

Sometimes we may feel that all of the demands of life have depleted our strength and there is no one to replenish it. But others don't feed our souls: God does.

> **TODAY'S READING**
> **Psalm 36:5–12**
>
> **You give them drink from your river of delights.**
>
> Psalm 36:8

In Psalm 36 we read about God's lovingkindness. It describes those who put their trust in Him and are abundantly satisfied. God gives them water from His "river of delights" (v. 8). He is the fountain of life!

We can go to God every day for the supply of our needs. As Charles Spurgeon wrote, "The springs of my faith and all my graces; the springs of my life and all my pleasures; the springs of my activity and all its right doings; the springs of my hope, and all its heavenly anticipations, all lie in thee, my Lord."

Let us be filled with His abundant supply. His fountain will never run dry. ●   *KEILA OCHOA*

Lord, I come to You with the confidence that You will fill me
with what I need.

God's love is abundant.

Please Come In

Jenny's house is situated on a little country lane, which is often used in rush hour by drivers who want to avoid the nearby main road and traffic lights. A few weeks ago workmen arrived to repair the badly damaged road surface, bringing with them large barriers and "No Entry" signs. "I was really worried at first," said Jenny, "thinking that I would be unable to get my car out until the road work was finished. But then I went to look at the signs more closely and realized that they said 'No Entry: Access for Residents Only.' No detours or barriers for me. I had the right to go in and out whenever I liked because I lived there. I felt very special!"

> **TODAY'S READING**
> **Hebrews 10:19–25**
>
> **Let us draw near to God . . . with the full assurance that faith brings.**
>
> Hebrews 10:22

In the Old Testament, access to God in the tabernacle and the temple was strictly limited. Only the high priest could go in through the curtain and offer sacrifices in the Most Holy Place, and then only once a year (LEV. 16:2–20; HEB. 9:25–26). But at the very moment Jesus died, the curtain of the temple was torn in two from top to bottom, showing that the barrier between man and God was destroyed forever (MARK 15:38).

Because of Christ's sacrifice for our sins, all those who love and follow Him can come into His presence at any time. He has given us the right of access. ✤

MARION STROUD

Lord, thank You for paying such a price to enable me to have unrestricted entry into Your presence!

Access to God's throne is always open.

Strangers and Foreigners

parked my bicycle, fingering my map of Cambridge for reassurance. Directions not being my strength, I knew I could easily get lost in this maze of roads bursting with historic buildings.

Life should have felt idyllic, for I had just married my Englishman and moved to the UK. But I felt adrift. When I kept my mouth closed I blended in, but when I spoke I immediately felt branded as an American tourist. I didn't yet know what my role was, and I quickly realized that blending two stubborn people into one shared life was harder than I had anticipated.

TODAY'S READING
Hebrews 11:8–16

He was looking forward to the city with foundations, whose architect and builder is God.

Hebrews 11:10

I related to Abraham, who left all that he knew as he obeyed the Lord's call to live as a foreigner and stranger in a new land (GEN. 12:1). He pressed through the cultural challenges while keeping faith in God, and 2,000 years later the writer to the Hebrews named him a hero (11:9). Like the other men and women listed in this chapter, Abraham lived by faith, longing for things promised, hoping and waiting for his heavenly home.

Perhaps you've always lived in the same town, but as Christ-followers we're all foreigners and strangers on this earth. By faith we press forward, knowing that God will lead and guide us, and by faith we believe He will never leave nor abandon us. By faith we long for home. ✒️   AMY BOUCHER PYE

Father God, I want to live by faith, believing Your promises and knowing that You welcome me into Your kingdom. Enlarge my faith, I pray.

God calls us to live by faith, believing that He will fulfill His promises.

Don't Quit!

I n 1952 **Florence Chadwick** attempted to swim 26 miles from the coast of California to Catalina Island. After 15 hours, a heavy fog began to block her view, she became disoriented, and she gave up. To her chagrin, Chadwick learned that she had quit just 1 mile short of her destination.

Two months later Chadwick tried a second time to swim to Catalina Island from the coast. Again a thick fog settled in, but this time she reached her destination, becoming the first woman to swim the Catalina Channel. Chadwick said she kept an image of the shoreline in her mind even when she couldn't see it.

When the problems of life cloud our vision, we have an opportunity to learn to see our goal with the eyes of faith. The New Testament letter to the Hebrews urges us to "run with perseverance the race marked out for us, fixing our eyes on Jesus, the pioneer and perfecter of faith" (12:1–2). When we feel like quitting, this is our signal to remember not only what Jesus suffered for us but what He now helps us to endure—until the day we see Him face to face. ❧

> TODAY'S READING
> **Hebrews 12:1–11**
>
> **Let us run with perseverance the race marked out for us, fixing our eyes on Jesus, the pioneer and perfecter of faith.**
>
> Hebrews 12:1–2

DENNIS FISHER

Dear Father, sometimes the challenges of life seem insurmountable.
Help me to fix my eyes on You and trust You.
I'm thankful You are bringing about Your good purposes in me.

We can finish strong when we focus on Christ.

Abigail's Reminder

David and 400 of his warriors thundered through the countryside in search of Nabal, a prosperous brute who had harshly refused to lend them help. David would have murdered him if he hadn't first encountered Abigail, Nabal's wife. She had packed up enough food to feed an army and traveled out to meet the troops, hoping to head off disaster. She respectfully reminded David that guilt would haunt him if he followed through with his vengeful plan (1 SAM. 25:31). David realized she was right and blessed her for her good judgment.

TODAY'S READING
1 Samuel 25:14–33

> **When the LORD takes pleasure in anyone's way, he causes their enemies to make peace with them.**
>
> Proverbs 16:7

David's anger was legitimate—he had protected Nabal's shepherds in the wilderness (VV.14–17) and had been repaid evil for good. However, his anger was leading him into sin. David's first instinct was to sink his sword into Nabal, even though he knew God did not approve of murder and revenge (EX. 20:13; LEV. 19:18).

When we've been offended, it's good to compare our instincts with God's intent for human behavior. We may be inclined to strike at people verbally, isolate ourselves, or escape through any number of ways. However, choosing a gracious response will help us avoid regret, and most important it will please God. When our desire is to honor God in our relationships, He is able to make even our enemies to be at peace with us (SEE PROV. 16:7). 🌀

JENNIFER BENSON SCHULDT

Lord, thank You for holding back Your anger and having mercy on me. Help me to walk in step with Your Spirit so that my actions please You in every situation.

We can endure life's wrongs because we know that God will make things right.

Self-Care

After my husband underwent heart surgery, I spent an anxious night by his hospital bed. Mid-morning, I remembered a scheduled haircut. "I'll have to cancel," I said, raking my fingers distractedly through my straggly hair.

"Mom, just wash your face and go to your appointment," my daughter said.

"No, no," I insisted. "It doesn't matter. I need to be *here*."

"I'll stay," Rosie said. "Self-care, Mom. . . . *Self-care*. You're of more use to Dad if you take care of yourself."

Moses was wearing himself out serving alone as judge over the Israelites.

TODAY'S READING
Exodus 18:14–24

Come with me by yourselves to a quiet place and get some rest. Mark 6:31

Jethro cautioned his son-in-law Moses: "You will only wear [yourself] out. The work is too heavy . . . you cannot handle it alone" (EX. 18:18). He then explained ways that Moses could delegate his work and share his heavy load with others.

Though it may seem paradoxical for the Christian, self-care is essential for a healthy life (MATT. 22:37–39; EPH. 5:29–30). Yes, we must love God first and love others as well, but we also need to get adequate rest to renew our body and spirit. Sometimes self-care means stepping away and graciously allowing others to help us with our burdens.

Jesus often slipped away to rest and pray (MARK 6:30–32). When we follow His example, we will be more effective in our relationships and better able to give care to others. ❧

CINDY HESS KASPER

Dear Lord, refresh my spirit today. Help me to bring balance to my life as I juggle my responsibilities. Thank You for Your love and care.

Don't try to do everything—take time to refresh your body and spirit.

My Personal Space

An industrial design graduate from a Singapore university was challenged in a workshop to come up with a novel solution to a common problem using only ordinary objects. She created a vest to protect one's personal space from being invaded while traveling in the crush of crowded public trains and buses. The vest was covered with long, flexible plastic spikes normally used to keep birds and cats away from plants.

TODAY'S READING
Luke 8:40–48

> We do not have a high priest who is unable to empathize with our weaknesses.
>
> Hebrews 4:15

Jesus knew what it was like to lose His personal space in the commotion of crowds desperate to see and touch Him. A woman who had suffered from constant bleeding for 12 years and could find no cure touched the fringe of His robe. Immediately, her bleeding stopped (LUKE 8:43–44).

Jesus's question, "Who touched me?" (V. 45) isn't as strange as it sounds. He felt power come out of Him (V. 46). That touch was different from those who merely happened to accidentally touch Him.

While we must admit that we do sometimes wish to keep our personal space and privacy, the only way we help a world of hurting people is to let them get close enough to be touched by the encouragement, comfort, and grace of Christ in us. ❧ *C. P. HIA*

Lord Jesus, I want to be near You and know You
so that when I'm in contact with others they can see You through me.

A Christian's life is the window through which others can see Jesus.

Looking Up

An article in the *Surgical Technology International* journal says that looking down at a smart phone with your head bent forward is the equivalent of having a 60-pound weight on your neck. When we consider that millions of people around the world spend an average of 2-4 hours daily reading and texting, the resulting damage to neck and spine becomes a growing health concern.

> **TODAY'S READING**
> **Psalm 146:1–10**
>
> **The LORD lifts up those who are bowed down.**
> Psalm 146:8

It is also easy to become spiritually bowed down by the burdens of life. How often we find ourselves discouraged by the problems we face and the needs of those we love. The psalmist understood this weight of concern yet saw hope as he wrote about "the Maker of heaven and earth, the sea, and everything in them—[who] remains faithful forever. He upholds the cause of the oppressed and gives food to the hungry. The LORD sets prisoners free, the LORD gives sight to the blind, the LORD lifts up those who are bowed down, the LORD loves the righteous" (PS. 146:6–8).

When we consider God's care, His great power, and His loving heart, we can begin to look up and praise Him. We can walk through each day knowing that "the LORD reigns forever . . . for all generations" (V. 10).

He lifts us up when we are bowed down. Praise the Lord! ✿

DAVID MCCASLAND

O Lord, lift our eyes to see Your power and love today
so we can raise our heads and our hearts in grateful praise to You.

Faith in God's goodness puts a song in your heart.

Deeply Loved

Years ago I had an office in Boston that looked out on the Granary Burying Ground where many prominent American heroes are buried. There one can find the gravestones for John Hancock and Samuel Adams, two signers of the Declaration of Independence, and just a few feet beyond that is Paul Revere's marker.

But no one really knows *where* in this burial ground each body is buried because the stones have been moved many times—sometimes to make the grounds more picturesque and other times so lawn mowers could fit between them. And while the Granary features approximately 2,300 markers, closer to 5,000 people are buried there! Even in death, it seems, some people are not fully known.

> **TODAY'S READING**
> **Matthew 6:25–34**
>
> **Your heavenly Father feeds [the birds of the air]. Are you not much more valuable than they?** Matthew 6:26

There may be times when we feel as if we are like those unmarked residents of the Granary, unknown and unseen. Loneliness can make us feel unseen by others—and maybe even by God. But we must remind ourselves that even though we may feel forgotten by our Creator God, we are not. God not only made us in His image (GEN. 1:26-27), but He also values each of us individually and sent His Son to save us (JOHN 3:16).

Even in our darkest hours, we can rest in the knowledge we are never alone, for our loving God is with us. ❧ *RANDY KILGORE*

Thank You, Lord, that You never leave me alone and that You know all about me. Make me aware of Your presence so I may share that comfort with others who are feeling alone too.

We are important because God loves us.

Positive Repetition

A **journalist had a** quirky habit of not using blue pens. So when his colleague asked him if he needed anything from the store, he asked for some pens. "But not blue pens," he said. "I don't want blue pens. I don't like blue. Blue is too heavy. So please purchase 12 ballpoint pens for me—anything but blue!" The next day his colleague passed him the pens—and they were all blue. When asked to explain, he said, "You kept saying 'blue, blue.' That's the word that left the deepest impression!" The journalist's use of repetition had an effect, but not the one he desired.

Moses, the lawgiver of Israel, also used repetition in his requests to his people. More than 30 times he urged his people to remain true to the law of their God. Yet the result was the opposite of what he asked for. He told them that obedience would lead them to life and prosperity, but disobedience would lead to destruction (DEUT. 30:15-18).

When we love God, we want to walk in His ways not because we fear the consequences but because it is our joy to please the One we love. That's a good word to remember. 🌾　　*POH FANG CHIA*

> **TODAY'S READING**
> **Deuteronomy 30:11-20**
>
> **I command you today to love the LORD your God, to walk in obedience to him.**
>
> Deuteronomy 30:16

Dear Lord, as we read Your inspired story,
may Your Spirit be our teacher. Help us to walk the path of obedience
as we hear the voice of Your heart.

Love for God will cause you to live for God.

When to Walk Away

When my father became a Christian in his old age, he fascinated me with his plan for overcoming temptation. Sometimes he just walked away! For example, whenever a disagreement between him and a neighbor began to degenerate into a quarrel, my father just walked away for a time rather than be tempted to advance the quarrel.

TODAY'S READING
Genesis 39:1–12

God is faithful; he will not let you be tempted beyond what you can bear.
1 Corinthians 10:13

One day he met with some friends who ordered *pito* (a locally brewed alcoholic beer). My father had formerly struggled with alcohol and had decided he was better off without it. So he simply stood up, said his goodbyes, and left the gathering of old friends for another day.

In Genesis, we read how Potiphar's wife tempted Joseph. He immediately recognized that giving in would cause him to "sin against God," so he fled (GEN. 39:9–12).

Temptation knocks often at our door. Sometimes it comes from our own desires, other times through the situations and people we encounter. As Paul told the Corinthians, "No temptation has overtaken you except what is common to mankind." But he also wrote, "God is faithful; he will not let you be tempted beyond what you can bear. But when you are tempted, he will also provide a way out so that you can endure it" (1 COR. 10:13).

The "way out" may include removing the objects of temptation or fleeing from them. Our best course of action may be to simply walk away. ❧   *LAWRENCE DARMANI*

Lord, please give me the wisdom and strength to know when to walk away from situations and people that tempt me to do wrong.

Every temptation is an opportunity to flee to God.

Ignore No More

I don't know how these people find me, but I keep getting more and more flyers in the mail from folks asking me to show up at their events so they can teach me about retirement benefits. It started several years ago when I began getting invitations to join an organization that works on behalf of retirees. These reminders all serve to say: "You're getting older. Get ready!"

I have ignored them all along, but soon enough I'm going to have to break down and go to one of their meetings. I really should be taking action on their suggestions.

TODAY'S READING
Philippians 1:27–30

The commands of the LORD are radiant, giving light to the eyes. Psalm 19:8

Sometimes I hear a similar reminder in the wisdom of Scripture. We know that what the passage says is true about us, but we are just not ready to respond. Maybe it's a passage like Romans 14:13 that says, "Let us stop passing judgment on one another." Or the reminder in 2 Corinthians 9:6, which tells us, "Whoever sows generously will also reap generously." Or this reminder in Philippians 1: "Stand firm in the one Spirit, striving together as one for the faith of the gospel without being frightened" (VV. 27–28).

As we read God's Word, we get vital reminders. Let's take these seriously as from the heart of the Father who knows what honors Him and is best for us. 🌱

DAVE BRANON

Thank You, Lord, for Your gentle reminders.
We know that the things You tell us to do in Your Word
are for our good and for Your glory. Help us to step up and do the things
that bring honor to Your name.

Holiness is simply Christ in us fulfilling
the will and commands of the Father.

Surprised by Grace

A woman from Grand Rapids, Michigan, fell asleep on the couch after her husband had gone to bed. An intruder sneaked in through the sliding door, which the couple had forgotten to lock, and crept through the house. He entered the bedroom where the husband was sleeping and picked up the television set. The sleeping man woke up, saw a figure standing there, and whispered, "Honey, come to bed." The burglar panicked, put down the TV, grabbed a stack of money from the dresser, and ran out.

TODAY'S READING
Acts 9:1–19

I became a servant of this gospel by the gift of God's grace. Ephesians 3:7

The thief was in for a big surprise! The money turned out to be a stack of Christian pamphlets with a likeness of a $20 bill on one side and an explanation of the love and forgiveness God offers to people on the other side. Instead of the cash he expected, the intruder got the story of God's love for him.

I wonder what Saul expected when he realized it was Jesus appearing to him on the road to Damascus, since he had been persecuting and even killing Jesus's followers? (ACTS 9:1–9). Saul, later called Paul, must have been surprised by God's grace toward him, which he called "a gift": "I became a servant of this gospel by the gift of God's grace given me through the working of his power" (EPH. 3:7).

Have you been surprised by God's gift of grace in your life as He shows you His love and forgiveness? 🌿 *ANNE CETAS*

Lord, Your grace is amazing to me.
I'm grateful that in spite of my sinfulness,
You offer Your love to me.

Never measure God's unlimited power by your limited expectations.

Full Sun

know better, but I still keep trying. The instructions on the label are clear: "Needs full sun." Our yard has mostly shade. It is not suitable for plants that need full sun. But I like the plant. I like its color, the shape of the leaves, the size, the scent. So I buy it, bring it home, plant it, and take really good care of it. But the plant is not happy at my house. My care and attention are not enough. It needs sunlight, which I cannot provide. I thought I could make up for lack of light by giving the plant some other kind of attention. But it doesn't work that way. Plants need what they need.

TODAY'S READING
Ephesians 5:1–16

Live as children of light. Ephesians 5:8

And so do people. Although we can survive for a while in less-than-ideal conditions, we can't thrive. In addition to our basic physical needs, we also have spiritual needs that can't be met by any substitute.

Scripture says that believers are children of light. This means that we need to live in the full light of God's presence to thrive (PS. 89:15). If we try to live in darkness, we will produce nothing but "fruitless deeds" (SEE EPH. 5:3–4, 11). But if we are living in the light of Jesus, the Light of the world, we will produce the fruit of His light, which is good, faithful, and true. 🌱   *JULIE ACKERMAN LINK*

Dear Lord, thank You for redeeming me and giving me new life.
Help me to live as a child of the Light.

Children of the Light walk in His light.

The Best Is Yet to Come

In our family, March means more than the end of winter. It means that the college basketball extravaganza called "March Madness" has arrived. As avid fans, we watch the tournament and enthusiastically root for our favorite teams. If we tune in early we get a chance to listen to the broadcasters talk about the upcoming game and to enjoy some of the pre-game drills where players shoot practice shots and warm up with teammates.

> **TODAY'S READING**
> **Colossians 3:1–11**
>
> **Set your minds on things above, not on earthly things.**
> Colossians 3:2

Our life on earth is like the pre-game in basketball. Life is interesting and full of promise, but it doesn't compare to what lies ahead. Just think of the pleasure of knowing that even when life is good, the best is yet to come! Or that when we give cheerfully to those in need, it's an investment in heavenly treasure. In times of suffering and sorrow, we can find hope as we reflect on the truth that a pain-free, tearless eternity awaits us. It's no wonder that Paul exhorts: "Set your minds on things above" (COL. 3:2).

The future God has promised us enables us to see all of life in new dimensions. While this may be a great life, the best life is still to come. It is a wonderful privilege to live *here* in the light of *there*. ✿

JOE STOWELL

Let us then be true and faithful, trusting, serving every day;
just one glimpse of Him in glory will the toils of life repay.
When we all get to heaven, what a day of rejoicing that will be!
ELIZA E. HEWITT

Living for the future puts today in perspective.

Stories in a Cabin

The vintage cabin, expertly constructed from hand-hewn logs, was worthy of a magazine cover. But the structure itself was only half the treasure. Inside, family heirlooms clung to the walls, infusing the home with memories. On the table sat a hand-woven egg basket, an ancient biscuit board, and an oil lamp. A weathered pork pie hat perched over the front door. "There's a story behind everything," the proud owner said.

TODAY'S READING
Hebrews 9:11–15

[Christ] went through the greater and more perfect tabernacle that is not made with human hands. Hebrews 9:11

When God gave Moses instructions for constructing the tabernacle, there was a "story" behind everything (EX. 25–27). The tabernacle had only one entrance, just as we have only one way to God (SEE ACTS 4:12). The thick inner curtain separated the people from the Most Holy Place where God's presence dwelt: Our sin separates us from God. Inside the Most Holy Place was the ark of the covenant, which symbolized God's presence. The high priest was a forerunner of the greater Priest to come—Jesus Himself. The blood of the sacrifices foreshadowed Christ's perfect sacrifice: "He entered the Most Holy Place once for all by his own blood, thus obtaining eternal redemption" (HEB. 9:12).

All these things told the story of Christ and the work He would accomplish on our behalf. He did it so that "those who are called may receive the promised eternal inheritance" (V. 15). Jesus invites us to be a part of His story. 🌱   *TIM GUSTAFSON*

What items have special meaning for me and why? What stories do I tell about them? How can they help point people to Jesus?

Jesus took our sin that we might have salvation.

God of My Strength

No one could have mistaken the ancient Babylonian soldiers for gentlemen. They were ruthless, resilient, and vicious, and they attacked other nations the way an eagle overtakes its prey. Not only were they powerful, they were prideful as well. They practically worshiped their own combat abilities. In fact, the Bible says that their "strength [was] their god" (HAB. 1:11).

> **TODAY'S READING**
> **Judges 7:1–8**
>
> **I will strengthen you and help you.**
> Isaiah 41:10

God did not want this kind of self-reliance to infect Israel's forces as they prepared to battle the Midianites. So He told Gideon, Israel's army commander, "You have too many men. I cannot deliver Midian into their hands, or Israel would boast against me, 'My own strength has saved me' " (JUDG. 7:2). As a result, Gideon discharged anyone who was fearful. Twenty-two thousand men hightailed it home, while 10,000 fighters stayed. God continued to downsize the army until only 300 men remained (VV. 3–7).

Having fewer troops meant that Israel was dramatically outnumbered—their enemies, who populated a nearby valley, were as "thick as locusts" (V. 12). Despite this, God gave Gideon's forces victory.

At times, God may allow our resources to dwindle so that we rely on His strength to keep going. Our needs showcase His power, but He is the One who says, "I will strengthen you and help you; I will uphold you with my righteous right hand" (ISA. 41:10). ✿

JENNIFER BENSON SCHULDT

Dear God, I am thankful for Your strength. You carry me when I am weak.
Help me to give You the credit for every victory in life.

God wants us to depend on His strength, not our own.

When the Water Blushed

Why did Jesus come to Earth before the invention of photography and video? Couldn't He have reached more people if everyone could see Him? After all, a picture is worth a thousand words.

"No," says Ravi Zacharias, who asserts that a word can be worth "a thousand pictures." As evidence, he quotes poet Richard Crashaw's magnificent line, "The conscious water saw its Master and blushed." In one simple line, Crashaw captures the essence of Jesus's first miracle (JOHN 2:1-11). Creation itself recognizes Jesus as the Creator. No mere carpenter could turn water to wine.

> TODAY'S READING
> **John 1:1–14**
>
> **In the beginning was the Word.... Through him all things were made.**
> John 1:1, 3

Another time, when Christ calmed a storm with the words, "Quiet! Be still," His stunned disciples asked, "Who is this? Even the wind and the waves obey him!" (MARK 4:39, 41). Later, Jesus told the Pharisees that if the crowd did not praise Him, "the stones will cry out" (LUKE 19:40). Even the rocks know who He is.

John tells us, "The Word became flesh and made his dwelling among us. We have seen His glory" (JOHN 1:14). Out of that eyewitness experience John also wrote, "We proclaim to you the one who existed from the beginning, whom we have heard and seen. . . . He is the Word of life" (1 JOHN 1:1 NLT). Like John, we can use our words to introduce others to Jesus whom wind and water obey. ✒

TIM GUSTAFSON

Jesus, we acknowledge You as the Creator who knows and loves His creation. Yet You wait for us to invite You into every aspect of our lives. Forgive us for those times we keep You at a safe distance. Today we choose to risk knowing You more completely.

The written Word reveals the Living Word.

Follow Me

Health clubs offer many different programs for those who want to lose weight and stay healthy. One fitness center caters only to those who want to lose at least 50 pounds and develop a healthy lifestyle. One member says that she quit her previous fitness club because she felt the slim and fit people were staring at her and judging her out-of-shape body. She now works out 5 days a week and is achieving healthy weight loss in a positive and welcoming environment.

> **TODAY'S READING**
> Mark 2:13–17
>
> **It is not the healthy who need a doctor, but the sick.** Mark 2:17

Two thousand years ago, Jesus came to call the spiritually unfit to follow Him. Levi was one such person. Jesus saw him sitting in his tax collector's booth and said, "Follow me" (MARK 2:14). His words captured Levi's heart, and he followed Jesus. Tax collectors were often greedy and dishonest in their dealings and were considered religiously unclean. When the religious leaders saw Jesus having dinner at Levi's house with other tax collectors, they asked, "Why does he eat with tax collectors and sinners?" (2:16). Jesus replied, "I have not come to call the righteous, but sinners" (2:17).

Jesus came to save sinners, which includes all of us. He loves us, welcomes us into His presence, and calls us to follow Him. As we walk with Him, we grow more and more spiritually fit. 🕊

MARVIN WILLIAMS

Read Acts 9:10-19 and see how one man obeyed God and welcomed someone who was considered spiritually unfit. What were the results? How can you reach out to those who need the Savior? How can you help your church become a more welcoming place for the spiritually unfit?

Jesus's arms of welcome are always open.

The Gallery of God

Psalm 100 is like a work of art that helps us celebrate our unseen God. While the focus of our worship is beyond view, His people make Him known.

Imagine the artist with brush and palette working the colorful words of this psalm onto a canvas. What emerges before our eyes is a world—"all the earth"—shouting for joy to the Lord (V. 1). Joy. Because it is the delight of our God to redeem us from death. "For the joy that was set before Him," Jesus endured the cross (HEB. 12:2 NKJV).

As our eyes move across the canvas we see an all-world choir of countless members singing "with gladness" and "joyful songs" (PS. 100:2). Our heavenly Father's heart is pleased when His people worship Him for who He is and what He has done.

> **TODAY'S READING**
> **Psalm 100**
>
> **The LORD is good and his love endures forever.**
> Psalm 100:5

Then we see images of ourselves, fashioned from dust in the hands of our Creator, and led like sheep into green pasture (V. 3). We, His people, have a loving Shepherd.

Finally, we see God's great and glorious dwelling place—and the gates through which His rescued people enter His unseen presence, while giving Him thanks and praise (V. 4).

What a picture, inspired by our God. Our good, loving, and faithful God. No wonder it will take forever to enjoy His greatness! 🍃

DAVE BRANON

Great God of heaven, thank You for life, for joy, for protection,
and for promising us a future with You forever. Help us to live with
thoughts of Your greatness always on our hearts and minds.

Nothing is more awesome than to know God.

Too Close

grew up in Oklahoma where severe weather is common from early spring through the end of summer. I recall one evening when the sky boiled with dark clouds, the TV weather forecaster warned of an approaching tornado, and the electricity went out. Very quickly, my parents, my sister, and I climbed down the wooden ladder into the storm cellar behind our house where we stayed until the storm passed by.

Today "storm chasing" has become a hobby for many people and a profitable business for others. The goal is to get as close as possible to a tornado without being harmed. Many storm chasers are skilled forecasters with accurate information, but I won't sign up for a tornado tour anytime soon.

In moral and spiritual areas of my life, however, I can foolishly pursue dangerous things God tells me to avoid because of His love for me, all the time believing I won't be harmed. A wiser approach is to read the book of Proverbs, which contains many positive ways to elude these snares of life.

"Trust in the LORD with all your heart and lean not on your own understanding," Solomon wrote. "In all your ways submit to him, and he will make your paths straight" (PROV. 3:5–6).

Our Lord is the master of the adventure of living, and following His wisdom leads us to fullness of life. ❦ *DAVID McCASLAND*

Father, Your wisdom leads us along the path of life.
Help us to follow Your guidance today.

Every temptation is an occasion to trust God.

The Olive Press

I f you visit the village of Capernaum beside the Sea of Galilee, you will find an exhibit of ancient olive presses. Formed from basalt rock, the olive press consists of two parts: a base and a grinding wheel. The base is large, round, and has a trough carved out of it. The olives were placed in this trough, and then the wheel, also made from heavy stone, was rolled over the olives to extract the oil.

TODAY'S READING
Mark 14:32–39

They went to a place called Gethsemane.
Mark 14:32

On the night before His death, Jesus went to the Mount of Olives overlooking the city of Jerusalem. There, in the garden called Gethsemane, He prayed to the Father, knowing what lay ahead of Him.

The word *Gethsemane* means "place of the olive press"— and that perfectly describes those first crushing hours of Christ's suffering on our behalf. There, "in anguish, he prayed . . . and his sweat was like drops of blood falling to the ground" (LUKE 22:44).

Jesus the Son suffered and died to take away "the sin of the world" (JOHN 1:29) and restore our broken relationship with God the Father. "Surely he took up our pain and bore our suffering. . . . He was pierced for our transgressions, he was crushed for our iniquities, the punishment that brought us peace was on him, and by his wounds we are healed" (ISA. 53:4–5).

Our hearts cry out in worship and gratitude. 🌿 *BILL CROWDER*

Father, help me understand what Your Son endured for me.
Help me appreciate the depths of love that would allow my Lord and
Christ to be crushed for my wrongs and my rescue.

*Gone my transgressions, and now I am free—all because Jesus was
wounded for me.* W. G. OVENS

Three-Word Obituary

Before **Stig Kernell** died, he told the local funeral home that he didn't want a traditional obituary. Instead, the Swedish man instructed them to publish only three words noting his passing: "I am dead." When Mr. Kernell died at age 92, that's exactly what appeared. The audacity and simplicity of his unusual death notice captured the attention of newspapers around the world. In a strange twist, the international curiosity about the man with the three-word obituary caused more attention to his death than he intended.

TODAY'S READING
Romans 8:28–39

Christ Jesus who died—more than that, who was raised to life—is at the right hand of God. Romans 8:34

When Jesus was crucified, the Lord's obituary could have read, "He is dead." But after 3 days, it would have been changed to front-page news saying, "He is risen!" Much of the New Testament is devoted to proclaiming and explaining the results of Christ's resurrection. "Christ Jesus who died—more than that, who was raised to life—is at the right hand of God and is also interceding for us. Who shall separate us from the love of Christ? . . . We are more than conquerors through him who loved us" (ROM. 8:34–37).

The three-word obituary of Jesus, "He is dead," has been transformed into an eternal anthem of praise to our Savior. He is risen! He is risen indeed! 🌱   *DAVID MCCASLAND*

Lord, we rejoice in Your great victory over sin and death
through Your resurrection. May we live in light of it every day.

Jesus sacrificed His life for ours.

Never Forsaken

Russian writer **Fyodor Dostoyevsky** said, "The degree of civilization in a society can be judged by entering its prisons." With that in mind, I read an online article describing "The Top 8 Deadliest Prisons in the World." In one of these prisons *every* prisoner is held in solitary confinement.

We are intended to live and relate in relationships and community, not in isolation. This is what makes solitary confinement such a harsh punishment.

TODAY'S READING
Psalm 22:1–10

Jesus cried out in a loud voice, . . . "My God, my God, why have you forsaken me?"

Matthew 27:46

Isolation is the agony Christ suffered when His eternal relationship with the Father was broken on the cross. We hear this in His cry captured in Matthew 27:46: "About three in the afternoon Jesus cried out in a loud voice, *'Eli, Eli, lema sabachthani?'* (which means, 'My God, my God, why have you forsaken me?')." As He suffered and died under the burden of our sins, Christ was suddenly alone, forsaken, isolated, cut off from His relationship with the Father. Yet His suffering in isolation secured for us the promise of the Father: "Never will I leave you; never will I forsake you" (HEB. 13:5).

Christ endured the agony and abandonment of the cross for us so that we would never be alone or abandoned by our God. Ever. ✸

BILL CROWDER

Father, thank You for making it possible for me to be Your child.
I will be eternally grateful for the price Jesus paid to make that
relationship possible. Thank You for the promise that You will
never abandon me.

Those who know Jesus are never alone.

It's Okay to Ask

I t's **perfectly natural** for fear and doubt to creep into our minds at times. "What if heaven isn't real after all?" "Is Jesus the only way to God?" "Will it matter in the end how I lived my life?" Questions like these should not be given quick or trite responses.

John the Baptist, whom Jesus called the greatest of the prophets (LUKE 7:28), had questions shortly before his execution (V. 19). He wanted to know for sure that Jesus was the Messiah and that his own ministry had therefore been valid.

Jesus's response is a comforting model for us to use. Instead of discounting the doubt or criticizing John, Jesus pointed to the miracles He was doing. As eyewitnesses, John's disciples could return with vivid assurances for their mentor.

> **TODAY'S READING**
> **Luke 7:18–28**
>
> **Go and tell John the things you have seen and heard: that the blind see, the lame walk, . . . the poor have the gospel preached to them.**
> Luke 7:22

But He did more—He used words and phrases (V. 22) drawn from Isaiah's prophecies of the coming Messiah (ISA. 35:4-6; 61:1), which were certain to be familiar to John.

Then, turning to the crowd, Jesus praised John (LUKE 7:24-28), removing any doubt that He was offended by John's need for reassurance after all he had seen (MATT. 3:13-17).

Questioning and doubting, both understandable human responses, are opportunities to remind, reassure, and comfort those who are shaken by uncertainty. 🌱   *RANDY KILGORE*

> When my poor soul in doubt is cast
> And darkness hides the Savior's face,
> His love and truth still hold me fast
> For He will keep me by His grace. *D. DEHAAN*

Christ's resurrection is the guarantee of our own.

Surprised!

Michelangelo Merisi da Caravaggio (1571–1610), an Italian artist, was known for his fiery temperament and unconventional technique. He used ordinary working people as models for his saints and was able to make viewers of his paintings feel they were a part of the scene. The *Supper at Emmaus* shows an innkeeper standing while Jesus and two of His followers are seated at a table when they recognize Him as the risen Lord (LUKE 24:31). One disciple is pushing himself to a standing position while the other's arms are outstretched and his hands open in astonishment.

> TODAY'S READING
> **Luke 24:13–35**
>
> **Then their eyes were opened and they recognized him.** Luke 24:31

Luke, who records these events in his gospel, tells us that the two men immediately returned to Jerusalem where they found the eleven disciples and others assembled together and saying, "'It is true! The Lord has risen and has appeared to Simon.' Then the two told what had happened on the way, and how Jesus was recognized by them when he broke the bread" (VV. 33–35).

Oswald Chambers said, "Jesus rarely comes where we expect Him; He appears where we least expect Him, and always in the most illogical connections. The only way a worker can keep true to God is by being ready for the Lord's surprise visits."

Whatever road we are on today, may we be ready for Jesus to make Himself known to us in new and surprising ways. 🌑

DAVID MCCASLAND

Lord Jesus, open our eyes to see You, the risen Christ,
alongside us and at work in the circumstances of our lives today.

To find the Lord Jesus Christ we must be willing to seek Him.

The Blacksmith and the King

I n 1878, when Scotsman Alexander Mackay arrived in what is now Uganda to serve as a missionary, he first set up a blacksmith forge among a tribe ruled by King Mutesa. Villagers gathered around this stranger who worked with his hands, puzzled because everyone "knew" that work was for women. At that time, men in Uganda never worked with their hands. They raided other villages to capture slaves, selling them to outsiders. Yet here was this foreign man at work forging farming tools.

TODAY'S READING
Exodus 31:1–11

Whatever you do, work at it with all your heart, as working for the Lord, not for human masters.

Colossians 3:23

Mackay's work ethic and life resulted in relationships with the villagers and gained him an audience with the king. Mackay challenged King Mutesa to end the slave trade, and he did.

In Scripture, we read of Bezalel and Oholiab, who were chosen and gifted by God to work with their hands designing the tent of meeting and all its furnishings for worship (EX. 31:1-11). Like Mackay, they honored and served God with their talent and labor.

We tend to categorize our work as either church work or secular. In truth, there is no distinction. God designs each of us in ways that make our contributions to the kingdom unique and meaningful. Even when we have little choice in where or how we work, God calls us to know Him more fully—and He will show us how to serve Him—right now. 🌐   *RANDY KILGORE*

Father, grant me an awareness of my place in Your work.
Help me to see You at work in the people and places where I
spend my time.

God will show us how to serve Him—wherever we are.

Wisdom and Grace

On April 4, 1968, American civil rights leader Dr. Martin Luther King Jr., was assassinated, leaving millions angry and disillusioned. In Indianapolis, a largely African-American crowd had gathered to hear Robert F. Kennedy speak. Many had not yet heard of Dr. King's death, so Kennedy had to share the tragic news. He appealed for calm by acknowledging not only their pain but his own abiding grief over the murder of his brother, President John F. Kennedy.

Kennedy then quoted a variation of an ancient poem by Aeschylus (526–456 BC):

Even in our sleep, pain which cannot forget falls drop by drop upon the heart until, in our own despair, against our will, comes wisdom through the awful grace of God.

"Wisdom through the awful grace of God" is a remarkable statement. It means that God's grace fills us with awe and gives us the opportunity to grow in wisdom during life's most difficult moments.

James wrote, "If any of you lacks wisdom, you should ask of God, who gives generously to all without finding fault, and it will be given to you" (JAMES 1:5). James says that this wisdom is grown in the soil of hardship (VV. 2–4), for there we not only learn from the wisdom of God, we rest in the grace of God. ✹ *BILL CROWDER*

> TODAY'S READING
> **James 1:1–8**
>
> **If any of you lacks wisdom, you should ask of God, who gives generously to all without finding fault.** James 1:5

Father, in the face of life's sometimes awful circumstances, may we find Your grace to be a source of awe and wonder. Instruct us in our trials, and carry us in Your arms when we are overwhelmed.

The darkness of trials only makes God's grace shine brighter.

Don't Walk Away

I n 1986, John Piper nearly quit as minister of a large church. At that time he admitted in his journal: "I am so discouraged. I am so blank. I feel like there are opponents on every hand." But Piper didn't walk away, and God used him to lead a thriving ministry that would eventually reach far beyond his church.

Although *success* is a word easily misunderstood, we might call John Piper successful. But what if his ministry had never flourished?

> **TODAY'S READING**
> Jeremiah 1:4–9
>
> **Before you were born I set you apart.** Jeremiah 1:5

God gave the prophet Jeremiah a direct call. "Before I formed you in the womb I knew you," God said. "Before you were born I set you apart" (JER. 1:5). God encouraged him not to fear his enemies, "for I am with you and will rescue you" (V. 8).

Jeremiah later lamented his commission with ironic language for a man with a prenatal calling. "Alas, my mother, that you gave me birth; a man with whom the whole land strives and contends!" (15:10).

God did protect Jeremiah, but his ministry never thrived. His people never repented. He saw them slaughtered, enslaved, and scattered. Yet despite a lifetime of discouragement and rejection, he never walked away. He knew that God didn't call him to success but to faithfulness. He trusted the God who called him. Jeremiah's resilient compassion shows us the heart of the Father, who yearns for everyone to turn to Him. 🌿 *TIM GUSTAFSON*

Do you sense a call from God? Where in your calling have you encountered discouragement? How do you define success, and how do you react to it when you experience it?

Beware of giving up too soon. Our emotions are not reliable guides. JOHN PIPER

The Hollywood Hills Cross

One of the most recognizable images in the US is the "HOLLYWOOD" sign in Southern California. People from all over the globe come to "Tinseltown" to gaze at cement footprints of stars and perhaps catch a glimpse of celebrities who might pass by. It's hard for these visitors to miss the sign anchored in the foothills nearby.

TODAY'S READING
1 Corinthians 1:18–31

May I never boast except in the cross of our Lord Jesus Christ. Galatians 6:14

Less well known in the Hollywood hills is another easily recognized symbol —one with eternal significance. Known as the Hollywood Pilgrimage Memorial Monument, this 32-foot cross looks out over the city. The cross was placed there in memory of Christine Wetherill Stevenson, a wealthy heiress who in the 1920s established the Pilgrimage Theatre (now the John Anson Ford Theatre). The site served as the venue for *The Pilgrimage Play*, a drama about Christ.

The two icons showcase an interesting contrast. Movies good and bad will come and go. Their entertainment value, artistic contributions, and relevance are temporary at best.

The cross, however, reminds us of a drama eternal in scope. The work of Christ is a story of the loving God who pursues us and invites us to accept His offer of complete forgiveness. The high drama of Jesus's death is rooted in history. His resurrection conquered death and has an eternal impact for all of us. The cross will never lose its meaning and power. ❧ *DENNIS FISHER*

Thank You, Father, for the eternal significance of the cross.
Help us to understand and appreciate the love that caused Your Son
to embrace His cross for our sakes.

To know the meaning of the cross, you must know the One who died there.

His Plans or Ours?

When my husband was 18 years old, he started a car-cleaning business. He rented a garage, hired helpers, and created advertising brochures. The business prospered. His intention was to sell it and use the proceeds to pay for college, so he was thrilled when a buyer expressed interest. After some negotiations, it seemed that the transaction would happen. But at the last minute, the deal collapsed. It wouldn't be until several months later that his plan to sell the business would succeed.

> TODAY'S READING
> **1 Chronicles 17:1–20**
>
> **"Who am I, LORD God…that you have brought me this far?"** 1 Chronicles 17:16

It's normal to be disappointed when God's timing and design for our lives do not match our expectations. When David wanted to build the Lord's temple, he had the right motives, the leadership ability, and the resources. Yet God said he could not undertake the project because he had killed too many people in battle (1 CHRON. 22:8).

David could have shaken his fist at the sky in anger. He could have pouted or plowed ahead with his own plans. But he humbly said, "Who am I, LORD God . . . that you have brought me this far?" (17:16). David went on to praise God and affirm his devotion to Him. He valued his relationship with God more than his ambition.

What is more important—achieving our hopes and dreams, or our love for God? ✿

JENNIFER BENSON SCHULDT

Dear heavenly Father, I commit all of my plans to You.
Thank You for bringing me this far. You mean more to me than
anything in the world.

True satisfaction is found in yielding ourselves to the will of God.

In Transition

People post obituary notices on billboards and concrete block walls in Ghana regularly. Headlines such as *Gone Too Soon, Celebration of Life,* and *What a Shock!* announce the passing away of loved ones and the approaching funerals. One I read—*In Transition*—points to life beyond the grave.

When a close relative or friend dies, we sorrow as Mary and Martha did for their brother Lazarus (JOHN 11:17–27). We miss the departed so much that our hearts break and we weep, as Jesus wept at the passing of His friend (V. 35).

TODAY'S READING
John 11:17–27

We will be with the Lord forever.

1 Thessalonians 4:17

Yet, it was at this sorrowful moment Jesus made a delightful statement on life after death: "I am the resurrection and the life. The one who believes in me will live, even though they die; and whoever lives by believing in me will never die" (V. 25).

On the basis of this we give departed believers only a temporary farewell. For they "will be with the Lord forever," Paul emphasizes (1 THESS. 4:17). Of course, farewells are painful, but we can rest assured that they are in the Lord's safe hands.

In Transition suggests that we are only changing from one situation to another. Though life on earth ends for us, we will continue to live forever and better in the next life where Jesus is. "Therefore encourage one another with these words" (V. 18). 🌱

LAWRENCE DARMANI

It is because of You, Jesus, that we have hope and are sure of a forever life. We're grateful.

Because of Jesus, we can live forever.

Take Heart!

I like to watch birds at play, so years ago I built a small sanctuary in our backyard to attract them. For several months I enjoyed the sight of my feathered friends feeding and flitting about—until a Cooper's Hawk made my bird refuge his private hunting reserve.

Such is life: Just about the time we settle down to take our ease, something or someone comes along to unsettle our nests. Why, we ask, must so much of life be a vale of tears?

I've heard many answers to that old question, but lately I'm satisfied with just one: "All the discipline of the world is to make [us] children, that God may be revealed to [us]" (George MacDonald, *Life Essential*). When we become like children, we begin trusting, resting solely in the love of our Father in heaven, seeking to know Him and to be like Him.

> TODAY'S READING
> **2 Corinthians 4:8–18**
>
> **In this world you will have trouble. But take heart! I have overcome the world.** John 16:33

Cares and sorrow may follow us all the days of our lives, but "we do not lose heart. . . . For our light and momentary troubles are achieving for us an eternal glory that far outweighs them all. So we fix our eyes not on what is seen, but on what is unseen, since what is seen is temporary, but what is unseen is eternal" (2 COR. 4:16–18).

Can we not rejoice, then, with such an end in view? ❧

DAVID ROPER

Lord, we do rejoice even in our struggles because we are rejoicing in who You are and Your good purposes for us. You are powerful, loving, in control, and eternal. We trust You and love You.

Heaven's delights will far outweigh earth's difficulties.

Sweet Reminders

When the tomb of Egyptian King Tutankhamen was discovered in 1922, it was filled with things ancient Egyptians thought were needed in the afterlife. Among items such as golden shrines, jewelry, clothing, furniture, and weapons was a pot filled with honey—still edible after 3,200 years!

> TODAY'S READING
> Exodus 3:7–17
>
> **Gracious words are a honeycomb, sweet to the soul and healing to the bones.** Proverbs 16:24

Today we think of honey primarily as a sweetener, but in the ancient world it had many other uses. Honey is one of the only foods known to have all the nutrients needed to sustain life, so it was eaten for nutrition. In addition, honey has medicinal value. It is one of the oldest known wound dressings because it has properties that prevent infection.

When God rescued the children of Israel from Egyptian captivity, He promised to lead them to a "land flowing with milk and honey" (EX. 3:8, 17), a metaphor for abundance. When their journey was prolonged due to sin, God fed them bread (manna) that tasted like honey (16:31). The Israelites grumbled about having to eat the same food for so long, but it's likely that God was kindly reminding them of what they would enjoy in the Promised Land.

God still uses honey to remind us that His ways and words are sweeter than the honeycomb (PS. 19:10). So then the words we speak should also be like the honey we eat—both sweet and healing. 🌱

JULIE ACKERMAN LINK

Read these verses about the use of words: Proverbs 12:18; Proverbs 13:3; Ephesians 4:29; Colossians 3:8. Which truths might God want you to put into practice in your life today?

Spend time counting your blessings, not airing your complaints.

Who Am I Working For?

Henry worked 70 hours a week. He loved his job and brought home a sizeable paycheck to provide good things for his family. He always had plans to slow down but he never did. One evening he came home with great news—he had been promoted to the highest position in his company. But no one was home. Over the years, his children had grown up and moved out, his wife had found a career of her own, and now the house was empty. There was no one to share the good news with.

Solomon talked about the need to keep a balance in life with our work. He wrote, "Fools fold their hands and ruin themselves" (ECCL. 4:5). We don't want to go to the extreme of being lazy, but neither do we want to fall into the trap of being a workaholic. "Better one handful with tranquillity than two handfuls with toil and chasing after the wind" (V. 6). In other words, it is better to have less and enjoy it more. Sacrificing relationships at the altar of success is unwise. Achievement is fleeting, while relationships are what make our life meaningful, rewarding, and enjoyable (VV. 7–12).

We can learn to work to live and not live to work by choosing to apportion our time wisely. The Lord can give us this wisdom as we seek Him and trust Him to be our Provider. ✿

POH FANG CHIA

> TODAY'S READING
> **Ecclesiastes 4:4–16**
>
> "For whom am I toiling," he asked, "and why am I depriving myself of enjoyment?"
>
> Ecclesiastes 4:8

Lord, show me if my priorities are skewed and where I need to make changes. Thank You for the gift of family and friends.

To spend time wisely, invest it in eternity.

Resisting the Trap

A Venus flytrap can digest an insect in about 10 days. The process begins when an unsuspecting bug smells nectar on the leaves that form the trap. When the insect investigates, it crawls into the jaws of the plant. The leaves clamp shut within half a second and digestive juices dissolve the bug.

This meat-eating plant reminds me of the way sin can devour us if we are lured into it. Sin is hungry for us. Genesis 4:7 says, "If you do not do what is right, sin is crouching at your door; it desires to have you." God spoke these words to Cain just before he killed his brother Abel.

> TODAY'S READING
> **Genesis 4:1–8**
>
> **Sin is crouching at your door; it desires to have you, but you must rule over it.** Genesis 4:7

Sin may try to entice us by tempting us with a new experience, convincing us that living right doesn't matter, or appealing to our physical senses. However, there is a way for us to rule over sin instead of letting it consume our lives. The Bible says, "Walk by the Spirit, and you will not gratify the desires of the flesh" (GAL. 5:16). When we face temptation, we don't face it alone. We have supernatural assistance. Relying on God's Spirit supplies the power to live for Him and others. ❧

JENNIFER BENSON SCHULDT

Dear God, at times I let down my guard and indulge in sin.
Please help me to listen to Your warnings and obey Your Word.
Protect me from my own impulses and conform me to Your image.
Thank You for Your work in me.

We fall into temptation when we don't flee from it.

Heart Check

When commuting into Chicago on the train, I always followed the "unwritten codes of conduct"—such as, no conversations with people sitting next to you if you don't know them. That was tough on a guy like me who has never met a stranger. I love talking to new people! Although I kept the code of silence, I realized that you can still learn something about people based on the section of the newspaper they read. So I'd watch to see what they turned to first: The business section? Sports? Politics? Current events? Their choices revealed their interests.

TODAY'S READING
Luke 12:22-34

Where your treasure is, there your heart will be also. Luke 12:34

Our choices are always revealing. Of course, God doesn't need to wait to see our choices in order for Him to know what's in our hearts. But the things that occupy our time and attention are telling. As Jesus said, "Where your treasure is, there your heart will be also" (LUKE 12:34). Regardless of what we want Him to think of us, the true condition of our heart becomes clear based on how we use our time, our money, and our talents. When we invest these resources in the things He cares about, then it reveals that our hearts are in tune with His.

God's heart is with the needs of people and the advancement of His kingdom. What do your choices tell Him and others about where your heart is? 🌿

JOE STOWELL

Lord, I want my heart to be in tune with Yours.
Forgive me for giving it to things of far less value, and teach me the joy
of investing my time in opportunities to serve You. Thank You.

Where is your treasure?

This Is the Day

n 1940, **Dr. Virginia Connally**, age 27, braved opposition and criticism to become the first female physician in Abilene, Texas. A few months before her 100th birthday in 2012, the Texas Medical Association presented her with its Distinguished Service Award, Texas's highest physician honor. Between those two landmark events, Dr. Connally has enthusiastically embraced a passion for spreading the gospel around the world through her many medical mission trips while living a life of service to God and to others—one day at a time.

TODAY'S READING
Psalm 118:19–29

This is the day the LORD has made; we will rejoice and be glad in it. Psalm 118:24 NKJV

Dr. Connally's pastor, Phil Christopher, said, "Every day for her is a gift." He recalled a letter in which she wrote, "Every tour, trip, effort, I wonder if this will be my last and ultimate? Only God knows. And this is enough."

The psalmist wrote, "This is the day the LORD has made; we will rejoice and be glad in it" (PS. 118:24 NKJV). So often we focus on the disappointments of yesterday or the uncertainties of tomorrow and miss God's matchless gift to us: Today!

Dr. Connally said of her journey with Christ, "As you live a life of faith, you're not looking for the results. I was just doing the things that God planted in my life and heart."

God made today. Let's celebrate it and make the most of every opportunity to serve others in His name. 🌱 *DAVID MCCASLAND*

Lord, thank You for today. May I embrace it as Your gift,
celebrate Your faithfulness, and live this day fully for You.

Welcome each day as a gift from God.

Great Sacrifice

W.T. Stead, an innovative English journalist at the turn of the 20th century, was known for writing about controversial social issues. Two of the articles he published addressed the danger of ships operating with an insufficient ratio of lifeboats to passengers. Ironically, Stead was aboard the *Titanic* when it struck an iceberg in the North Atlantic on April 15, 1912. According to one report, after helping women and children into lifeboats, Stead sacrificed his own life by giving up his life vest and a place in the lifeboats so others could be rescued.

> TODAY'S READING
> Hebrews 10:5–18
>
> **The Lord Jesus Christ...gave himself for our sins to rescue us.**
> Galatians 1:3–4

There is something very stirring about self-sacrifice. No greater example of that can be found than in Christ Himself. The writer of Hebrews says, "This Man, after He had offered one sacrifice for sins forever, sat down at the right hand of God. . . . For by one offering He has perfected forever those who are being sanctified" (HEB. 10:12, 14 NKJV). In his letter to the Galatians, Paul opened with words describing this great sacrifice: "The Lord Jesus Christ . . . gave himself for our sins to rescue us from the present evil age" (GAL. 1:3–4).

Jesus's offering of Himself on our behalf is the measure of His love for us. That willing sacrifice continues to rescue men and women and offer assurance of eternity with Him. ❧ *BILL CROWDER*

God of love and grace, words can never capture the wonder of the sacrifice that Christ offered on our behalf. May our love respond to You with faith and worship—for Your Son who was slain is worthy of our praise.

Jesus laid down His life to show His love for us.

Unconventional Tactics

I n 1980, a woman hopped on a subway during the Boston Marathon. No big deal, except for one small detail. She was supposed to be *running* the marathon! Later, witnesses saw her jump into the race less than a mile from the finish line. She finished well ahead of all the other female runners, and oddly, she wasn't winded or even sweating much. For a brief time she looked like the winner.

TODAY'S READING
2 Chronicles 20:1–13

We do not know what to do, but our eyes are on you. 2 Chronicles 20:12

In a conflict long ago, a people who were losing a battle found a more honorable way to win. When messengers told King Jehoshaphat, "A vast army is coming against you from Edom," he was terrified (2 CHRON. 20:2–3). But instead of turning to typical military tactics, Jehoshaphat turned to God. He acknowledged God's supremacy and admitted his own fear and confusion. "We do not know what to do, but our eyes are on you" (V. 12). Then the king chose singers to lead the army into battle. Instead of a war cry, they sang of God's love (V. 21). The result was startling. Their enemies turned on each other (VV. 22–24). In the end, "The kingdom of Jehoshaphat was at peace, for his God had given him rest on every side" (V. 30).

Life can ambush us with overwhelming challenges. Yet our fear and uncertainties give us the opportunity to turn to our all-powerful God. He specializes in the unconventional. 🌿

TIM GUSTAFSON

Lord, You are not the source of confusion or fear,
but of strength and peace. We exchange our panicky plans for Your
amazing answers. Encourage us as we wait for You.

Our God is never predictable, but He is unfailingly reliable.

Chameleon Crawl

When we think of the chameleon, we probably think of its ability to change color according to its surroundings. But this lizard has another interesting characteristic. On several occasions I've watched a chameleon walk along a pathway and wondered how it ever reached its destination. Reluctantly, the chameleon stretches out one leg, seems to change its mind, attempts again, and then carefully plants a hesitant foot, as if afraid the ground will collapse under it. That was why I couldn't help laughing when I heard someone say, "Do not be a

TODAY'S READING
Acts 2:42–47

Every day they continued to meet together. Acts 2:46

chameleon church member who says, 'Let me go to church today; no, let me go next week; no, let me wait for a while!'"

"The house of the LORD" at Jerusalem was King David's place of worship, and he was far from being a "chameleon" worshiper. Rather, he rejoiced with those who said, "Let us go to the house of the LORD" (PS. 122:1). The same was true for believers in the early church. "They devoted themselves to the apostles' teaching and to fellowship, to the breaking of bread and to prayer. . . . Every day they continued to meet together in the temple courts" (ACTS 2:42, 46).

What a joy it is to join with others in worship and fellowship! Praying and worshiping together, studying the Scriptures together, and caring for one another are essential for our spiritual growth and unity as believers. 🕊 *LAWRENCE DARMANI*

Before our Father's throne we pour our ardent prayers; our fears,
our hopes, our aims are one, our comforts and our cares.
JOHN FAWCETT

Worshiping together brings strength and joy.

The Apple of His Eye

A friend's baby was suffering seizures, so they sped to the hospital in an ambulance, the mother's heart racing as she prayed for her daughter. Her fierce love for this child hit her afresh as she held her tiny fingers, recalling too how much more the Lord loves us and how we are "the apple of His eye."

TODAY'S READING
Zechariah 2

> **Whoever touches you touches the apple of his eye.**
>
> Zechariah 2:8

The prophet Zechariah employs this phrase in his word to God's people who had returned to Jerusalem after their captivity in Babylon. He calls them to repent, to rebuild the temple, and to renew their hearts of love for the true God. For the Lord loves His people greatly; they are the apple of His eye.

Hebrew scholars suggest this phrase from Zechariah 2 denotes one's reflection in the pupil of another's eye, with the word "apple" emerging because it's a common spherical object. So with eyes being precious and fragile, they need protecting, and that's how the Lord wants to love and protect His people— by holding them close to His heart.

The Lord who dwells in our midst pours out His love on us—even, amazingly, far more than a loving mother who does all she can for her ailing child. We are the apple of His eye, His beloved. 🌾

AMY BOUCHER PYE

Father God, You love us so much that You gave us Your only Son to die that we might live. May we receive Your love this day and live in it.

A parent's love for a child reflects our Father's love for us.

The God Who Paints

Nezahualcoyotl (1402-1472) may have had a difficult name to pronounce, but his name is full of significance. It means "Hungry Coyote," and this man's writings show a spiritual hunger. As a poet and ruler in Mexico before the arrival of the Europeans, he wrote, "Truly the gods, which I worship, are idols of stone that do not speak nor feel. . . . Some very powerful, hidden and unknown god is the creator of the entire universe. He is the only one that can console me in my affliction and help me in such anguish as my heart feels; I want him to be my helper and protection."

> **TODAY'S READING**
> **Psalm 42**
>
> **My soul thirsts for God, for the living God.** Psalm 42:2

We cannot know if Nezahualcoyotl found the Giver of life. But during his reign he built a pyramid to the "God who paints things with beauty," and he banned human sacrifices in his city.

The writers of Psalm 42 cried out, "My soul thirsts for God, for the living God" (V. 2). Every human being desires the true God, just as "the deer pants for streams of water" (V. 1).

Today there are many Hungry Coyotes who know that the idols of fame, money, and relationships can't fill the void in their souls. The Living God has revealed Himself through Jesus, the only One who gives us meaning and fulfillment. This is good news for those who are hungry for the God who paints things with beauty. ❧

KEILA OCHOA

Lord, You are the One my soul needs. Only You can bring meaning and fulfillment to my life. You are the One my heart cries out for. I put my hope in You.

Beneath all of our longings is a deep desire for God.

God's Way

We really needed to hear from God. Having been asked to foster two young children as an emergency measure just for 3 months, a decision had to be made about their future. With three older children of our own, becoming foster parents to preschoolers didn't seem to fit with our life plan and having our family almost double in size had been hard work. Our book of daily readings by the veteran missionary Amy Carmichael directed us to some unfamiliar verses in Numbers 7.

> TODAY'S READING
> **Numbers 7:1–9**
>
> **They were to carry on their shoulders the holy things, for which they were responsible.**
>
> Numbers 7:9

"I wonder how the Kohathites felt?" Amy wrote. "All the other priests had ox-carts to carry their parts of the tabernacle through the desert. But the sons of Kohath had to trudge along the rocky tracks and through the burning sand, with the 'holy things for which they were responsible' on their shoulders. Did they ever grumble inwardly, feeling that the other priests had an easier task? Perhaps! But God knows that some things are too precious to be carried on ox-carts and then He asks us to carry them on our shoulders."

My husband and I knew this was our answer. We had often thought of sponsoring a child from an undeveloped country, but we hadn't done so. That would have been easier, much like the ox-cart. Now we had two needy children in our own home to carry "on our shoulders" because they were so precious to Him.

God has different plans for each of us. We might feel that others have an easier assignment, or a more glamorous role to play. But if our loving Father has handpicked us for our task, who are we to whisper, "I can't do this"? ❧   *MARION STROUD*

God uses ordinary people to carry out His extraordinary plans.

Jesus Wept

was engrossed in a book when a friend bent over to see what I was reading. Almost immediately, she recoiled and looked at me aghast. "What a gloomy title!" she said. I was reading "The Glass Coffin" in *Grimm's Fairy Tales,* and the word *coffin* disturbed her. Most of us don't like to be reminded of our mortality. But the reality is that out of 1,000 people, 1,000 people will die.

Death always elicits a deep emotional response. It was at the funeral of one of His dear friends that Jesus displayed strong emotions. When He saw Mary, whose brother had recently died, "he was deeply moved in spirit and troubled" (JOHN 11:33). Another translation says, "a deep anger welled up within him" (NLT).

Jesus was troubled—even angry—but at what? Possibly, He was indignant at sin and its consequences. God didn't make a

> **TODAY'S READING**
> **John 11:1–4, 38–44**
>
> **The sting of death is sin.... But thanks be to God! He gives us the victory through our Lord Jesus Christ.**
>
> 1 Corinthians 15:56–57

world filled with sickness, suffering, and death. But sin entered the world and marred God's beautiful plan.

The Lord comes alongside us in our grief, weeping with us in our sorrow (V. 35). But more than that, Christ defeated sin and death by dying in our place and rising from the dead (1 COR. 15:56–57).

Jesus promises, "The one who believes in me will live, even though they die" (JOHN 11:25). As believers we enjoy fellowship with our Savior now, and we look forward to an eternity with Him where there will be no more tears, pain, sickness, or death. ❧

POH FANG CHIA

Christ's empty tomb guarantees our victory over death.

The Spirit Delivers

Until recently, many towns in rural Ireland didn't use house numbers or postal codes. So if there were three Patrick Murphys in town, the newest resident with that name would not get his mail until it was first delivered to the other two Patrick Murphys who had lived there longer. "My neighbors would get it first," said Patrick Murphy (the newest resident). "They'd have a good read, and they'd go, 'No, it's probably not us.' " To end all this mail-delivery confusion, the Irish government recently instituted its first postal-code system which will ensure the proper delivery of the mail.

Sometimes when we pray we feel like we need help delivering to God what is on our heart. We may not know the right words to say or how to express our deep longings. The apostle Paul says in Romans 8 that the Holy Spirit helps us and intercedes for us by taking our unspeakable

> TODAY'S READING
> **Romans 8:19–27**
>
> **The Spirit helps us in our weakness. We do not know what we ought to pray for, but the Spirit himself intercedes for us through wordless groans.** Romans 8:26

"groanings" and presenting them to the Father. "We do not know what we ought to pray for, but the Spirit himself intercedes for us through wordless groans" (v. 26). The Spirit always prays according to God's will, and the Father knows the mind of the Spirit.

Be encouraged that God hears us when we pray and He knows our deepest needs. ❧

MARVIN WILLIAMS

Thank You, Father, for giving me Your Spirit to help me when I pray.
Thank You for hearing my prayers and for loving me.

When you can't put your prayers into words, God hears your heart.

God's Enduring Word

At the beginning of World War II, aerial bombings flattened much of Warsaw, Poland. Cement blocks, ruptured plumbing, and shards of glass lay strewn across the great city. In the downtown area, however, most of one damaged building still stubbornly stood. It was the Polish headquarters for the British and Foreign Bible Society. Still legible on a surviving wall were these words: "Heaven and earth will pass away, but my words will never pass away" (MATT. 24:35).

TODAY'S READING
Psalm 119:89–96

Heaven and earth will pass away, but my words will never pass away.
Matthew 24:35

Jesus made that statement to encourage His disciples when they asked Him about the "end of the age" (V. 3). But His words also give us courage in the midst of our embattled situation today. Standing in the rubble of our shattered dreams, we can still find confidence in God's indestructible character, sovereignty, and promises.

The psalmist wrote: "Your word, LORD, is eternal; it stands firm in the heavens" (PS. 119:89). But it is more than the word of the Lord; it is His very character. That is why the psalmist could also say, "Your faithfulness continues through all generations" (V. 90).

As we face devastating experiences, we can define them either in terms of despair or of hope. Because God will not abandon us to our circumstances, we can confidently choose hope. His enduring Word assures us of His unfailing love. *DENNIS FISHER*

Thank You, Lord, for the gift of Your Word. Thank You for its truth,
its timelessness, and the guidance You give us by that Word.
Help us believe and trust everything You say.

We can trust God's unchanging Word.

Relief for the Troubled

One of my favorite scenes in literature occurs when a feisty aunt confronts an evil stepfather over the abuse of her nephew, David Copperfield. This scene takes place in Charles Dickens's novel named after the main character.

When David Copperfield shows up at his aunt's house, his stepfather is not far behind. Aunt Betsy Trotwood is not pleased to see the malicious Mr. Murdstone. She recounts a list of offenses and does not let him slither out of his responsibility for each act of cruelty. Her

> TODAY'S READING
> **2 Thessalonians 1:3–12**
>
> **[God will] give relief to you who are troubled.**
>
> 2 Thessalonians 1:7

charges are so forceful and truthful that Mr. Murdstone—a normally aggressive person—finally leaves without a word. Through the strength and goodness of Aunt Betsy's character, David finally receives justice.

There is Someone else who is strong and good, and who will one day right the wrongs in our world. When Jesus returns, He will come down from heaven with a group of powerful angels. He will "give relief to you who are troubled," and He will not ignore those who have created problems for His children (2 THESS. 1:6–7). Until that day, Jesus wants us to stand firm and have courage. No matter what we endure on earth, we are safe for eternity. ❧

JENNIFER BENSON SCHULDT

Dear God, please protect us and give us wisdom through Your Holy Spirit. Help us to be just and fair in everything we do so that we are good representatives for You.

One day God will right every wrong.

Greater than the Mess

A **major theme of** the Old Testament book of 2 Samuel could easily be "Life is a mess!" It has all the elements of a blockbuster TV miniseries. As David sought to establish his rule as king of Israel, he faced military challenges, political intrigue, and betrayal by friends and family members. And David himself was certainly not without guilt as his relationship with Bathsheba clearly showed (CHS. 11–12).

> **TODAY'S READING**
> **2 Samuel 22:26–37**
>
> **You, LORD, are my lamp; the LORD turns my darkness into light.** 2 Samuel 22:29

Yet near the end of 2 Samuel we find David's song of praise to God for His mercy, love, and deliverance. "You, LORD, are my lamp; the LORD turns my darkness into light" (22:29).

In many of his difficulties, David turned to the Lord. "With your help I can advance against a troop [run through a barricade]; with my God I can scale a wall" (V. 30).

Perhaps we identify with David's struggles because he, like us, was far from perfect. Yet he knew that God was greater than the most chaotic parts of his life.

With David we can say, "As for God, his way is perfect: the Lord's word is flawless; he shields all who take refuge in him" (V. 31). And that includes us!

Life is messy, but God is greater than the mess. ❧

DAVID MCCASLAND

Lord, we cannot read about the failures and difficulties of others
without being reminded of our own. We bring them all to You,
seeking forgiveness and Your power for a fresh start.

It's not too late to make a fresh start with God.

Meant to Be Understood

I enjoy visiting museums such as the National Gallery in London and the State Tretyakov Gallery in Moscow. While most of the art is breathtaking, some of it confuses me. I look at seemingly random splashes of color on canvas and realize I have no idea what I am seeing—even though the artist is a master at his craft.

TODAY'S READING
Romans 15:1–6

Sometimes we can feel the same way about the Scriptures. We wonder, *Is it even possible to understand them? Where do I start?* Perhaps Paul's words can give us some help: "Everything that was written in the past was written to teach us, so that through the endurance taught in the Scriptures and the encouragement they provide we might have hope" (ROM. 15:4).

> **Everything that was written in the past was written to teach us.** Romans 15:4

God has given us the Scriptures for our instruction and encouragement. He has also given us His Spirit to help us to know His mind. Jesus said that He was sending the Spirit to "guide [us] into all the truth" (JOHN 16:13). Paul affirms this in 1 Corinthians 2:12, saying, "What we have received is not the spirit of the world, but the Spirit who is from God, so that we may understand what God has freely given us."

With the help of the Spirit, we can approach the Bible with confidence, knowing that through its pages God wants us to know Him and His ways. 🍂

BILL CROWDER

Father, thank You for giving us Your Son to bring us into relationship with You. Thank You for giving us the Scriptures so that we can know You better. And thank You for giving us Your Spirit to guide us into the truth of what we need to know about You and Your great love.

Read the Bible to get to know its Author.

Storms on the Horizon

Our son, Josh, is a commercial salmon fisherman in Kodiak, Alaska. Some time ago he sent me a photograph he took of a tiny vessel a few hundred yards ahead of his boat moving through a narrow pass. Ominous storm clouds loom on the horizon. But a rainbow, the sign of God's providence and loving care, stretches from one side of the pass to the other, encircling the little boat.

TODAY'S READING
Matthew 8:23–28

The photograph reflects our earthly voyage: We sail into an uncertain future, but we are surrounded by the faithfulness of God!

> **What kind of man is this? Even the winds and the waves obey him!**
>
> Matthew 8:27

Jesus's disciples were surrounded by a storm, and He used the experience to teach them about the power and faithfulness of God (MATT. 8:23–27). We seek answers for the uncertainties of life. We watch the future growing closer and wonder what will happen to us there. Puritan poet John Keble captured this in one of his poems in which he watched the future as it drew near. But as he watched he was "waiting to see what God will do."

Whether young or old we all face uncertain futures. Heaven answers: God's love and goodness encircle us no matter what awaits us. We wait and see what God will do! 🌿 *DAVID ROPER*

What do you need to trust God with today?

We sail into the uncertain future surrounded by the faithfulness of God!

An Amazing Love

The final major historic acts of the Old Testament are described in Ezra and Nehemiah as God allowed the people of Israel to return from exile and resettle in Jerusalem. The City of David was repopulated with Hebrew families, a new temple was built, and the wall was repaired.

And that brings us to Malachi. This prophet, who was most likely a contemporary of Nehemiah, brings the written portion of the Old Testament to a close. Notice the first thing he said to the people of Israel: "'I have loved you,' says the LORD." And look at their response: "How have you loved us?" (1:2).

> **TODAY'S READING**
> **Malachi 1:1–10; 4:5–6**
>
> **"I have loved you,"**
> **says the LORD.**
> Malachi 1:2

Amazing, isn't it? Their history had proven God's faithfulness, yet after hundreds of years in which God continually provided for His chosen people in both miraculous and mundane ways, they wondered how He had shown His love. As the book continues, Malachi reminds the people of their unfaithfulness (SEE VV. 6–8). They had a long historical pattern of God's provision for them, followed by their disobedience, followed by God's discipline.

It was time, soon, for a new way. The prophet hints at it in Malachi 4:5–6. The Messiah would be coming. There was hope ahead for a Savior who would show us His love and pay the penalty once and for all for our sin.

That Messiah indeed has come! Malachi's hope is now a reality in Jesus. 🌱   *DAVE BRANON*

Thank You, Father, for the story You told in Your Word of the people of Israel. It reminds us to be grateful for what You have done for us. Thank You for loving us so much You sent us Jesus.

Those who put their trust in Jesus will have eternal life.

The Fragrance of Christ

Which of the five senses brings back your memories most sharply? For me it is definitely the sense of smell. A certain kind of sun oil takes me instantly to a French beach. The smell of chicken mash brings back childhood visits to my grandmother. A hint of pine says "Christmas," and a certain kind of aftershave reminds me of my son's teenage years.

Paul reminded the Corinthians that they were the aroma of Christ: "For we are to God the pleasing aroma of Christ" (2 COR. 2:15). He may have been referring to

TODAY'S READING
2 Corinthians 2:14–17

We are to God the pleasing aroma of Christ. 2 Corinthians 2:15

Roman victory parades. The Romans made sure everyone knew they had been victorious by burning incense on altars throughout the city. For the victors, the aroma was pleasing; for the prisoners it meant certain slavery or death. So as believers, we are victorious soldiers. And when the gospel of Christ is preached, it is a pleasing fragrance to God.

As the aroma of Christ, what perfumes do Christians bring with them as they walk into a room? It's not something that can be bought in a bottle or a jar. When we spend a lot of time with someone, we begin to think and act like that person. Spending time with Jesus will help us spread a pleasing fragrance to those around us. 🌿

MARION STROUD

Lord, please shape my thoughts and actions so people may sense
that I have been with You.

When we walk with God, people will notice.

Doing Right in God's Sight

"**C**owboy builders**"** is a term many British homeowners use for tradespeople who do shoddy construction work. The term is bandied about with fear or regret, often because of bad experiences.

No doubt there were rogue carpenters, masons, and stonecutters in biblical times, but tucked away in the story of King Joash repairing the temple is a line about the complete honesty of those who oversaw and did the work (2 KINGS 12:15).

TODAY'S READING
2 Kings 12:1–15

Joash did what was right . . . all the years Jehoiada the priest instructed him. 2 Kings 12:2

However, King Joash "did what was right in the eyes of the LORD" (V. 2) only when Jehoiada the priest instructed him. As we see in 2 Chronicles 24:17–27, after Jehoiada died Joash turned from the Lord and was persuaded to worship other gods.

The mixed legacy of a king who enjoyed a season of fruitfulness only while under the spiritual counsel of a godly priest makes me stop and think. What will our legacies be? Will we continue to grow and develop in our faith throughout our lives, producing good fruit? Or will we become distracted by the things of this world and turn to modern-day idols—such as comfort, materialism, and self-promotion? ✺

AMY BOUCHER PYE

Go deeper: How does this passage compare with Jesus's letter
to the church at Ephesus in Revelation 2?
How do these passages apply to your life?

Living well and doing right require perseverance and spiritual direction.

The Restoration Business

Adam Minter is in the junk business. The son of a junkyard owner, he circles the globe researching junk. In his book *Junkyard Planet*, he chronicles the multibillion-dollar industry of waste recycling. He notes that entrepreneurs around the world devote themselves to locating discarded materials such as copper wire, dirty rags, and plastics and repurposing them to make something new and useful.

TODAY'S READING
Philippians 3:1–8

> **I have suffered the loss of all things, and count them as rubbish, that I may gain Christ.**
>
> Philippians 3:8 NKJV

After the apostle Paul turned his life over to the Savior, he realized his own achievements and abilities amounted to little more than trash. But Jesus transformed it all into something new and useful. Paul said, "Whatever were gains to me I now consider loss for the sake of Christ. What is more, I consider everything a loss because of the surpassing worth of knowing Christ Jesus my Lord, for whose sake I have lost all things. I consider them garbage, that I may gain Christ" (PHIL. 3:7–8). Having been trained in Jewish religious law, he had been an angry and violent man toward those who followed Christ (ACTS 9:1–2). After being transformed by Christ, the tangled wreckage of his angry past was transformed into the love of Christ for others (2 COR. 5:14–17).

If you feel that your life is just an accumulation of junk, remember that God has always been in the restoration business. When we turn our lives over to Him, He makes us into something new and useful for Him and others. 🌱　　　DENNIS FISHER

Are you wondering how to become a new person? Romans 3:23 and 6:23 tell us that when we admit we are sinners and ask for God's forgiveness, He gives us the free gift of eternal life that was paid for by the death and resurrection of Jesus. Talk to him about your need.

Christ makes all things new.

Shine Through

A **little girl wondered** what a saint might be. One day her mother took her to a great cathedral to see the gorgeous stained-glass windows with scenes from the Bible. When she saw the beauty of it all she cried out loud, "Now I know what saints are. They are people who let the light shine through!"

Some of us might think that saints are people of the past who lived perfect lives and did Jesus-like miracles. But when a translation of Scripture uses the word *saint*, it is actually referring to anyone who belongs to God through faith in

> **TODAY'S READING**
> **Matthew 5:13–16**
>
> **Let your light shine before others.**
>
> Matthew 5:16

Christ. In other words, saints are people like us who have the high calling of serving God while reflecting our relationship with Him wherever we are and in whatever we do. That is why the apostle Paul prayed that the eyes and understanding of his readers would be opened to think of themselves as the treasured inheritance of Christ and saints of God (EPH. 1:18).

So what then do we see in the mirror? No halos or stained glass. But if we are fulfilling our calling, we will look like people who, maybe even without realizing it, are letting the rich colors of the love, joy, peace, patience, kindness, gentleness, faithfulness, and self-control of God shine through. ❧   *KEILA OCHOA*

Lord, You are the light of the world.
Thank You for wanting to shine that light in our lives.
Cleanse me today so that I may let Your light shine through.

Saints are people through whom God's light shines.

Just What I Need

As I stood in the back of the room at a senior citizens' center in Palmer, Alaska, listening to my daughter's high school choir sing "It Is Well with My Soul," I wondered why she, the choir director, had chosen that song. It had been played at her sister Melissa's funeral, and Lisa knew it was always tough for me to hear it without having an emotional response.

My musings were interrupted when a man sidled up next to me and said, "This is just what I need to hear." I introduced myself and then asked why he needed this song. "I lost my son Cameron last week in a motorcycle accident," he said.

Wow! I was so focused on myself that I never considered the needs of others, and God was busy using that song exactly where He wanted it to be used. I took my new friend Mac, who worked at the center, aside, and we talked about God's care in this toughest time in his life.

All around us are people in need, and sometimes we have to set aside our own feelings and agendas to help them. One way we can do that is to remember how God has comforted us in our trials and troubles "so that we can comfort those in any trouble with the comfort we ourselves receive from God" (2 COR. 1:4). How easy it is to be engrossed in our own concerns and forget that someone right next to us might need a prayer, a word of comfort, a hug, or gift of mercy in Jesus's name. ✪ *DAVE BRANON*

> TODAY'S READING
> **2 Corinthians 1:3–7**
>
> **We can comfort those in any trouble with the comfort we ourselves receive from God.**
>
> 2 Corinthians 1:4

Lord, help me to see where help is needed, and help me to provide that help. Thank You for the comfort You give; help me to share it.

Comfort received should be comfort shared.

Out of the Ruins

In the **Jewish Quarter** of Jerusalem you'll find Tiferet Yisrael Synagogue. Built in the 19th century, the synagogue was dynamited by commandos during the 1948 Arab-Israeli War.

For years the site lay in ruins. Then, in 2014, rebuilding began. As city officials set a piece of rubble as the cornerstone, one of them quoted from Lamentations: "Restore us to yourself, LORD, that we may return; renew our days as of old" (5:21).

Lamentations is Jeremiah's funeral song for Jerusalem. With graphic imagery the prophet describes the impact of war on his city. Verse 21 is his heartfelt prayer for God to intervene. Still, the prophet wonders if that is even possible. He con-cludes his anguished song with this fearful caveat: "unless you have utterly rejected us and are angry with us beyond measure" (v. 22). Decades later, God did answer that prayer as the exiles returned to Jerusalem.

> TODAY'S READING
> **Lamentations 5:8–22**
>
> **He has granted us new life to rebuild the house of our God and repair its ruins.** Ezra 9:9

Our lives too may seem to be in ruins. Troubles of our own making and conflicts we can't avoid may leave us devastated. But we have a Father who understands. Gently, patiently, He clears away the rubble, repurposes it, and builds something better. It takes time, but we can always trust Him. He special-izes in rebuilding projects. ❧

TIM GUSTAFSON

Lord, You have reclaimed us, and You are remaking us.
Thank You for Your love and Your care despite our self-centered and
destructive ways. Thank You for true forgiveness and unity in You.

God will one day restore all the beauty lost before.

Prayer Marathon

Do you struggle to maintain a consistent prayer life? Many of us do. We know that prayer is important, but it can also be downright difficult. We have moments of deep communion with God and then we have times when it feels like we're just going through the motions. Why do we struggle so in our prayers?

The life of faith is a marathon. The ups, the downs, and the plateaus in our prayer life are a reflection of this race. And just as in a marathon we need to keep running, so we keep praying. The point is: Don't give up!

TODAY'S READING
1 Thessalonians 5:16–28

Pray continually.
1 Thessalonians 5:17

That is God's encouragement too. The apostle Paul said, "pray continually" (1 THESS. 5:17), "keep on praying" (ROM. 12:12 NLT), and "devote yourselves to prayer" (COL. 4:2). All of these statements carry the idea of remaining steadfast and continuing in the work of prayer.

And because God, our heavenly Father, is a personal being, we can develop a time of close communion with Him, just as we do with our close human relationships. A. W. Tozer writes that as we learn to pray, our prayer life can grow "from the initial most casual brush to the fullest, most intimate communion of which the human soul is capable." And that's what we really want—deep communication with God. It happens when we keep praying. 🌿

POH FANG CHIA

Dear Father, we often struggle to spend time with You.
Help us to make the time, and help us sense Your goodness
and presence.

There is never a day when we don't need to pray.

No Greater Joy

Bob and Evon Potter were a fun-loving couple with three young sons when their life took a wonderful new direction. In 1956 they attended a Billy Graham Crusade in Oklahoma City and gave their lives to Christ. Before long, they wanted to reach out to others to share their faith and the truth about Christ, so they opened their home every Saturday night to high school and college students who had a desire to study the Bible. A friend invited me and I became a regular at the Potters' house.

TODAY'S READING
3 John 1:1–8

I have no greater joy than to hear that my children are walking in the truth. 3 John 1:4

This was a serious Bible study that included lesson preparation and memorizing Scripture. Surrounded by an atmosphere of friendship, joy, and laughter, we challenged each other and the Lord changed our lives during those days.

I stayed in touch with the Potters over the years and received many cards and letters from Bob who always signed them with these words: "I have no greater joy than to hear that my children are walking in the truth" (3 JOHN 1:4). Like John writing to his "dear friend Gaius" (V. 1), Bob encouraged everyone who crossed his path to keep walking with the Lord.

A few years ago I attended Bob's memorial service. It was a joyful occasion filled with people still walking the road of faith—all because of a young couple who opened their home and their hearts to help others find the Lord. ✿ *DAVID MCCASLAND*

Thank You, Lord, for the people who have encouraged me
to keep walking in Your truth. May I honor them by helping someone
along that road today.

Be a voice of encouragement to someone today.

The Promised Spirit

Tenacity and audacity—**Elisha** had heaps of both. Having spent time with Elijah, he witnessed the Lord working through the prophet by performing miracles and by speaking truth in an age of lies. Second Kings 2:1 tells us that Elijah is about to be taken "up to heaven," and Elisha doesn't want him to leave.

The time came for the dreaded separation, and Elisha knew he needed what Elijah had if he was going to successfully continue the ministry. So he made a daring demand: "Let me inherit a double portion of your spirit" (2 KINGS 2:9). His bold request was a reference to the double portion given the firstborn son or heir under the law (DEUT. 21:17). Elisha wanted to be recognized as the heir of Elijah. And God said yes.

TODAY'S READING
2 Kings 2:5–12

"Let me inherit a double portion of your spirit," Elisha replied. 2 Kings 2:9

Recently one of my mentors—a woman who spread the good news of Jesus—died. Having battled ill health for years, she was ready to enjoy her eternal feast with the Lord. Those of us who loved her were grateful at the thought of her newfound freedom from pain and that she could enjoy God's presence, but we grieved the loss of her love and example. Despite her departure, she did not leave us alone. We too had God's presence.

Elisha gained a double portion of Elijah's spirit—a tremendous privilege and blessing. We who live after the life, death, and resurrection of Jesus have the promised Holy Spirit. The triune God makes His home with us! ❧ *AMY BOUCHER PYE*

Dear Lord, we want to be more like You.
Help us to be witnesses of Your Spirit within us.

When Jesus ascended to His Father, He sent His Spirit.

Unseen, Yet Loved

Like others in the blogging community, I'd never met the man known to us as BruceC. Yet when his wife posted a note to the group to let us know that her husband had died, a string of responses from distant places showed we all knew we had lost a friend.

BruceC had often opened his heart to us. He talked freely about his concern for others and what was important to him. Many of us felt like we knew him. We would miss the gentle wisdom that came from his years in law enforcement and his faith in Christ.

TODAY'S READING
1 Peter 1:1–9

Though you have not seen him, you love him. 1 Peter 1:8

In recalling our online conversations with BruceC, I gained a renewed appreciation for words written by a first-century witness of Jesus. In the first New Testament letter the apostle Peter wrote, he addressed readers scattered throughout the Roman Empire: "Though you have not seen [Christ], you love him" (1 PETER 1:8).

Peter, as a personal friend of Jesus, was writing to people who had only heard about the One who had given them reason for so much hope in the middle of their troubles. Yet, as a part of the larger community of believers, they loved Him. They knew that at the price of His own life, He had brought them into the everlasting family of God. ❧   *MART DEHAAN*

Lord, we have never seen You, yet we believe in You and love You.
Strengthen our love for our brothers and sisters in Christ
who love You as well. Make us one community in You.

Our love for Christ is only as real as our love for our neighbor.

Keep Climbing!

Richard needed a push, and he got one. He was rock climbing with his friend Kevin, who was the belayer (the one who secures the rope). Exhausted and ready to quit, Richard asked Kevin to lower him to the ground. But Kevin urged him on, saying he had come too far to quit. Dangling in midair, Richard decided to keep trying. Amazingly, he was able to reconnect with the rock and complete the climb because of his friend's encouragement.

> TODAY'S READING
> **1 Thessalonians 4:1–12**
>
> **Encourage one another daily.**
> Hebrews 3:13

In the early church, followers of Jesus encouraged one another to continue to follow their Lord and to show compassion. In a culture riddled with immorality, they passionately appealed to one another to live pure lives (ROM. 12:1; 1 THESS. 4:1). Believers encouraged one another daily, as God prompted them to do so (ACTS 13:15). They urged each other to intercede for the body (ROM. 15:30), to help people stay connected to the church (HEB. 10:25), and to love more and more (1 THESS. 4:10).

Through His death and resurrection, Jesus has connected us to one another. Therefore, we have the responsibility and privilege with God's enablement to encourage fellow believers to finish the climb of trusting and obeying Him. ❧ MARVIN WILLIAMS

When was the last time you needed to urge someone to keep following Jesus? Who has encouraged you or stirred you to pursue holiness, to keep praying, or to enlarge your love for Jesus and others?

Encourage one another and build each other up. 1 THESSALONIANS 5:11

Our Divine Defense

Under Nehemiah's supervision, the Israelite workers were rebuilding the wall around Jerusalem. When they were nearly half finished, however, they learned that their enemies were plotting to attack Jerusalem. This news demoralized the already exhausted workers.

Nehemiah had to do something. First, he prayed and posted numerous guards in strategic places. Then, he armed his workers. "Those who carried materials did their work with one hand and held a weapon in the other, and each of the builders wore his sword at his side as he worked" (NEH. 4:17–18).

> **TODAY'S READING**
> **Nehemiah 4:7–18**
>
> **Take . . . the sword of the Spirit, which is the word of God.**
> Ephesians 6:17

We who are building God's kingdom need to arm ourselves against the attack of our spiritual enemy, Satan. Our protection is the sword of the Spirit, which is God's Word. Memorizing Scripture and meditating on it enable us to "take [our] stand against the devil's schemes" (EPH. 6:11). If we think that working for God doesn't matter, we should turn to the promise that what we do for Jesus will last for eternity (1 COR. 3:11–15). If we fear we've sinned too greatly for God to use us, we must remember we've been forgiven by the power of Jesus's blood (MATT. 26:28). And if we're worried we might fail if we try to serve God, we can recall that Jesus said we will bear fruit as we abide in Him (JOHN 15:5).

God's Word is our divine defense! ❧   *JENNIFER BENSON SCHULDT*

God, thank You for the Bible. I believe that Your Word is alive and active.
Please help me to remember it when I am worried or fearful,
when I need encouragement and inspiration.

God's Word is a divine defense against attacks from the Enemy.

Start Afresh

When I was growing up, one of my favorite books was *Anne of Green Gables* by Lucy Maud Montgomery. In one amusing passage, young Anne, by mistake, adds a skin medication instead of vanilla to the cake she is making. Afterward, she exclaims hopefully to her stern-faced guardian, Marilla, "Isn't it nice to think that tomorrow is a new day with no mistakes in it yet?"

I like that thought: tomorrow is a new day—a new day when we can start afresh. We all make mistakes. But when it comes to sin, God's forgiveness is what enables us to start each morning with a clean slate. When we repent, He chooses to remember our sins no more (JER. 31:34; HEB. 8:12).

TODAY'S READING
Psalm 86:5–15

His compassions never fail. They are new every morning; great is your faithfulness.

Lamentations 3:22–23

Some of us have made wrong choices in our lives, but our past words and deeds need not define our future in God's eyes. There is always a fresh start. When we ask for His forgiveness, we take a first step toward restoring our relationship with Him and with others. "If we confess our sins, he is faithful and just and will forgive us our sins and purify us from all unrighteousness" (1 JOHN 1:9).

God's compassion and faithfulness are new every morning (LAM. 3:23), so we can start afresh each day. 🌿 *CINDY HESS KASPER*

Thank You for this new day, Lord. Forgive me for doing those things in the past that I shouldn't have done, and for not doing those things that I should have done. Set my feet on Your right path today.

Each new day gives us new reasons to praise the Lord.

Ambassador of Love

I n my work as a chaplain, some people occasionally ask if I am willing to give them some additional spiritual help. While I'm happy to spend time with anyone who asks for help, I often find myself doing more learning than teaching. This was especially true when one painfully honest new Christian said to me with resignation, "I don't think it's a good idea for me to read the Bible. The more I read what God expects from me, the more I judge others who aren't doing what it says."

As he said this, I realized that I was at least partly responsible for instilling this judgmental spirit in him. At that time, one of the first things I did with those new to faith in Jesus was to introduce them to things they should no longer be doing. In other words, instead of showing them God's love and letting the Holy Spirit reshape them, I urged them to "behave like a believer."

> **TODAY'S READING**
> **John 3:9–21**
>
> **For God did not send his Son into the world to condemn the world, but to save the world through him.** John 3:17

Now I was gaining a new appreciation for John 3:16–17. Jesus's invitation to believe in Him in verse 16 is followed by these words. "For God did not send his Son into the world to condemn the world, but to save the world through him."

Jesus didn't come to condemn us. But by giving these new Christians a checklist of behaviors, I was teaching them to condemn themselves, which then led them to judge others. Instead of being agents of condemnation, we are to be ambassadors of God's love and mercy. 🌱

RANDY KILGORE

Father, help me not to judge others today. Let me learn this until it changes me into someone more like You.

***If Jesus didn't come to condemn the world,
that's probably not our mission either!***

Not Forgotten

At her mother's 50th birthday celebration with hundreds of people present, firstborn daughter Kukua recounted what her mother had done for her. The times were hard, Kukua remembered, and funds were scarce in the home. But her single mother deprived herself of personal comfort, selling her precious jewelry and other posses-sions in order to put Kukua through high school. With tears in her eyes, Kukua said that no matter how difficult things were, her mother never abandoned her or her siblings.

TODAY'S READING
Isaiah 49:13–21

I will not forget you! Isaiah 49:15

God compared His love for His people with a mother's love for her child. When the people of Israel felt abandoned by God during their exile, they complained: "The LORD has forsaken me, the Lord has forgotten me" (ISA. 49:14). But God said, "Can a mother forget the baby at her breast and have no compassion on the child she has borne? Though she may forget, I will not forget you!" (V. 15).

When we are distressed or disillusioned, we may feel aban-doned by society, family, and friends, but God does not aban-don us. It is a great encouragement that the Lord says, "I have engraved you on the palms of my hands" (V. 16) to indicate how much He knows and protects us. Even if people forsake us, God will never forsake His own. ❧

LAWRENCE DARMANI

Thank You, Lord, that I am Yours forever.
I'm thankful that I won't have to walk through any experience alone.

God never forgets us.

Resting and Waiting

t was high noon. Jesus, foot-weary from His long journey, was resting beside Jacob's well. His disciples had gone into the city of Sychar to buy bread. A woman came out of the city to draw water ... and found her Messiah. The account tells us that she quickly went into the city and invited others to come hear "a man who told me everything I ever did" (JOHN 4:29).

The disciples came back bringing bread. When they urged Jesus to eat, He said to them, "My food ... is to do the will of him who sent me and to finish his work" (V. 34).

Now I ask you: What work had Jesus been doing? He'd been resting and waiting by the well.

TODAY'S READING
John 4:4–14

"My food," said Jesus, "is to do the will of him who sent me and to finish his work."

John 4:34

I find great encouragement in this story for I am living with physical limitations. This passage tells me that I do not have to scurry about—worrying myself about doing the will of my Father and getting His work done. In this season of life, I can rest and wait for Him to bring His work to me.

Similarly, your tiny apartment, your work cubicle, your prison cell, or your hospital bed can become a "Jacob's well," a place to rest and to wait for your Father to bring His work to you. I wonder who He'll bring to you today? 🕊 *DAVID ROPER*

Lord, our circumstances can often threaten to overwhelm us.
Today, help us to see You in all of life. We are learning to trust You
as You do Your work.

If you want a field of service, look around you.

Always in His Care

Veteran news reporter Scott Pelley never goes on assignment without his travel essentials—a shortwave radio, camera, indestructible suitcase, laptop computer, phone, and an emergency locator beacon that works anywhere. "You extend the antenna, push two buttons, and it sends a signal to a satellite connected to the National Oceanic and Atmospheric Administration," Pelley says. "It tells them who and where I am. Depending on what country you're in, they'll either send a rescue team—or not" (*AARP The Magazine*). Pelley has never needed to use the beacon, but he never travels without it.

TODAY'S READING
Psalm 139:1–18

You know when I sit and when I rise; you perceive my thoughts from afar.

Psalm 139:2

But when it comes to our relationship with God, we don't need radios, phones, or emergency beacons. No matter how precarious our circumstances become, He already knows who and where we are. The psalmist celebrated this as he wrote, "You have searched me, LORD, and you know me. . . . You are familiar with all my ways" (PS. 139:1–3). Our needs are never hidden from God, and we are never separated from His care.

Today, we can say with confidence, "If I rise on the wings of the dawn, if I settle on the far side of the sea, even there your hand will guide me, your right hand will hold me fast" (VV. 9–10).

The Lord knows who we are, where we are, and what we need. We are always in His care. ❧

DAVID MCCASLAND

O Lord, we praise You for Your never-ending love and your never-failing care.

We are always in His care.

Is He Good?

"I **don't think God** is good," my friend told me. She had been praying for years about some difficult issues, but nothing had improved. Her anger and bitterness over God's silence grew. Knowing her well, I sensed that deep down she believed God is good, but the continual pain in her heart and God's seeming lack of interest caused her to doubt. It was easier for her to get angry than to bear the sadness.

TODAY'S READING
Genesis 3:1–8

He said to the woman, "Did God really say …?"

Genesis 3:1

Doubting God's goodness is as old as Adam and Eve (GEN. 3). The serpent put that thought in Eve's mind when he suggested that God was withholding the fruit from her because "God knows that when you eat from it your eyes will be opened, and you will be like God, knowing good and evil" (V. 5). In pride, Adam and Eve thought they, rather than God, should determine what was good for them.

Years after losing a daughter in death, James Bryan Smith found he was able to affirm God's goodness. In his book *The Good and Beautiful God*, Smith wrote, "God's goodness is not something I get to decide upon. I am a human being with limited understanding." Smith's amazing comment isn't naïve; it arises out of years of processing his grief and seeking God's heart.

In times of discouragement, let's listen well to each other and help each other see the truth that God is good. 🕮 *ANNE CETAS*

Lord, we will praise You in our difficult times like the psalmist did. You know us, and we turn to You because we know You are good.

The LORD is good to all; he has compassion on all he has made. PSALM 145:9

Time to Grow

n Debbie's new home, she discovered an abandoned plant in a dark corner of the kitchen. The dusty and ragged leaves looked like those of a moth orchid, and she imagined how pretty the plant would look once it had sent up new bloom-bearing stems. She moved the pot into a spot by the window, cut off the dead leaves, and watered it thoroughly. She bought plant food and applied it to the roots. Week after week she inspected the plant, but no new shoots appeared. "I'll give it another month," she told her husband, "and if nothing has happened by then, out it goes."

TODAY'S READING
Galatians 6:1–10

At the proper time we will reap a harvest if we do not give up.

Galatians 6:9

When decision day came, she could hardly believe her eyes. Two small stems were poking out from among the leaves! The plant she'd almost given up on was still alive.

Do you ever get discouraged by your apparent lack of spiritual growth? Perhaps you frequently lose your temper or enjoy that spicy piece of gossip you just can't resist passing on. Or perhaps you get up too late to pray and read your Bible, in spite of resolving to set the alarm earlier.

Why not tell a trusted friend about the areas of your life in which you want to grow spiritually and ask that person to pray for and encourage you to be accountable? Be patient. You will grow as you allow the Holy Spirit to work in you. ✹ *MARION STROUD*

Please give me patience, dear Lord, with myself and with others.
Help me to cooperate with the Holy Spirit as He shapes my desires
and helps me to grow.

Each small step of faith is a giant step of growth.

The Bread that Satisfies

learned to recite the Lord's Prayer as a boy in primary school. Every time I said the line, "Give us today our daily bread" (MATT. 6:11), I couldn't help but think about the bread that we got only occasionally at home. Only when my father returned from his trip into town did we have a loaf of bread. So asking God to give us our daily bread was a relevant prayer to me.

TODAY'S READING
Luke 10:38–11:4

Give us each day our daily bread.
Luke 11:3

How curious I was when years later I discovered the booklet *Our Daily Bread*. I knew the title came from the Lord's Prayer, but I also knew it couldn't be talking about the loaf of bread from the baker's shop. I discovered as I read the booklet regularly that this "bread," full of Scripture portions and helpful notes, was spiritual food for the soul.

It was spiritual food that Mary chose when she sat at the feet of Jesus and listened attentively to His words (LUKE 10:39). While Martha wearied herself with concern about physical food, Mary was taking time to be near their guest, the Lord Jesus, and to listen to Him. May we take that time as well. He is the Bread of Life (JOHN 6:35), and He feeds our hearts with spiritual food. He is the Bread that satisfies. 🌿 *LAWRENCE DARMANI*

I sit before You now, Lord, and want to learn from You.
My heart is open to hear from You in Your Word.

"I am the bread of life." JESUS

Great Literature

Recently I came across an article describing what constitutes great literature. The author suggested that great literature "changes you. When you are done reading, you're a different person."

In that light, the Word of God will always be classified as great literature. Reading the Bible challenges us to be better. Stories of biblical heroes inspire us to be courageous and persevering. The wisdom and prophetic books warn of the danger of living by our fallen instincts. God spoke through various writers to pen life-changing psalms for our benefit. The teachings of Jesus shape our character to become more like Him. The writings of Paul orient our minds and lives to holy living. As the Holy Spirit brings these Scriptures to our minds, they become powerful agents for change in our lives.

> **TODAY'S READING**
> **Psalm 119:97–104**
>
> **How sweet are your words . . . , sweeter than honey to my mouth!** Psalm 119:103

The writer of Psalm 119 loved God's Word for its transforming influence in his life. He recognized that the ancient Scriptures handed down from Moses made him wise and more understanding than his teachers (V. 99). It kept him from evil (V. 101). No wonder he exclaimed, "Oh, how I love your law! I meditate on it all day long," and "How sweet are your words to my taste, sweeter than honey to my mouth!" (VV. 97, 103).

Welcome to the joy of loving great literature, especially the life-changing power of God's Word! ✒   *JOE STOWELL*

Lord, thank You for Your Word and its powerful influence in my life.
Help me learn to put its truth into practice.

The Spirit of God uses the Word of God to change the people of God.

Chili Peppers

"**My mother gave us** chili peppers before we went to bed," said Samuel, recalling his difficult childhood in sub-Saharan Africa. "We drank water to cool our mouths, and then we would feel full." He added, "It did not work well."

Government upheaval had forced Samuel's father to flee for his life, leaving their mother as the family's sole provider. Sam's brother had sickle cell anemia, and they couldn't afford medical care. Their mother took them to church, but it didn't mean much to Sam. *How could God allow our family to suffer like this?* he wondered.

Then one day a man learned about their plight and brought them some medicine to help with treatment. "On Sunday we will go to this man's church," his mother announced. Right away Sam sensed something different about this church. They celebrated their relationship with Jesus by living His love.

> TODAY'S READING
> **James 1:22–27**
>
> **Religion that God our Father accepts as pure and faultless is this: to look after orphans and widows in their distress.**
>
> James 1:27

That was three decades ago. Today in this part of the world, Sam has started more than 20 churches, a large school, and a home for orphans. He's continuing the legacy of true religion taught by James, the brother of Jesus, who urged us not to "merely listen to the word" but to "do what it says" (JAMES 1:22). "Religion that God our Father accepts as pure and faultless is this: to look after orphans and widows in their distress" (V. 27).

There's no telling what a simple act of kindness done in Jesus's name can do. ❧

TIM GUSTAFSON

Sometimes the best witness is kindness.

God's Dwelling Place

James Oglethorpe (1696–1785) was a British general and member of Parliament who had a vision for a great city. Charged with settling the state of Georgia in North America, he planned the city of Savannah according to that vision. He designed a series of squares, each having a green space and designated areas for churches and shops, with the rest reserved for housing. The visionary thinking of Oglethorpe is seen today in a beautiful, well-organized city that is considered a jewel of the American South.

TODAY'S READING
Revelation 21:1–7

There will be no more death or mourning or crying or pain. Revelation 21:4

In Revelation 21, John received a vision of a different city—the New Jerusalem. What he said of this city was less about its design and more about the character of who was there. When John described our eternal home, he wrote, "I heard a loud voice from the throne saying, 'Look! God's dwelling place is now among the people, and he will dwell with them'" (v. 3). And because of *who* was there—God Himself—this dwelling place would be notable for what was *not* there. Quoting from Isaiah 25:8, John wrote, "He will wipe every tear from their eyes. There will be no more death" (v. 4).

No more death! Nor will there be any more "mourning or crying or pain." All our sorrow will be replaced by the wonderful, healing presence of the God of the universe. This is the home Jesus is preparing for all who turn to Him for forgiveness. 🌼

BILL CROWDER

Thank You, Father, that Your Son is preparing a place for us to live with You. Thank You that it will be more than just a wonderful place. It is where we will live with You and know You forever.

While You prepare a place for us, Lord, prepare us for that place.

Paddling Home

I like Reepicheep, C. S. Lewis's tough little talking mouse in the Chronicles of Narnia series. Determined to reach the "utter East" and join the great lion Aslan [symbolic of Christ], Reepicheep declares his resolve: "While I may, I sail East in *Dawn Treader*. When she fails me, I row East in my coracle [small boat]. When that sinks, I shall paddle East with my four paws. Then, when I can swim no longer, if I have not yet reached Aslan's Country, there shall I sink with my nose to the sunrise."

Paul put it another way: "I press on toward the goal" (PHIL. 3:14). His goal was to be like Jesus. Nothing else mattered. He admitted that he had much ground to cover but he would not give up until he attained that to which Jesus had called him.

TODAY'S READING
Philippians 3:12–16

One thing I do: Forgetting what is behind and straining toward what is ahead.

Philippians 3:13

None of us are what we should be, but we can, like the apostle, press and pray toward that goal. Like Paul we will always say, "I have not yet arrived." Nevertheless, despite weakness, failure, and weariness we must press on (V. 12). But everything depends on God. Without Him we can do nothing!

God is with you, calling you onward. Keep paddling! ✒

DAVID ROPER

Lord, help us learn that we do not press on toward our goal
by our own effort but through prayer and the guidance of the Holy Spirit.
Apart from You, we can do nothing. Work in us today, we pray.

God provides the power we need to persevere.

Why Me?

Ruth was a foreigner. She was a widow. She was poor. In many parts of the world today she would be considered a nobody—someone whose future doesn't hold any hope.

However, Ruth found favor in the eyes of a relative of her deceased husband, a rich man and the owner of the fields where she chose to ask for permission to glean grain. In response to his kindness, Ruth asked, "What have I done to deserve such kindness? . . . I am only a foreigner" (RUTH 2:10 NLT).

> **TODAY'S READING**
> **Ruth 2:1–11**
>
> **Why have I found such favor in your eyes?** Ruth 2:10

Boaz, the good man who showed Ruth such compassion, answered her truthfully. He had heard about her good deeds toward her mother-in-law, Naomi, and how she chose to leave her country and follow Naomi's God. Boaz prayed that God, "under whose wings" she had come for refuge, would bless her (1:16; 2:11–12; SEE PS. 91:4). As her kinsman redeemer (RUTH 3:9), when Boaz married Ruth he became her protector and part of the answer to his prayer.

Like Ruth, we were foreigners and far from God. We may wonder why God would choose to love us when we are so undeserving. The answer is not in us, but in Him. "God showed his great love for us by sending Christ to die for us while we were still sinners" (ROM. 5:8 NLT). Christ has become our Redeemer. When we come to Him in salvation, we are under His protective wings. ❧

KEILA OCHOA

Dear Lord, I don't know why You love me, but I don't doubt Your love.
I thank You and worship You!

Gratefulness is the heart's response to God's undeserved love.

No Worries

A **comfortable plane ride** was about to get bumpy. The voice of the captain interrupted in-flight beverage service and asked passengers to make sure their seatbelts were fastened. Soon the plane began to roll and pitch like a ship on a wind-whipped ocean. While the rest of the passengers were doing their best to deal with the turbulence, a little girl sat through it all reading her book. After the plane landed, she was asked why she had been able to be so calm. She responded, "My daddy is the pilot and he's taking me home."

TODAY'S READING
Mark 4:35–5:1

Let us go over to the other side.
Mark 4:35

Though Jesus's disciples were seasoned fishermen, they were terrified the day a storm threatened to swamp their boat. They were following Jesus's instructions. Why was this happening? (MARK 4:35–38). He was with them but He was asleep at the stern of the craft. They learned that day that it is not true that when we do as our Lord says there will be no storms in our lives. Yet because He was with them, they also learned that storms don't stop us from getting to where our Lord wants us to go (5:1).

Whether the storm we encounter today is the result of a tragic accident, a loss of employment, or some other trial, we can be confident that all is not lost. Our Pilot can handle the storm. He will get us home. ❧

C.P. HIA

What storms are you encountering today? Perhaps you have lost a loved one or are facing a serious illness. Perhaps you are having difficulty finding a job. Ask the Lord to strengthen your faith and take you safely through the storm to the other side.

We don't need to fear the storm with Jesus as our anchor.

When the Woods Wake Up

Through cold, snowy winters, the hope of spring sustains those of us who live in Michigan. May is the month when that hope is rewarded. The transformation is remarkable. Limbs that look lifeless on May 1 turn into branches that wave green leafy greetings by month's end. Although the change each day is imperceptible, by the end of the month the woods in my yard have changed from gray to green.

God has built into creation a cycle of rest and renewal. What looks like death to us is rest to God. And just as rest is preparation for renewal, death is preparation for resurrection.

I love watching the woods awaken every spring, for it reminds me that death is a temporary condition and that its purpose is to prepare for new life, a new beginning, for something even better. "Unless a kernel of wheat falls to the ground and dies, it remains only a single seed. But if it dies, it produces many seeds" (JOHN 12:24).

While pollen is a springtime nuisance when it coats my furniture and makes people sneeze, it reminds me that God is in the business of keeping things alive. And after the pain of death, He promises a glorious resurrection for those who believe in His Son. ◗

> TODAY'S READING
> **John 11:14–27**
>
> **I am the resurrection and the life. The one who believes in me will live, even though they die.**
> John 11:25

JULIE ACKERMAN LINK

Read these encouraging verses that remind us of the hope of resurrection: 1 Corinthians 15:35–58.

Every new leaf of springtime is a reminder of our promised resurrection.

Like Sheep

One of my daily chores when I lived with my grandfather in northern Ghana was taking care of sheep. Each morning I took them out to pasture and returned by evening. That was when I first noticed how stubborn sheep can be. Whenever they saw a farm, for instance, their instinct drove them right into it, getting me in trouble with the farmers on a number of occasions.

TODAY'S READING
Isaiah 53:1–6

> **We all, like sheep, have gone astray, each of us has turned to our own way.** Isaiah 53:6

Sometimes when I was tired from the heat and resting under a tree, I observed the sheep dispersing into the bushes and heading for the hills, causing me to chase after them and scratching my skinny legs in the shrubs. I had a hard time directing the animals away from danger and trouble, especially when robbers sometimes raided the field and stole stray sheep.

So I quite understand when Isaiah says, "We all, like sheep, have gone astray, each of us has turned to our own way" (53:6). We stray in many ways: desiring and doing what displeases our Lord, hurting other people by our conduct, and being distracted from spending time with God and His Word because we are too busy or lack interest. We behave like sheep in the field.

Fortunately for us, we have the Good Shepherd who laid down His life for us (JOHN 10:11) and who carries our sorrows and our sins (ISA. 53:4–6). And as our shepherd, He calls us back to safe pasture that we might follow Him more closely. 🍂

LAWRENCE DARMANI

Shepherd of my soul, I do wander at times. I'm grateful that You're always seeking me to bring me back to Your side.

If you want God to lead you, be willing to follow.

Flowing Peace

" 'm not surprised you lead retreats," said an acquaintance in my exercise class. "You have a good aura." I was jolted but pleased by her comment, because I realized that what she saw as an "aura" in me, I understood to be the peace of Christ. As we follow Jesus, He gives us the peace that transcends understanding (PHIL. 4:7) and radiates from within—though we may not even be aware of it.

Jesus promised His followers this peace when, after their last supper together, He prepared them for His death and resurrection. He told them that

TODAY'S READING
John 14:16–27

Peace I leave with you; my peace I give you. John 14:27

though they would have trouble in the world, the Father would send them the Spirit of truth to live with them and be in them (JOHN 14:16–17). The Spirit would teach them, bringing to mind His truths; the Spirit would comfort them, bestowing on them His peace. Though soon they would face trials—including fierce opposition from the religious leaders and seeing Jesus executed—He told them not to be afraid. The Holy Spirit's presence would never leave them.

Although as God's children we experience hardship, we too have His Spirit living within and flowing out of us. God's peace can be His witness to everyone we meet—whether at a local market, at school or work, or in the gym. ☙ *AMY BOUCHER PYE*

Father, Son, and Holy Spirit, thank You for welcoming me
into Your circle of love. May I share Your peace with someone
in my community today.

When we keep our mind on God, His Spirit keeps our mind at peace.

He Walked in Our Shoes

To help his staff of young architects understand the needs of those for whom they design housing, David Dillard sends them on "sleepovers." They put on pajamas and spend 24 hours in a senior living center in the same conditions as people in their 80s and 90s. They wear earplugs to simulate hearing loss, tape their fingers together to limit manual dexterity, and exchange eyeglasses to replicate vision problems. Dillard says, "The biggest benefit is [that] when I send 27-year-olds out, they come back with a heart 10 times as big. They meet people and understand their plights" (RODNEY BROOKS, *USA TODAY*).

> **TODAY'S READING**
> **Hebrews 2:10–18**
>
> **Because he himself suffered when he was tempted, he is able to help those who are being tempted.** Hebrews 2:18

Jesus lived on this earth for 33 years and shared in our humanity. He was made like us, "fully human in every way" (HEB. 2:17), so He knows what it's like to live in a human body on this earth. He understands the struggles we face and comes alongside with understanding and encouragement.

"Because [Jesus] himself suffered when he was tempted, he is able to help those who are being tempted" (V. 18). The Lord could have avoided the cross. Instead, He obeyed His Father. Through His death, He broke the power of Satan and freed us from our fear of death (VV. 14–15).

In every temptation, Jesus walks beside us to give us courage, strength, and hope along the way. 🌀   *DAVID MCCASLAND*

Lord Jesus, thank You for "walking in our shoes" on this earth
and for being with us. May we experience Your presence today.

Jesus understands.

Can't Die but Once

Born into slavery and badly treated as a young girl, Harriet Tubman (C. 1822–1913) found a shining ray of hope in the Bible stories her mother told. The account of Israel's escape from slavery under Pharaoh showed her a God who desired freedom for His people.

Harriet found freedom when she slipped over the Maryland state line and out of slavery. She couldn't remain content, however, knowing so many were still trapped in captivity. So she led more than a dozen rescue missions to free those still in slavery, dismissing the personal danger. "I can't die but once," she said.

> **TODAY'S READING**
> **Matthew 10:26–32**
>
> **Do not be afraid of those who kill the body but cannot kill the soul.** Matthew 10:28

Harriet knew the truth of the statement: "Do not be afraid of those who kill the body but cannot kill the soul" (MATT. 10:28). Jesus spoke those words as He sent His disciples on their first mission. He knew they would face danger, and not everyone would receive them warmly. So why expose the disciples to the risk? The answer is found in the previous chapter. "When he saw the crowds, [Jesus] had compassion on them, because they were harassed and helpless, like sheep without a shepherd" (9:36).

When Harriet Tubman couldn't forget those still trapped in slavery, she showed us a picture of Christ, who did not forget us when we were trapped in our sins. Her courageous example inspires us to remember those who remain without hope in the world. 🍂

TIM GUSTAFSON

May we find our peace and purpose in You, Lord,
and share You with others.

True freedom is found in knowing and serving Christ.

Praise from Pure Hearts

During my friend Myrna's travels to another country, she visited a church for worship. She noticed that as people entered the sanctuary they immediately knelt and prayed, facing away from the front of the church. My friend learned that people in that church confessed their sin to God before they began the worship service.

This act of humility is a picture to me of what David said in Psalm 51: "My sacrifice, O God, is a broken spirit; a broken and contrite heart you, God, will not despise" (V. 17). David was describing his own remorse and repentance for his sin of adultery with Bathsheba. Real sorrow for sin involves adopting God's view of what we've done—seeing it as clearly wrong, disliking it, and not wanting it to continue.

> TODAY'S READING
> **Psalm 51:7–17**
>
> **A broken and contrite heart you, God, will not despise.** Psalm 51:17

When we are truly broken over our sin, God lovingly puts us back together. "If we confess our sins, he is faithful and just and will forgive us our sins and purify us from all unrighteousness" (1 JOHN 1:9). This forgiveness produces a fresh sense of openness with Him and is the ideal starting point for praise. After David repented, confessed, and was forgiven by God, he responded by saying, "Open my lips, Lord, and my mouth will declare your praise" (PS. 51:15).

Humility is the right response to God's holiness. And praise is our heart's response to His forgiveness. 🖋 *JENNIFER BENSON SCHULDT*

Dear God, help me never to excuse or minimize my sin.
Please meet me in my brokenness, and let nothing hold me back
from praising Your name.

Praise is the song of a soul set free.

Knowing and Doing

Chinese philosopher Han Feizi made this observation about life: "Knowing the facts is easy. Knowing how to act based on the facts is difficult."

A rich man with that problem once came to Jesus. He knew the law of Moses and believed he had kept the commandments since his youth (MARK 10:20). But he seems to be wondering what additional facts he might hear from Jesus. "'Good teacher,' he asked, 'what must I do to inherit eternal life?'" (V. 17).

Jesus's answer disappointed the rich man. He told him to sell his possessions, give the money to the poor, and follow Him (V. 21). With these few words Jesus exposed a fact the man didn't want to hear. He loved and relied on his wealth more than he trusted Jesus. Abandoning the security of his money to follow Jesus was too great a risk, and he went away sad (V. 22).

> **TODAY'S READING**
> **Mark 10:17–27**
>
> **With man this is impossible, but not with God; all things are possible with God.** Mark 10:27

What was the Teacher thinking? His own disciples were alarmed and asked, "Who then can be saved?" He replied, "With man this is impossible, but not with God; all things are possible with God" (V. 27). It takes courage and faith. "If you declare with your mouth, 'Jesus is Lord,' and believe in your heart that God raised him from the dead, you will be saved" (ROM. 10:9). 🌐

POH FANG CHIA

God, thank You for the good news of Jesus. Give us the courage to act on what we know to be true, and to accept the salvation offered through Jesus. Thank You that You will give us the strength to act on the facts.

Believe in the Lord Jesus, and you will be saved. ACTS 16:31

Not a Simple Story

Life seems straightforward in the laws of the Old Testament. Obey God and get blessed. Disobey Him and expect trouble. It's a satisfying theology. But is it that simple?

King Asa's story seems to fit the pattern. He led his people away from false gods and his kingdom thrived (2 CHRON. 15:1–19). Then late in his reign, he depended on himself instead of God (16:2–7) and the rest of his life was marked by war and illness (V. 12).

It's easy to look at that story and draw a simple conclusion. But when the prophet Hanani warned Asa, he said that God will "strengthen those whose hearts are fully committed to him" (16:9). Why do our hearts need strengthening? Because doing the right thing may require courage and perseverance.

> TODAY'S READING
> **2 Chronicles 16:7–14**
>
> **The eyes of the LORD range throughout the earth to strengthen those whose hearts are fully committed to him.**
>
> 2 Chronicles 16:9

Job got the starring role in a cosmic tragedy. His crime? "He [was] blameless and upright" (JOB 1:8). Joseph, falsely accused of attempted rape, languished in prison for years—to serve God's good purposes (GEN. 39:19–41:1). And Jeremiah was beaten and put in stocks (JER. 20:2). What was the prophet's offense? Telling the truth to rebellious people (26:15).

Life is not simple, and God's ways are not our ways. Making the right decision may come at a cost. But in God's eternal plan, His blessings arrive in due time. ✿

TIM GUSTAFSON

Lord, thank You for the examples of courage and obedience in Your Word.
Help us learn from their mistakes and from their wise choices, as we
make our choice to serve You.

God helps those who depend on Him.

Lord, Help!

I **was so happy** for my friend when she told me she was going to be a mum! Together we counted the days until the birth. But when the baby suffered a brain injury during delivery, my heart broke and I didn't know *how* to pray. All I knew was *who* I should pray to—God. He is our Father, and He hears us when we call.

I knew that God was capable of miracles. He brought Jairus's daughter back to life (LUKE 8:49–55) and in so doing also healed the girl of whatever disease had robbed her of life. So I asked Him to bring healing for my friend's baby too.

But what if God doesn't heal? I wondered. *Surely He doesn't lack the power. Could it be He doesn't care?* I thought of Jesus's suffering on the cross and the explanation that "God demonstrates his own love for us in this: While we were still sinners, Christ died for us" (ROM. 5:8). Then I remembered the questions of Job and how he learned to see the wisdom of God as shown in the creation around him (JOB 38–39).

Slowly I saw how God calls us to Him in the details of our lives. In God's grace, my friend and I learned together what it means to call on the Lord and to trust Him—whatever the outcome. ❧

POH FANG CHIA

> **TODAY'S READING**
> Hebrews 4:14–16
>
> **Let us then approach God's throne of grace with confidence, so that we may receive mercy and find grace to help us in our time of need.** Hebrews 4:16

Lord, to whom can I go but You! I trust You with my life and the lives of my loved ones. I'm grateful You always hear my cry.

When life knocks you down, you're in the perfect position to pray!

Strength for the Weary

O n a beautiful, sunny day, I was walking in a park and feeling very weary in spirit. It wasn't just one thing weighing me down—it seemed to be everything. When I stopped to sit on a bench, I noticed a small plaque placed there in loving memory of a "devoted husband, father, brother, and friend." Also on the plaque were these words, "But they who wait for the Lord shall renew their strength; they shall mount up with wings like eagles; they shall run and not be weary, they shall walk and not faint" (ISA. 40:31 ESV).

TODAY'S READING
Isaiah 40:27–31

Those who hope in the LORD will renew their strength. Isaiah 40:31

Those familiar words came to me as a personal touch from the Lord. Weariness—whether physical, emotional, or spiritual—comes to us all. Isaiah reminds us that although we become tired, the Lord, the everlasting God, the Creator of the ends of the earth "will not grow tired or weary" (V. 28). How easily I had forgotten that in every situation "[the Lord] gives strength to the weary and increases the power of the weak" (V. 29).

What's it like on your journey today? If fatigue has caused you to forget God's presence and power, why not pause and recall His promise. "Those who hope in the LORD will renew their strength" (V. 31). Here. Now. Right where we are. ✒

DAVID MCCASLAND

Lord, thank You that You do not grow weary.
Give me the strength to face whatever situation I am in today.

When life's struggles make you weary, find strength in the Lord.

You Have Purpose

On a hot day in western Texas, my niece Vania saw a woman standing by a stoplight and holding up a sign. As she drove closer, she tried to read what the sign said, assuming it was a request for food or money. Instead, she was surprised to see these three words:

"You Have Purpose"

God has created each of us for a specific purpose. Primarily that purpose is to bring honor to Him, and one way we do that is by meeting the needs of others (1 PETER 4:10–11).

A mother of young children may find purpose in wiping runny noses and telling her kids about Jesus. An employee in an unsatisfying job might find his purpose in doing his work conscientiously, remembering it is the Lord he is serving (COL. 3:23–24). A woman who has lost her sight still finds purpose in praying for her children and grandchildren and influencing them to trust God.

Psalm 139 says that before we were born "all the days ordained for [us] were written in [His] book" (V. 16). We are "fearfully and wonderfully made" to bring glory to our Creator (V. 14).

Never forget: You have purpose! 🌿

CINDY HESS KASPER

> TODAY'S READING
> **1 Peter 4:7–11**
>
> **If anyone serves, they should do so with the strength God provides, so that in all things God may be praised through Jesus Christ.**
>
> 1 Peter 4:11

Lord, it often seems that our lives swing from drudgery to challenges we don't want. Today help us to see You in the midst of whatever faces us. Show us a small glimpse of the purpose and meaning You bring to everything.

Even when everything seems meaningless,
God still has a purpose for your life.

The Beauty of Rome

The glory of the Roman Empire offered an expansive backdrop for the birth of Jesus. In 27 BC Rome's first emperor, Caesar Augustus, ended 200 years of civil war and began to replace rundown neighborhoods with monuments, temples, arenas, and government complexes. According to Roman historian Pliny the Elder, they were "the most beautiful buildings the world has ever seen."

TODAY'S READING
John 17:1–5

Now this is eternal life: that they may know you, the only true God. John 17:3

Yet even with her beauty, the Eternal City and its empire had a history of brutality that continued until Rome fell. Thousands of slaves, foreigners, revolutionaries, and army deserters were crucified on roadside poles as a warning to anyone who dared to defy the power of Rome.

What irony that Jesus's death on a Roman cross turned out to reveal an eternal glory that made the pride of Rome look like the momentary beauty of a sunset!

Who could have imagined that in the public curse and agony of the cross we would find the eternal glory of the love, presence, and kingdom of our God?

Who could have foreseen that all heaven and earth would one day sing, "Worthy is the Lamb, who was slain, to receive power and wealth and wisdom and strength and honor and glory and praise!" (REV. 5:12). 🌿

MART DEHAAN

Father in heaven, please help us to reflect the heart of Your sacrifice for the world. May Your love become our love, Your life our life, and Your glory our never-ending joy.

The Lamb who died is the Lord who lives!

Broken to Be Made New

During World War II my dad served with the US Army in the South Pacific. During that time Dad rejected any idea of religion, saying, "I don't need a crutch." Yet the day came when his attitude toward spiritual things would change forever. Mom had gone into labor with their third child, and my brother and I went to bed with the excitement of soon seeing our new brother or sister. When I got out of bed the next morning, I excitedly asked Dad, "Is it a boy or a girl?" He replied, "It was a little girl but she was born dead." We began to weep together at our loss.

> **TODAY'S READING**
> **Psalm 119:71–75**
>
> I know, LORD, that your laws are righteous, and that in faithfulness you have afflicted me.
>
> Psalm 119:75

For the first time, Dad took his broken heart to Jesus in prayer. At that moment he felt an overwhelming sense of peace and comfort from God, though his daughter would always be irreplaceable. Soon he began to take an interest in the Bible and continued to pray to the One who was healing his broken heart. His faith grew through the years. He became a strong follower of Jesus—serving Him as a Bible-study teacher and a leader in his church.

Jesus is not a crutch for the weak. He is the source of new spiritual life! When we're broken, He can make us new and whole (PS. 119:75). 🌿

DENNIS FISHER

What is on your heart that you need to talk with God about?
Bring Him your brokenness and ask Him to make you whole.

Brokenness can lead to wholeness.

Tell It!

The year was 1975 and something significant had just happened to me. I needed to find my friend Francis, with whom I shared a lot of personal matters, and tell him about it. I found him in his apartment hurriedly preparing to go out, but I slowed him down. The way he stared at me, he must have sensed that I had something important to tell him. "What is it?" he asked. So I told him simply, "Yesterday I surrendered my life to Jesus!"

Francis looked at me, sighed heavily, and said, "I've felt like doing the same for a long time now." He asked me to share what happened, and I told him how the previous day someone had explained the gospel to me and how I asked Jesus to come into my life. I still remember the tears in his eyes as he too prayed to receive Jesus's forgiveness. No longer in a hurry, he and I talked and talked about our new relationship with Christ.

> **TODAY'S READING**
> **Mark 5:1–20**
>
> **The man went away and began to tell … how much Jesus had done for him.** Mark 5:20

After Jesus healed the man with an evil spirit, He told him, "Go home to your own people and tell them how much the Lord has done for you, and how he has had mercy on you" (MARK 5:19). The man didn't need to preach a powerful sermon; he simply needed to share his story.

No matter what our conversion experience is, we can do what that man did: "[He] went away and began to tell … how much Jesus had done for him." ❂

LAWRENCE DARMANI

What has Jesus done for you? Tell it!

Let the redeemed of the LORD tell their story. PSALM 107:2

Better by Far

A siren wailed outside a little boy's house. Unfamiliar with the sound, he asked his mother what it was. She explained that it was meant to alert people of a dangerous storm. She said that if people did not take cover, they might die as a result of the tornado. The boy replied, "Mommy, why is that a bad thing? If we die, don't we meet Jesus?"

TODAY'S READING
Philippians 1:12–26

> **I desire to depart and be with Christ, which is better by far.** Philippians 1:23

Little children don't always understand what it means to die. But Paul, who had a lifetime of experience, wrote something similar: "I desire to depart and be with Christ, which is better by far" (PHIL. 1:23). The apostle was under house arrest at the time, but his statement wasn't fueled by despair. He was rejoicing because his suffering was causing the gospel to spread (VV. 12–14).

So why would Paul be torn between a desire for life and death? Because to go on living would mean "fruitful labor." But if he died he knew he would enjoy a special kind of closeness with Christ. To be absent from our bodies is to be home with the Lord (2 COR. 5:6–8).

People who believe in the saving power of Jesus's death and resurrection will be with Him forever. It's been said, "All's well that ends in heaven." Whether we live or die, we win. "For to me, to live is Christ and to die is gain" (PHIL. 1:21). 🌐

JENNIFER BENSON SCHULDT

Dear Jesus, help me to keep my eyes on You, whether I face difficulty in life or death. Let me find security and peace in You.

*Belief in Jesus's death and resurrection brings
the assurance of life with Him forever.*

What Really Matters

Two men sat down to review their business trip and its results. One said he thought the trip had been worthwhile because some meaningful new relationships had begun through their business contacts. The other said, "Relationships are fine, but selling is what matters most." Obviously they had very different agendas.

TODAY'S READING
Philippians 2:1–11

In humility value others above yourselves, not looking to your own interests but each of you to the interests of others.

Philippians 2:3–4

It is all too easy—whether in business, family, or church—to view others from the perspective of how they can benefit us. We value them for what we can get from them, rather than focusing on how we can serve them in Jesus's name. In his letter to the Philippians, Paul wrote, "Do nothing out of selfish ambition or vain conceit. Rather, in humility value others above yourselves, not looking to your own interests but each of you to the interests of the others" (PHIL. 2:3–4).

People are not to be used for our own benefit. Because they are loved by God and we are loved by Him, we love one another. His love is the greatest love of all. ❷

BILL CROWDER

Teach me, Lord, to see people as You do—bearing Your image,
being worthy of Your love, and needing Your care.
May Your great love find in my heart a vessel
through which that love can be displayed.

Joy comes from putting another's needs ahead of our own.

Our New Name

She called herself a worrier, but when her child was hurt in an accident, she learned how to escape that restricting label. As her child was recovering, she met each week with friends to talk and pray, asking God for help and healing. Through the months as she turned her fears and concerns into prayer, she realized that she was changing from being a *worrier* to a prayer *warrior*. She sensed that the Lord was giving her a new name. Her identity in Christ was deepening through the struggle of unwanted heartache.

> **TODAY'S READING**
> **Revelation 2:12–17**
>
> **I will also give that person a white stone with a new name written on it.**
> Revelation 2:17

In Jesus's letter to the church at Pergamum, the Lord promises to give to the faithful a white stone with a new name on it (REV. 2:17). Biblical commentators have debated over the meaning, but most agree that this white stone points to our freedom in Christ. In biblical times, juries in a court of law used a white stone for a not-guilty verdict and a black stone for guilty. A white stone also gained the bearer entrance into such events as banquets; likewise, those who receive God's white stone are welcomed to the heavenly feast. Jesus's death brings us freedom and new life—and a new name.

What new name do you think God might give to you? 🌱

AMY BOUCHER PYE

May I live out my new identity, sharing Your love and joy.
Show me how You have made me into a new creation.

Followers of Christ have a brand-new identity.

Take Notice

While standing in a checkout line, I was estimating my bill and trying to keep my son from wandering away. I barely noticed when the woman ahead of me shuffled toward the exit, leaving all of her items behind. The clerk confided that the woman didn't have enough money to pay her bill. I felt terrible; if only I had been aware of her situation earlier, I would have helped her.

In the book of Ruth, Boaz became aware of Ruth's plight when he saw her gleaning in his fields (2:5). He learned that she was recently widowed and was the breadwinner for herself and her mother-in-law. Boaz saw her need for protection and warned his harvesters to leave her alone (V. 9). He supplied her with extra food by instructing his workers to let grain fall purposely (V. 16). Boaz even addressed Ruth's emotional needs by comforting her (VV. 11–12). When Naomi heard about this, she said, "Blessed be the one who took notice of you" (V. 19).

Are you aware of the needs of the people around you—in your church, neighborhood, or under your own roof? Today, consider how you might help bear someone's burden. Then you will be fulfilling God's plan for you (GAL. 6:2; EPH. 2:10). 🌢

JENNIFER BENSON SCHULDT

Help me Lord, to notice
The hurting, sick, and lost;
Guide me as I help them
Regardless of the cost.
SCHULDT

God works through us to meet the needs of those around us.

Tears and Laughter

Last year at a retreat I reconnected with some friends I hadn't seen in a long time. I laughed with them as we enjoyed the reunion, but I also cried because I knew how much I had missed them.

On the last day of our time together we celebrated the Lord's Supper. More smiles and tears! I rejoiced over the grace of God, who had given me eternal life and these beautiful days with my friends. But again I cried as I was sobered by what it had cost Jesus to deliver me from my sin.

TODAY'S READING
Ezra 3:7–13

No one could distinguish the sound of the shouts of joy from the sound of weeping. Ezra 3:13

I thought about Ezra and that wonderful day in Jerusalem. The exiles had returned from captivity and had just completed rebuilding the foundation of the Lord's temple. The people sang for joy, but some of the older priests cried (EZRA 3:10–12). They were likely remembering Solomon's temple and its former glory. Or were they grieving over their sins that had led to the captivity in the first place?

Sometimes when we see God at work we experience a wide range of emotions, including joy when we see God's wonders and sorrow as we remember our sins and the need for His sacrifice.

The Israelites were singing and weeping, the noise was heard far away (V. 13). May our emotions be expressions of our love and worship to our Lord, and may they touch those around us. 🌱

KEILA OCHOA

Lord, You welcome our sorrow and our joy, our tears and our laughter.
We bring all of our emotions in their raw honesty to You. May we praise
You with our whole being.

Both tears and smiles bring God praise.

Repeat After Me

When Rebecca stood on stage to speak at a conference, her first sentence into the microphone echoed around the room. It was a bit unsettling for her to hear her own words come back at her, and she had to adjust to the faulty sound system and try to ignore the echo of every word she spoke.

Imagine what it would be like to hear everything we say repeated! It wouldn't be so bad to hear ourselves repeat "I love you" or "I was wrong" or "Thank You, Lord" or "I'm praying for you." But not all of our words are beautiful or gentle or kind. What about those angry outbursts or demeaning comments that no one wants to hear once, let alone twice—those words that we would really rather take back?

> **TODAY'S READING**
> **Psalm 141**
>
> **Take control of what I say, O LORD, and guard my lips.**
>
> Psalm 141:3 NLT

Like the psalmist David, we long to have the Lord's control over our words. He prayed, "Take control of what I say, O LORD, and guard my lips" (PS. 141:3 NLT). And thankfully, the Lord wants to do that. He can help us control what we say. He can guard our lips.

As we learn to adjust to our own sound system by paying careful attention to what we say and praying about the words we speak, the Lord will patiently teach us and even empower us to have self-control. And best of all, He forgives us when we fail and is pleased with our desire for His help. ✍ *ANNE CETAS*

Can you think of something you said recently that you would like to take back? Ask the Lord to help you become aware of careless words.

Part of self-control is mouth-control.

God of the Ordinary

Hearing testimonies about how God did something spectacular in someone else's life can challenge us. While we may rejoice to hear about answers to prayer, we may also wonder why God hasn't done anything amazing for us lately.

It's easy to think that if God showed up in astonishing ways for us like He did for Abraham, then we would be more inspired to be faithful servants of God. But then we remember that God showed up for Abraham every 12 to 14 years, and most of Abraham's journey was rather ordinary (SEE GEN. 12:1–4; 15:1–6; 16:16–17:12).

> **TODAY'S READING**
> **Genesis 12:1–4; 17:1–2**
>
> He will not let you be tempted beyond what you can bear.
>
> 1 Corinthians 10:13

God's work is usually done behind the scenes in the ordinary things of life. As our text says, "He will not let you be tempted beyond what you can bear. But when you are tempted, he will also provide a way out" (1 COR. 10:13). Every day God is busy shielding us from devastating onslaughts of Satan that would otherwise leave us helplessly defeated. And when temptation hits, He is making exit ramps for us so we can escape.

When we put our head on the pillow at night, we should pause to thank God for the amazing things He has done for us that day in the midst of our ordinary lives. So, instead of longing for Him to do something spectacular for you, thank Him! He already has. ✍

JOE STOWELL

Lord, help me to be constantly aware that Your power and presence are with me even in the ordinary times in my life. Thank You for Your amazing work on my behalf that I know nothing about.

God is always in control behind the scenes, even on "ordinary" days.

True Communication

Walking in my North London neighborhood, I can hear snatches of conversation in many languages—Polish, Japanese, Hindi, Croatian, and Italian, to name a few. This diversity feels like a taste of heaven, yet I can't understand what they're saying. As I step into the Russian café or the Polish market and hear the different accents and sounds, I sometimes reflect on how wonderful it must have been on the day of Pentecost when people of many nations could understand what the disciples were saying.

On that day, pilgrims gathered together in Jerusalem to celebrate the festival of the harvest. The Holy Spirit rested on the believers so that when they spoke, the hearers (who had come from all over the known world) could understand them in their own languages (ACTS 2:5–6). What a miracle that these strangers from different lands could understand the praises to God in their own tongues! Many were spurred on to find out more about Jesus.

> **TODAY'S READING**
> **Acts 2:1–12**
>
> **A crowd came together in bewilderment, because each one heard their own language being spoken.** Acts 2:6

We may not speak or understand many languages, but we know that the Holy Spirit equips us to connect with people in other ways. Amazingly, we are God's hands and feet—and mouth—to further His mission. Today, how might we—with the Spirit's help—reach out to someone unlike us? 🌐 *AMY BOUCHER PYE*

Lord, give us eyes to see those around us as You see them. Give us ears to hear their stories; give us hearts to share Your love.

Love is the language everybody understands.

Some Assembly Required

Around our home, the words "some assembly required" have been the cause of great frustration (mine) and great humor (my family). When my wife and I first married, I attempted to make simple home repairs—with disastrous results. A repaired shower handle worked perfectly—if the plan was for the water to run between the walls. My fiascoes continued after we had children, when I assured my wife, Cheryl, I "don't need instructions" to put these "simple" toys together. Wrong!

Gradually, I learned my lesson and began to pay strict attention to the instructions and things went together as they should. Unfortunately, the longer things went well, the more confident I became, and soon I was again ignoring instructions with predictably disastrous results.

TODAY'S READING
Judges 2:7–19

Whenever the LORD raised up a judge for them, he was with the judge and saved them out of the hands of their enemies. Judges 2:18

The ancient Israelites struggled with a similar tendency: they would forget God, ignoring His instructions to avoid following after Baal and the other gods of the region (JUDG. 2:12). This produced disastrous results, until God, in His mercy, raised up judges to rescue them and bring them back to Himself (2:18).

God has reasons for all of the instructions He's given us to keep our affections on Him. Only by a daily awareness of His loving presence can we resist the temptation to "construct" our lives our own way. What great gifts He has given us in His Word and His presence! ❧

RANDY KILGORE

Lord, keep me close to You this day. Remind me of Your presence through Your Word and prayer and the leading of the Holy Spirit.

Our greatest privilege is to enjoy God's presence.

Abba, Father

The scene belonged on a funny Father's Day card. As a dad muscled a lawn mower ahead of him with one hand, he expertly towed a child's wagon behind him with the other. In the wagon sat his three-year-old daughter, delighted at the noisy tour of their yard. This might not be the safest choice, but who says men can't multitask?

If you had a good dad, a scene like that can invoke fantastic memories. But for many, "Dad" is an incomplete concept. Where are we to turn if our fathers are gone, or if they fail us, or even if they wound us?

King David certainly had his short-comings as a father, but he understood the paternal nature of God. "A father to the fatherless," he wrote, "a defender of widows, is God in his holy dwelling. God sets the lonely in families" (PS. 68:5-6). The apostle Paul expanded on that idea: "The Spirit you received brought about your adoption to sonship." Then, using the Aramaic word for *father*—a term young children would use for their dad—Paul added, "By him we cry, '*Abba*, Father'" (ROM. 8:15). This is the same word Jesus used when He prayed in anguish to His Father the night He was betrayed (MARK 14:36).

What a privilege to come to God using the same intimate term for "father" that Jesus used! Our *Abba* Father welcomes into His family anyone who will turn to Him. ● 　　TIM GUSTAFSON

> **TODAY'S READING**
> **Romans 8:12–17**
>
> **A father to the fatherless, a defender of widows, is God in his holy dwelling.**
> Psalm 68:5

Heavenly Father, I want to be part of Your family. I believe that Your only Son Jesus died for my sins. Please forgive me and help me.

A good father reflects the love of the heavenly Father.

Defeat or Victory?

Each year on June 18 the great Battle of Waterloo is recalled in what is now Belgium. On that day in 1815, Napoleon's French army was defeated by a multinational force commanded by the Duke of Wellington. Since then, the phrase "to meet your Waterloo" has come to mean "to be defeated by someone who is too strong for you or by a problem that is too difficult for you."

When it comes to our spiritual lives, some people feel that ultimate failure is inevitable and it's only a matter of time until each of us will "meet our Waterloo." But John refuted that pessimistic view when he wrote to followers of Jesus: "Everyone born of God overcomes the world. This is the victory that has overcome the world, even our faith" (1 JOHN 5:4).

> **TODAY'S READING**
> 1 John 5:1–13
>
> **Everyone born of God overcomes the world. This is the victory that has overcome the world, even our faith.** 1 John 5:4

John weaves this theme of spiritual victory throughout his first letter as he urges us not to love the things this world offers, which will soon fade away (2:15-17). Instead, we are to love and please God, "And this is what he promised us—eternal life" (2:25).

While we may have ups and downs in life, and even some battles that feel like defeats, the ultimate victory is ours in Christ as we trust in His power. 🌐 *DAVID MCCASLAND*

Lord Jesus, Your ultimate victory in this fallen world is assured, and You ask us to share in it each day of our lives. By Your grace, enable us to overcome the world through faith and obedience to You.

When it comes to problems, the way out is to trust God on the way through.

Marathon Reading

When the sun came up on the first day of the seventh month in 444 BC, Ezra started reading the law of Moses (what we know as the first five books of the Bible). Standing on a platform in front of the people in Jerusalem, he read it straight through for the next six hours.

Men, women, and children had gathered at the entrance to the city known as the Water Gate to observe the Festival of Trumpets—one of the feasts prescribed for them by God. As they listened, four reactions stand out.

They stood up in reverence for the Book of the Law (NEH. 8:5). They praised God by lifting their hands and saying "Amen." They bowed down in humble worship (V. 6). Then they listened carefully as the Scriptures were both read and explained to them (V. 8). What an amazing day as the book that "the Lord had commanded for Israel" (V. 1) was read aloud inside Jerusalem's newly rebuilt walls!

> TODAY'S READING
> Nehemiah 8:1–8
>
> **They read from the Book of the Law of God, making it clear and giving the meaning so that the people understood what was being read.**
>
> Nehemiah 8:8

Ezra's marathon reading session can remind us that God's words to us are still meant to be a source of praise, worship, and learning. When we open the Bible and learn more about Christ, let's praise God, worship Him, and seek to discover what He is saying to us now. ✝

DAVE BRANON

Lord, thank You for this amazing book we call the Bible. Thank You for inspiring its creation by the writers You chose to pen its words. Thank You for preserving this book through the ages so we can learn Your people's story and the good news of Your love.

The goal of Bible study is not just learning but living.

Hoo-ah!

The US Army's expression "hoo-ah" is a guttural response barked when troops voice approval. Its original meaning is lost to history, but some say it is derived from an old acronym HUA—Heard, Understood, and Acknowledged. I first heard the word in basic training.

Many years later it found its way into my vocabulary again when I began to meet on Wednesday mornings with a group of men to study the Scriptures. One morning one of the men—a former member of the 82nd Airborne Division—was reading one of the psalms and came to the notation *selah* that occurs throughout the psalms. Instead of reading "*selah*," however, he growled *hoo-ah*, and that became our word for *selah* ever after.

TODAY'S READING
Psalm 68:7–10,19–20

Blessed be the Lord, who daily loads us with benefits, the God of our salvation! *Selah.* Psalm 68:19 NKJV

No one knows for certain what *selah* actually means. Some say it is only a musical notation. It often appears after a truth that calls for a deep-seated, emotional response. In that sense *hoo-ah* works for me.

This morning I read Psalm 68:19: "Blessed be the Lord, who daily [day to day] loads us with benefits, the God of our salvation! *Selah*" (NKJV).

Imagine that! Every single morning God loads us up on His shoulders and carries us through the day. *He* is our salvation. Thus safe and secure in Him, we've no cause for worry or for fear. "Hoo-ah!" I say. ❧

DAVID ROPER

Day by day and with each passing moment, strength I find to meet my trials here. Trusting in my Father's wise bestowment, I've no cause for worry or for fear. LINA SANDELL BERG

Worship is giving God the best that He has given you. OSWALD CHAMBERS

Learning to Love

Love does more than make "the world go round," as an old song says. It also makes us immensely vulnerable. From time to time, we may say to ourselves: "Why love when others do not show appreciation?" or "Why love and open myself up to hurt?" But the apostle Paul gives a clear and simple reason to pursue love: "These three remain: faith, hope and love. But the greatest of these is love. Follow the way of love" (1 COR. 13:13–14:1).

> **TODAY'S READING**
> **1 Corinthians 13**
>
> **Follow the way of love.** 1 Corinthians 14:1

"Love is an activity, the essential activity of God himself," writes Bible commentator C. K. Barrett, "and when men love either Him or their fellow-men, they are doing (however imperfectly) what God does." And God is pleased when we act like Him.

To begin following the way of love, think about how you might live out the characteristics listed in 1 Corinthians 13:4–7. For example, how can I show my child the same patience God shows me? How can I show kindness and respect for my parents? What does it mean to look out for the interests of others when I am at work? When something good happens to my friend, do I rejoice with her or am I envious?

As we "follow the way of love," we'll find ourselves often turning to God, the source of love, and to Jesus, the greatest example of love. Only then will we gain a deeper knowledge of what true love is and find the strength to love others like God loves us. 🌱

POH FANG CHIA

God, thank You that You are love and that You love me so much.
Help me to love others the way Jesus showed us so that the
whole world will know I am Your child.

***Love comes from God. Everyone who loves has been born of God
and knows God.*** 1 JOHN 4:7

A Remote Location

Tristan da Cunha Island is famous for its isolation. It is the most remote inhabited island in the world, thanks to the 288 people who call it home. The island is located in the South Atlantic Ocean, 1,750 miles from South Africa—the nearest mainland. Anyone who might want to drop by for a visit has to travel by boat for seven days because the island has no airstrip.

TODAY'S READING
Mark 8:1–13

> **My God will meet all your needs according to the riches of his glory in Christ Jesus.**
> Philippians 4:19

Jesus and His followers were in a somewhat remote area when He produced a miraculous meal for thousands of hungry people. Before His miracle, Jesus said to His disciples, "[These people] have already been with me three days and have nothing to eat. If I send them home hungry, they will collapse on the way" (MARK 8:2–3). Because they were in the countryside where food was not readily available, they had to depend fully on Jesus. They had nowhere else to turn.

Sometimes God allows us to end up in desolate places where He is our only source of help. His ability to provide for us is not necessarily linked with our circumstances. If He created the entire world out of nothing, God can certainly meet our needs—whatever our circumstances—out of the riches of His glory, in Christ Jesus (PHIL. 4:19). ❖

JENNIFER BENSON SCHULDT

Dear God, thank You for all that You have provided through Your Son, Jesus Christ. You know what my needs are. Please reassure me of Your care and power.

We can trust God to do what we cannot do.

Serving Christ

"**'m a secretary,"** a friend told me. "When I tell people this, they sometimes look at me with a certain pity. But when they find out who I am secretary for, they open their eyes with admiration!" In other words, society often defines some jobs as less important than others, unless those jobs happen to relate in some way to rich or famous people.

For the child of God, however, any occupation, regardless of the earthly boss, can be held proudly because we serve the Lord Jesus.

In Ephesians 6, Paul talks to servants and masters. He reminds both groups that we serve one Master who is in heaven. So we need to do everything with

> TODAY'S READING
> **Ephesians 6:5–9**
>
> **Obey [your earthly masters] . . . as slaves of Christ, doing the will of God from your heart.** Ephesians 6:6

sincerity of heart, integrity, and respect because we are serving and working for Christ Himself. As the apostle Paul reminds us, "Serve wholeheartedly, as if you were serving the Lord, not people" (EPH. 6:7).

What a privilege to serve God in everything we do, whether answering a phone or driving a car or doing housework or running a business. Let us work with a smile today, remembering that no matter what we are doing, we are serving God. 🌸 *KEILA OCHOA*

Lord Jesus, I want to serve You in everything I do.
Help me, as I begin each day, to remember this.

Serving shows our love for God.

His Loving Presence

Our hearts sank when we learned that our good friend Cindy had been diagnosed with cancer. Cindy was a vibrant person whose life blessed all who crossed her path. My wife and I rejoiced when she went into remission, but a few months later her cancer returned with a vengeance. In our minds she was too young to die. Her husband told me about her last hours. When she was weak and hardly able to talk, Cindy whispered to him, "Just be with me." What she wanted more than anything in those dark moments was his loving presence.

> **TODAY'S READING**
> **Hebrews 13:1–6**
>
> **Never will I leave you.** Hebrews 13:5

The writer to the Hebrews comforted his readers by quoting Deuteronomy 31:6, where God told His people: "Never will I leave you; never will I forsake you" (HEB. 13:5). In the darkest moments of life, the assurance of His loving presence gives us confidence that we are not alone. He gives us the grace to endure, the wisdom to know He is working, and the assurance that Christ can "empathize with our weaknesses" (4:15).

Together let's embrace the blessing of His loving presence so we can confidently say, "The Lord is my helper; I will not be afraid" (13:6). ❧

JOE STOWELL

Lord, thank You for the promise that You will never leave me.
May the reality of Your constant supporting presence fill my heart with
comfort, confidence, and courage.

There is peace in the presence of God.

A Firm Place to Stand

The historic riverwalk area of Savannah, Georgia, is paved with mismatched cobblestones. Local residents say that centuries ago the stones provided ballast for ships as they crossed the Atlantic Ocean. When cargo was loaded in Georgia, the ballast stones were no longer needed, so they were used to pave the streets near the docks. Those stones had accomplished their primary job—stabilizing the ship through dangerous waters.

TODAY'S READING
Psalm 40:1–5

> He lifted me out of the slimy pit; out of the mud and mire, he set my feet on a rock and gave me a firm place to stand.
>
> Psalm 40:2

The days in which we live can feel as turbulent as the high seas. Like sailing ships of old, we need stability to help us navigate our way through the storms of life. David faced danger as well, and he celebrated the character of God for providing him with stability after he had endured a desperate time. He declared, "He lifted me out of the slimy pit; out of the mud and mire, he set my feet on a rock, and gave me a firm place to stand" (PS. 40:2). David's experience was one of conflict, personal failure, and family strife, yet God gave him a place to stand. So David sang "a hymn of praise to our God" (V. 3).

In times of difficulty, we too can look to our powerful God for the stability only He brings. His faithful care inspires us to say with David, "Many, Lord my God, are the wonders you have done, the things you planned for us" (V. 5). ❂   *BILL CROWDER*

My hope is built on nothing less than Jesus' blood and righteousness;
I dare not trust the sweetest frame, but wholly lean on Jesus' name.
On Christ, the solid rock, I stand—all other ground is sinking sand.
EDWARD MOTE

**When the world around us is crumbling,
Christ is the solid Rock on which we stand.**

Shocking Honesty

When the minister asked one of his elders to lead the congregation in prayer, the man shocked everyone. "I'm sorry, Pastor," he said, "but I've been arguing with my wife all the way to church, and I'm in no condition to pray." The next moment was *awkward*. The minister prayed. The service moved on. Later, the pastor vowed never to ask anyone to pray publicly without first asking privately.

That man demonstrated astonishing honesty in a place where hypocrisy would have been easier. But there is a larger lesson about prayer here. God is a loving Father. If I as a husband do not respect and honor my wife—a cherished daughter of God—why would her heavenly Father hear my prayers?

TODAY'S READING
1 Peter 3:7-12

Treat her as you
should so your
prayers will not
be hindered.
1 Peter 3:7 NLT

The apostle Peter made an interesting observation about this. He instructed husbands to treat their wives with respect and as equal heirs in Christ "so that nothing will hinder your prayers" (1 PETER 3:7). The underlying principle is that our relationships affect our prayer life.

What would happen if we exchanged the Sunday smiles and the façade of religiosity for refreshing honesty with our brothers and sisters? What might God do through us when we pray and learn to love each other as we love ourselves? ❦

TIM GUSTAFSON

Father, You love all of Your children, but so often we fight and disagree.
Help us learn to interact with love and respect in all our relationships so
the world will see the difference You make. Teach us to pray.

Prayer is simply an honest conversation with God.

No Drifting

At the end of one school semester, my wife and I picked up our daughter from her school 100 kilometers (60 miles) away. On our way back home we detoured to a nearby beach resort for snacks. While enjoying our time there, we watched the boats at the seashore. Usually they are anchored to prevent them from drifting away, but I noticed one boat drifting unhindered among the others—slowly and steadily making its way out to sea.

TODAY'S READING
Hebrews 2:1–4

> We must pay the most careful attention...so that we do not drift away. Hebrews 2:1

As we drove home, I reflected on the timely caution given to believers in the book of Hebrews: "We must pay the most careful attention, therefore, to what we have heard, so that we do not drift away" (HEB. 2:1). We have good reason to stay close. The author of Hebrews says that while the Mosaic law was reliable and needed to be obeyed, the message of the Son of God is far superior. Our salvation is "so great" in Jesus that He shouldn't be ignored (V. 3).

Drifting in our relationship with God is hardly noticeable at first; it happens gradually. However, spending time talking with Him in prayer and reading His Word, confessing our wrongs to Him, and interacting with other followers of Jesus can help us stay anchored in Him. As we connect with the Lord regularly, He will be faithful to sustain us, and we can avoid drifting away. ✒

LAWRENCE DARMANI

What do you know about Jesus that keeps you wanting to be near Him?

To avoid drifting away from God, stay anchored to the Rock.

Leaving the Past Behind

Chris Baker is a tattoo artist who transforms symbols of pain and enslavement into works of art. Many of his clients are former gang members and victims of human trafficking who have been marked with identifying names, symbols, or codes. Chris transforms these into beautiful art by tattooing over them with new images.

Jesus does for the soul what Chris Baker does for the skin—He takes us as we are and transforms us. The Bible says, "Anyone who belongs to Christ has become a new person. The old life is gone; a new life has begun!" (2 COR. 5:17 NLT). Before knowing Christ, we follow our desires wherever they lead us, and our lifestyles reflect this. When we repent and begin to walk with Christ, the passions and pitfalls that once dominated our lives is the "old life" (1 COR. 6:9–11) that fades away as we are transformed. "All this is from God, who reconciled us to himself through Christ" (2 COR. 5:18).

Still, life as a "new person" isn't always easy. It can take time to disconnect from old habits. We may struggle with ideas that were foundational to our old way of life. Yet over time, God's Holy Spirit works in us, giving us inner strength and an understanding of Christ's love. As God's beautiful new creations, we're free to leave the past behind. ✒

JENNIFER BENSON SCHULDT

> **TODAY'S READING**
> 2 Corinthians 5:12–21
>
> **Anyone who belongs to Christ has become a new person.**
>
> 2 Corinthians 5:17 NLT

Jesus, thank You for the power of Your death and resurrection. Your victory over sin means that I can be forgiven and can enjoy a new life in You.

To enjoy the future, accept God's forgiveness for the past.

Our Way of Life

I was struck by a phrase I heard quoted from a contemporary Bible translation. When I Googled the phrase "our way of life" to locate the passage, many of the results focused on things people felt were threatening their expected way of living. Prominent among the perceived threats were climate change, terrorism, and government policies.

What really is our way of life as followers of Jesus? I wondered. Is it what makes us comfortable, secure, and happy, or is it something more?

Paul reminded the Christians in Ephesus of the remarkable way God had transformed their lives. "God, who is rich in mercy, out of the great love with which he loved us even when we were dead through our trespasses, made us alive together with Christ—by grace you have been saved" (EPH. 2:4–5 NRSV). The result is that we are "created in Christ Jesus for good works, which God prepared beforehand to be our way of life" (V. 10 NRSV).

Doing good works, helping others, giving, loving, and serving in Jesus's name—these are to be our way of life. They are not optional activities for believers, but the very reason God has given us life in Christ.

In a changing world, God has called and empowered us to pursue a life that reaches out to others and honors Him. ✒

> **TODAY'S READING**
> **Ephesians 2:1–10**
>
> **We are what he has made us, created in Christ Jesus for good works, which God prepared beforehand to be our way of life.**
> Ephesians 2:10 NRSV

DAVID MCCASLAND

Father, thank You for the incredible riches of Your love and mercy. You rescued us from our dead way of living and made us alive with Christ.

Let your light shine before others, that they may see your good deeds and glorify your Father in heaven. MATTHEW 5:16

Called by Name

When I first meet a new group of students in the college composition class I teach, I already know their names. I take the time to familiarize myself with their names and photos on my student roster, so when they walk into my classroom I can say, "Hello, Jessica," or "Welcome, Trevor." I do this because I know how meaningful it is when someone knows and calls us by name.

> TODAY'S READING
> **John 10:1–11**
>
> **He calls his own sheep by name.**
> John 10:3

Yet to truly know someone, we need to know more than that person's name. In John 10, we can sense the warmth and care Jesus, the Good Shepherd, has for us when we read that He "calls his own sheep by name" (V. 3). He knows even more than our name. He knows our thoughts, longings, fears, wrongs, and deepest needs. Because He knows our deepest needs, He has given us our very life—our eternal life—at the cost of His own. As He says in verse 11, He "lays down his life for the sheep."

You see, our sin separated us from God. So Jesus, the Good Shepherd, became the Lamb and sacrificed Himself, taking our sin on Himself. When He gave His life for us and then was resurrected, He redeemed us. As a result, when we accept His gift of salvation through faith, we are no longer separated from God.

Give thanks to Jesus! He knows your name and your needs! 🌱

DAVE BRANON

Dear Lord, thank You for knowing my name and for knowing exactly what I need. Thank You for dying for my sin and for rising from the grave to defeat death and give me eternal life with You.

God's knowledge of us knows no bounds.

Out in the Cold

In desperation, a woman called the housing assistance center where I worked. A heating problem had turned her rental home into a freezer with furniture. Panicked, she asked me how she would care for her children. I hurriedly replied with the scripted official response: "Just move into a hotel and send the landlord the bill." She angrily hung up on me.

I knew the textbook answer to her question, but I had completely missed her heart. She wanted someone to understand her fear and desperation. She needed to know she wasn't alone. In essence, I had left her out in the cold.

TODAY'S READING
Job 11:7–20

To God belong wisdom and power; counsel and understanding are his. Job 12:13

After Job had lost everything, he had friends with answers but little understanding. Zophar told him all he needed to do was live wholeheartedly for God. Then "life will be brighter than noonday," he said (11:17). That counsel wasn't well received, and Job responded with scathing sarcasm: "Wisdom will die with you!" (12:2). He knew the dissatisfying taste of textbook answers to real-world problems.

It's easy to be critical of Job's friends for their failure to see the big picture. But how often are we too quick with answers to questions we don't truly understand? People do want answers. But more than that, they want to know we hear and understand. They want to know we care. 🌿 *TIM GUSTAFSON*

Father, help us to be a friend first before we offer advice to others.
Thank You for the privilege of sharing our hearts with You in prayer.
Thank You for sending us Your Holy Spirit so that we will never be alone.

Before people want to hear what you say,
they want to know that you care.

Come Sit a Spell

When I was a kid, our family made a monthly excursion from Ohio to West Virginia to visit my maternal grandparents. Every time we arrived at the door of their farmhouse, Grandma Lester would greet us with the words, "Come on in and sit a spell." It was her way of telling us to make ourselves comfortable, stay a while, and share in some "catching up" conversation.

Life can get pretty busy. In our action-oriented world, it's hard to get to know people. It's tough to find time to ask someone to "sit a spell" with us. We can get more done if we text each other and get right to the point.

> **TODAY'S READING**
> **Luke 19:1–9**
>
> **Zaccheus, come down immediately. I must stay at your house today.** Luke 19:5

But look at what Jesus did when He wanted to make a difference in the life of a tax collector. He went to Zaccheus's house to "sit a spell." His words, "I must stay at your house" indicate that this was no quick stopover (LUKE 19:5). Jesus spent time with him, and Zaccheus's life was turned around because of this time with Jesus.

On the front porch of my grandmother's house were several chairs—a warm invitation to all visitors to relax and talk. If we're going to get to know someone and to make a difference in their life—as Jesus did for Zaccheus—we need to invite them to "come sit a spell." ❧

DAVE BRANON

Dear Lord, as I look around at those who share this life with me, help me to make time to spend with them—for encouragement, challenge, and perhaps just plain conversation.

The best gift you can give to others may be your time.

Waiting on God

was sitting with a group of passengers on an airport shuttle heading to our connecting flight when the bus driver was told to "hold in place." It looked like we would miss our flight, and this was more than one passenger could handle. He exploded at the driver, insisting he ignore his orders or "risk the wrath of a lawsuit." Just then an airline employee came dashing up carrying a briefcase. Looking at the angry man, the airline employee triumphantly held up the briefcase. When he had caught his breath, he said, "You left your briefcase. I heard you mention how important your meeting was, and I figured you would need this."

TODAY'S READING
2 Peter 3:8–15

[The Lord] is patient with you, not wanting anyone to perish, but everyone to come to repentance.

2 Peter 3:9

Sometimes I find myself impatient with God, especially about His return. I wonder, *What can He be waiting on?* The tragedies around us, the suffering of people we love, and even the stresses of daily life all seem bigger than the fixes on the horizon.

Then someone tells their story of having just met Jesus, or I discover God is still at work in the messes. It reminds me of what I learned that day on the shuttle. There are stories and details God knows that I don't. It reminds me to trust Him and to remember that the story isn't about me. It's about God's plan to give time to others who don't yet know His Son (2 PETER 3:9). ❦

RANDY KILGORE

I'm thankful You are patiently waiting for more people to trust in You before You return. Help me to be patient too.

Wait and witness till Jesus returns.

Join the Cry

A **women's prayer group** in my country holds regular monthly prayer sessions for Ghana and other African countries. When asked why they pray so incessantly for the nations, their leader Gifty Dadzie remarked, "Look around, listen to and watch the news. Our nations are hurting: war, disaster, diseases, and violence threaten to overshadow God's love for humanity and His blessing upon us. We believe God intervenes in the affairs of nations, so we praise Him for His blessings and cry for His intervention."

The Bible reveals that God indeed intervenes in the affairs of nations (2 CHRON. 7:14). And when God intervenes, He uses ordinary people. We may not be assigned huge tasks, but we can play our part to help bring about peace and the righteousness that exalts a nation (PROV. 14:34). We can do that through prayer. The apostle Paul wrote, "I urge, then, first of all, that petitions, prayers, intercession and thanksgiving be made for all people—for kings and all those in authority, that we may live peaceful and quiet lives in all godliness and holiness" (1 TIM. 2:1–2).

As the psalmist exhorted the ancient Israelites to "pray for the peace of Jerusalem" (PS. 122:6), so may we pray for the peace and healing of our nations. When we pray in humility, turn from wickedness, and seek God, He hears us. 🌿 *LAWRENCE DARMANI*

> **TODAY'S READING**
> **Psalm 122:6–9**
>
> **I urge…that petitions, prayers, intercession and thanksgiving be made for all people.** 1 Timothy 2:1

Lord, we pray today for the peace of our nations. We ask for Your intervention as we turn to You in confession and repentance. We praise You for Your blessing and Your provision.

Prayer for those in authority is both a privilege and a duty.

Coming Alongside

Her thirty classmates and their parents watched as Mi'Asya nervously walked to the podium to speak at her fifth grade graduation ceremony. When the principal adjusted the microphone to Mi'Asya's height, she turned her back to the microphone and the audience. The crowd whispered words of encouragement: "Come on, honey, you can do it." But she didn't budge. Then a classmate walked to the front and stood by her side. With the principal on one side of Mi'Asya and her friend on the other, the three read her speech together. What a beautiful example of support!

Moses needed help and support in the middle of a battle with the Amalekites (EX. 17:10–16). "As long as Moses held up his hands [with the staff of God in his hands], the Israelites were winning, but whenever he lowered his hands, the Amalekites were winning" (V. 11). When Aaron and Hur saw what was happening, they stood beside Moses, "one on one side, one on the other," and supported his arms when he grew tired. With their support, victory came by sunset.

> TODAY'S READING
> **Exodus 17:8–16**
>
> **Aaron and Hur held [Moses's] hands up—one on one side, one on the other.** Exodus 17:12

We all need the support of one another. As brothers and sisters in the family of God, we have so many opportunities to encourage one another on our shared journey of faith. And God is right here in our midst giving us His grace to do that. 🕊

ANNE CETAS

Who could you help today? Or do you need support yourself?
Who could you ask?

Hope can be ignited by a spark of encouragement.

Strengthening the Heart

The neighborhood fitness center where I have worked out for years closed down last month, and I had to join a new gym. The former place was a warm, friendly facility, patronized by those who liked to socialize while they worked out. We hardly ever broke a sweat. The new gym is a hard-core facility filled with serious men and women, earnestly invested in building better bodies. I watch these people strain and toil. Their bodies look strong, but I wonder if their hearts are being strengthened with grace.

TODAY'S READING
1 Timothy 4:6–11

It is good for our hearts to be strengthened by grace. Hebrews 13:9

The heart is a muscle—the muscle that keeps the other muscles going. It's good to build and tone our other muscles, but the essential thing is doing whatever keeps the heart strong.

So it is with our spiritual heart. We strengthen and tone the heart through the Word of truth by receiving its message of God's goodness and grace. Keeping our spiritual heart strong and fit must be our first priority, the one thing we do above all others.

Paul would agree: "Train yourself for godliness; for while bodily training is of some value, godliness is of value in every way, as it holds promise for the present life and also for the life to come" (1 TIM. 4:7–8 ESV). 🌾

DAVID ROPER

> May I feed on Your goodness every day, Lord,
> so my heart will grow stronger through the Spirit.

God's training is designed to grow us in faith.

Important Reminders

Anthropologist **Anthony Graesch** says that the outside of a refrigerator reveals what's important to people. During a research study of families in Los Angeles, Graesch and his colleagues noted an average of 52 items posted on the fridge—including school schedules, family photos, children's drawings, and magnets. Graesch calls the refrigerator "a repository of family memory."

The Lord may use a tangible item like a photo, keepsake, or Scripture verse to remind us of His faithfulness and the call to obey His Word. When Moses addressed the Israelites just before they entered the land of Canaan, he urged them to keep all the commands God had given them. "Impress them on your children. Talk about them when you sit at home and when you walk along the road.... Write them on the doorframes of your houses and on your gates" (DEUT. 6:7, 9).

Giving God's Word a visible place of honor in their homes and lives was a powerful daily reminder to "be careful that you do not forget the LORD, who brought you ... out of the land of slavery" (V. 12).

Today the Lord encourages us to remember that as we obey His Word, we can depend on His faithful care for all that lies ahead. ❧

DAVID MCCASLAND

> TODAY'S READING
> **Deuteronomy 6:1–12**
>
> **These commandments that I give you today are to be on your hearts.**
> Deuteronomy 6:6

Father, we are grateful for every reminder of Your faithfulness
and loving care. May we honor You by obeying Your Word.

Daily blessings are reminders of God's faithfulness.

Our Chief Task

When a British scholar called on the world's religions to work together for worldwide unity, people everywhere applauded. Pointing out that the major religions share a belief in the Golden Rule, she suggested, "The chief task of our time is to build a global society where people of all persuasions can live together in peace and harmony."

> **TODAY'S READING**
> Matthew 7:12–23
>
> **I am the way and the truth and the life. No one comes to the Father except through me.** John 14:6

Jesus cited the Golden Rule in His Sermon on the Mount: "Do to others what you would have them do to you" (MATT. 7:12). In the same sermon, He said, "Love your enemies and pray for those who persecute you"(5:44). Putting those radical commands into practice would indeed go a long way toward peace and harmony. But immediately following the Golden Rule, Jesus called for discernment. "Watch out for false prophets," He warned. "They come to you in sheep's clothing, but inwardly they are ferocious wolves" (7:15).

Respect for others and discernment of the truth go hand in hand. If we have the truth, we have a message worth telling. But God extends to everyone the freedom to choose Him or reject Him. Our responsibility is to lovingly present the truth and respect the personal choice of others just as God does.

Our respect for others is vital to winning their respect. It's an important step in gaining an opportunity to convey the message of Jesus, who said, "I am the way and the truth and the life" (JOHN 14:6). 🕊

TIM GUSTAFSON

Father in heaven, help us to see each individual as uniquely made in Your image and worthy of our love and respect. Show Your love through our lives in some small way today.

Love people; love the truth.

Everything We Need and More

n a field on the English countryside, G. K. Chesterton stood up from where he had been sitting and exploded with laughter. His outburst was so sudden and so loud that the cows could not take their eyes off him.

Just minutes before, the Christian writer and apologist had been miserable. That afternoon he had been wandering the hills, sketching pictures on brown paper using colored chalks. But he was dismayed to discover he had no white chalk, which he considered to be essential to his artwork. Soon, though, he began to laugh when he realized that the ground beneath him was porous limestone—the earth's equivalent of white chalk. He broke off a piece and resumed drawing.

TODAY'S READING
2 Peter 1:1–10

[God's] divine power has given us everything we need for a godly life. 2 Peter 1:3

Like Chesterton, who realized he "was sitting on an immense warehouse of white chalk," believers have God's unlimited spiritual resources within reach at all times. "His divine power has given us everything we need for a godly life through our knowledge of him" (2 PETER 1:3).

Maybe you feel you are lacking some important element necessary for godliness such as faith, grace, or wisdom. If you know Christ, you have everything you need and more. Through Jesus, you have access to the Father—the one who graciously provides believers with all things. ❧   *JENNIFER BENSON SCHULDT*

Dear Lord, forgive me for overlooking Your power and trying to
live in my own strength. I can't do it.
Thank You for providing everything I need.

God has unlimited power.

Language of Love

When my grandmother came to Mexico as a missionary, she had a hard time learning Spanish. One day she went to the market. She showed her shopping list to the girl helping her and said, "It's in two tongues *(lenguas)*." But she meant to say that she had written it in two languages *(idiomas)*. The butcher overheard them and assumed she wanted to purchase two cow tongues. My grandmother didn't realize it until she got home. She had never cooked beef tongue before!

> **TODAY'S READING**
> **James 3:1–12**
>
> **With the tongue we praise our Lord and Father, and with it we curse human beings, who have been made in God's likeness.** James 3:9

Mistakes are inevitable when we are learning a second language, including learning the new language of God's love. At times our speech is contradictory because we praise the Lord but then speak badly of others. Our old sinful nature opposes our new life in Christ. What comes out of our mouths shows us how much we need God's help.

Our old "tongue" must go away. The only way to learn the new language of love is by making Jesus the Lord of our speech. When the Holy Spirit works in us, He gives us self-control to speak words that please the Father. May we surrender every word to Him! "Set a guard over my mouth, LORD; keep watch over the door of my lips" (PS. 141:3). ❂   *KEILA OCHOA*

Lord Jesus, take control of my mouth today.
Forgive me for careless, thoughtless, and angry words.
Let my words bless You and others.

May the words we speak point others to Jesus.

A Lesson Learned

Mary was widowed and facing serious health challenges when her daughter invited her to move into the new "granny apartment" attached to her home. Although it would involve leaving friends and the rest of her family many miles away, Mary rejoiced in God's provision.

Six months into her new life, the initial joy and contentment threatened to slip away as she was tempted to grumble inwardly and doubt whether the move was really God's perfect plan. She missed her Christian friends, and her new church was too far away to get to independently.

> TODAY'S READING
> **Philippians 4:10–19**
>
> **I have learned to be content whatever the circumstances.**
>
> Philippians 4:11

Then she read something that the great 19th-century preacher Charles Spurgeon had written. "Now contentment is one of the flowers of heaven, and it must be cultivated," he pointed out. "Paul says … 'I have *learned* to be content,' as if he didn't know how at one time."

Mary concluded that if an ardent evangelist like Paul, confined to prison, abandoned by friends, and facing execution could learn contentment, then so could she.

"I realized that until I could learn this lesson, I wouldn't enjoy those things God had planned," she said. "So I confessed my inward grumbling and asked for His forgiveness. Soon after that a newly retired lady asked if I would be her prayer partner, and others offered me a ride to church. My needs for a 'soul friend' and greater mobility were wonderfully met." 🌱

MARION STROUD

Are there areas of life where you need to learn contentment?
Ask God to help you now.

God doesn't always change our circumstances, but He will change us.

The Easy Road?

Life's path is often difficult. So if we expect that God will always give us an easy road, we may be tempted to turn our back on Him when the terrain gets tough.

If you've ever considered doing that, think about the people of Israel. When they were given freedom from the Egyptians after hundreds of years of bondage, they took off for the Promised Land. But God didn't send them straight home. He "did not lead them on the road through the Philistine country, though that was shorter" (EX. 13:17). Instead He sent them on the hard road through the desert. In the short run, this helped them avoid wars (V. 17), but in the long run, there was something bigger at work.

God used that time in the desert to instruct and mature the people He had called to follow Him. The easy road would have led them to disaster. The long road prepared the nation of Israel for their successful entry into the Promised Land.

Our God is faithful, and we can trust Him to lead us and care for us no matter what we face. We may not understand the reason for the path we are on, but we can trust Him to help us grow in faith and maturity along the way. 🌾

DAVE BRANON

> **TODAY'S READING**
> **Exodus 13:17–22**
>
> **When Pharaoh let the people go, God did not lead them on the road through the Philistine country, though that was shorter.** Exodus 13:17

Lord, we cannot see the path ahead, so we must trust that
the way is right and that it is the best road for us to take.
Please encourage us, and teach us as we let You direct our path.

God's timing is always right—wait patiently for Him.

Something I Should Know?

During a concert, singer-songwriter David Wilcox responded to a question from the audience about how he composes songs. He said there are three aspects to his process: a quiet room, an empty page, and the question, "Is there something I should know?" It struck me as a wonderful approach for followers of Jesus as we seek the Lord's plan for our lives each day.

TODAY'S READING
Matthew 14:22–36

He went up on a mountainside by himself to pray.

Matthew 14:23

Throughout Jesus's public ministry, He took time to be alone in prayer. After feeding 5,000 people with five loaves of bread and two fish, He sent His disciples to cross the Sea of Galilee by boat while He dismissed the crowd (MATT. 14:22). "After [Jesus] had dismissed them, he went up on a mountainside by himself to pray. Later that night, he was there alone" (V. 23).

If the Lord Jesus saw the need to be alone with His Father, how much more do we need a daily time of solitude to pour out our hearts to God, ponder His Word, and prepare to follow His directions. A quiet room—anywhere we can focus on the Lord without distractions. An empty page—a receptive mind, a blank sheet of paper, a willingness to listen. Is there something I should know? "Lord, speak to me by Your Spirit, Your written Word, and the assurance of Your direction."

From that quiet hillside, Jesus descended into a violent storm, knowing exactly what His Father wanted Him to do (VV. 24–27). ❧   *DAVID MCCASLAND*

Taking time to be with God is the best place to find strength.

From Mourning to Dancing

"**W**e're cutting your job." A decade ago those words sent me reeling when the company I worked for eliminated my position. At the time, I felt shattered, partly because my identity was so intertwined with my role as editor. Recently I felt a similar sadness when I heard that my freelance job was ending. But this time I didn't feel rocked at my foundation, because over the years I have seen God's faithfulness and how He can turn my mourning to joy.

> **TODAY'S READING**
> **Isaiah 61:1–4**
>
> **He has sent me ... to bestow on [those who grieve] a crown of beauty instead of ashes, the oil of joy instead of mourning.** Isaiah 61:1, 3

Though we live in a fallen world where we experience pain and disappointment, the Lord can move us from despair to rejoicing, as we see in Isaiah's prophecy about the coming of Jesus (ISA. 61:1–3). The Lord gives us hope when we feel hopeless; He helps us to forgive when we think we can't; He teaches us that our identity is in Him and not in what we do. He gives us courage to face an unknown future. When we wear the rags of "ashes," He gently gives us a coat of praise.

When we face loss, we shouldn't run from the sadness, but neither do we want to become bitter or hardened. When we think about God's faithfulness over the years, we know that He's willing and able to turn our grief to dancing once again—to give us sufficient grace in this life and full joy in heaven. ❧

AMY BOUCHER PYE

Father God, You turned Jesus's pain on the cross into our best gift ever. Deepen my faith that I may welcome Your life-changing love into my life.

God can bring times of growth out of our times of heartache.

Unexpected

n the midday heat of summer, while traveling in the American South, my wife and I stopped for ice cream. On the wall behind the counter we saw a sign reading, "Absolutely No Snowmobiling." The humor worked because it was so unexpected.

TODAY'S READING
Matthew 10:35–42

Whoever finds their life will lose it, and whoever loses their life for my sake will find it.

Matthew 10:39

Sometimes saying the unexpected has the most effect. Think of this in regard to a statement by Jesus: "Whoever finds their life will lose it, and whoever loses their life for my sake will find it" (MATT. 10:39). In a kingdom where the King is a servant (MARK 10:45), losing your life becomes the only way to find it. This is a startling message to a world focused on self-promotion and self-protection.

In practical terms, how can we "lose our life"? The answer is summed up in the word *sacrifice*. When we sacrifice, we put into practice Jesus's way of living. Instead of grasping for our own wants and needs, we esteem the needs and well-being of others.

Jesus not only taught about sacrifice but He also lived it by giving Himself for us. His death on the cross became the ultimate expression of the heart of the King who lived up to His own words: "Greater love has no one than this: to lay down one's life for one's friends" (JOHN 15:13).

BILL CROWDER

Loving Father, teach me the heart of Christ, that I might more fully appreciate the sacrifice He has made for me and be willing to sacrifice myself for others.

Nothing is really lost by a life of sacrifice. HENRY LIDDON

The Gift and the Giver

t's only a keychain. Five little blocks held together by a shoe-lace. My daughter gave it to me years ago when she was seven. Today the lace is frayed and the blocks are chipped, but they spell a message that never grows old: "I ♥ DAD."

The most precious gifts are determined not by *what* went into them, but by *who* they are from. Ask any parent who ever received a bouquet of dandelions from a chubby hand. The best gifts are valued not in money but in love.

Zechariah understood that. We hear it in his prophetic song as he praised God for giving him and his wife Elizabeth their son John when they were well past their childbearing years (LUKE 1:67–79). Zechariah rejoiced because John was to be a prophet who would proclaim God's greatest gift to all people—the coming Messiah: "Because of God's tender mercy, the morning light from heaven is about to break upon us" (LUKE 1:78 NLT). Those words point to a gift given with so much love that it will even "shine on those living in darkness and in the shadow of death" (1:79).

> TODAY'S READING
> **Luke 1:67–79**
>
> **Because of God's tender mercy, the morning light from heaven is about to break upon us.**
> Luke 1:78 NLT

The sweetest gift we can receive is God's tender mercy—the forgiveness of our sins through Jesus. That gift cost Him dearly at the cross, but He offers it freely out of His deep love for us. ♥

JAMES BANKS

Jesus, thank You for Your gift of forgiveness and life through You.
I receive Your gift with joy.

Jesus is both the Gift and the Giver.

An Open Hand

I n 1891, **Biddy Mason** was laid to rest in an unmarked grave in Los Angeles. That wasn't unusual for a woman born into slavery, but it was remarkable for someone as accomplished as Biddy. After winning her freedom in a court battle in 1856, she combined her nursing skills with wise business decisions to make a small fortune. As she observed the plight of immigrants and prisoners, she reached out to them, investing in charity so frequently that people began lining up at her house for help. In 1872, just sixteen years out of slavery, she and her son-in-law financed the founding of

> TODAY'S READING
> **Acts 20:22–35**
>
> **It is more blessed to give than to receive.** Acts 20:35

the First African Methodist Episcopal Church in Los Angeles.

Biddy embodied the apostle Paul's words: "I showed you that by this kind of hard work we must help the weak, remembering the words the Lord Jesus himself said: 'It is more blessed to give than to receive'" (ACTS 20:35). Paul came from privilege, not slavery, yet he chose a life that would lead to his imprisonment and martyrdom so that he could serve Christ and others.

In 1988, benefactors unveiled a tombstone for Biddy Mason. In attendance were the mayor of Los Angeles and nearly 3,000 members of the little church that had begun in her home over a century earlier. Biddy once said, "The open hand is blessed, for it gives in abundance even as it receives." The hand that gave so generously received a rich legacy. ✦   *TIM GUSTAFSON*

Who in your life is struggling and could use a little help from you?
How can you reach out to that person or family today?

The open hand is blessed, for it gives in abundance even as it receives.
BIDDY MASON

Misplaced Trust

I **like watching birds,** an activity I developed while growing up in a forest village in Ghana where there were many different species of birds. In the city suburb where I now live, I recently observed the behavior of some crows that interested me. Flying toward a tree that had shed most of its leaves, the crows decided to take a rest. But instead of settling on the sturdy branches, they lighted on the dry and weak limbs that quickly gave way. They flapped their way out of danger—only to repeat the useless effort. Apparently their bird-sense didn't tell them that the solid branches were more trustworthy and secure resting places.

> TODAY'S READING
> **Psalm 20**
>
> **Some trust in chariots and some in horses, but we trust in the name of the LORD our God.** Psalm 20:7

How about us? Where do we place our trust? David observes in Psalm 20:7: "Some trust in chariots and some in horses, but we trust in the name of the LORD our God." Chariots and horses represent material and human assets. While these represent things that are useful in daily life, they don't give us security in times of trouble. If we place our trust in things or possessions or wealth, we will find that they eventually give way beneath us, as the branches gave way beneath the crows.

Those who trust in their chariots and horses can be "brought to their knees and fall," but those who trust in God will "rise up and stand firm" (20:8). 🌿   *LAWRENCE DARMANI*

Have you ever trusted someone or something and been disappointed or let down? Who or what was it? What do you trust in the most?

In a world of change, we can trust our unchanging God.

Marking Time

The military command, "Mark Time, March" means to march in place without moving forward. It is an active pause in forward motion while remaining mentally prepared and expectantly waiting the next command.

In everyday language, the term *marking time* has come to mean "motion without progress, not getting anywhere, not doing anything important while you wait." It conveys a feeling of idle, meaningless waiting.

In contrast, the word *wait* in the Bible often means "to look eagerly for, to hope, and to expect." The psalmist, when facing great difficulties, wrote: "O my God, I trust in You; let me not be ashamed; let not my enemies triumph over me. Indeed, let no one who waits on You be ashamed" (PS. 25:2-3 NKJV).

> **TODAY'S READING**
> **Psalm 25:1-15**
>
> **Let no one who waits on You be ashamed.**
>
> Psalm 25:3 NKJV

We often have no choice about the things we must wait for—a medical diagnosis, a job interview result, the return of a loved one—but we can decide *how* we wait. Rather than giving in to fear or apathy, we can continue to "march in place," actively seeking God's strength and direction each day.

"Show me Your ways, O LORD; teach me Your paths. Lead me in Your truth and teach me, for You are the God of my salvation; on You I wait all the day" (VV. 4-5 NKJV). 🍂   *DAVID MCCASLAND*

Lord, give me grace to embrace the pauses in my life,
and to be prepared to follow Your next command.

Waiting on God is active trust in Him.

He Understands

Some young children have trouble falling asleep at night. While there may be many reasons for this, my daughter explained one of them as I turned to leave her bedroom one evening. "I'm afraid of the dark," she said. I tried to relieve her fear, but I left a nightlight on so she could be sure that her room was monster-free.

I didn't think much more about my daughter's fear until a few weeks later when my husband went on an overnight business trip. After I settled into bed, the dark seemed to press in around me. I heard a tiny noise and jumped up to investigate. It turned out to be nothing but I finally understood my daughter's fear when I experienced it myself.

> TODAY'S READING
> **Psalm 27:1–8**
>
> **The LORD is my light and my salvation.** Psalm 27:1

Jesus understands our fears and problems because He lived on the earth as a human and endured the same types of trouble we face. "He was despised and rejected by mankind, a man of suffering, and familiar with pain" (ISA. 53:3). When we describe our struggles to Him, He doesn't brush us aside, minimize our feelings, or tell us to snap out of it—He relates to our distress. Somehow, knowing that He understands can dispel the loneliness that often accompanies suffering. In our darkest times, He is our light and our salvation. ✿

JENNIFER BENSON SCHULDT

Dear Jesus, I believe that You hear my prayers and that You understand my situation. You are the One who lights my darkness.

Jesus is our light in the darkest night.

Tactical Distractions

■ t became **painfully** clear the first time my wife and I collaborated on a writing project that procrastination was going to be a major obstacle. Her role was to edit my work and keep me on schedule; my role seemed to be to drive her crazy. Most times, her organization and patience outlasted my resistance to deadlines and direction.

I promised to have a certain amount of writing done by the end of one day. For the first hour, I plugged away diligently. Satisfied with what I'd accomplished so far, I decided to take a break. Before I knew it, my time was up. In trouble for sure, I thought of a way out. I set about doing a couple of chores my wife despised and which always netted me praise when I did them.

TODAY'S READING
Jonah 4

The LORD replied, "Is it right for you to be angry?"

Jonah 4:4

My plan failed.

I sometimes play the same games with God. He brings specific people into my life He wants me to serve or tasks He wants me to accomplish. Like Jonah, who went another way when God gave Him an assignment (JONAH 4:2), I need to set aside my own feelings. I often try to impress God with good deeds or spiritual activity when what He really wants is obedience to His priorities. Inevitably, my plan fails.

Are you dodging duties God makes clear He wants you to tackle? Trust me: Real contentment comes from doing it in His strength and in His way. 🌿

RANDY KILGORE

Loving Father, help us to recognize our busyness and distractions
for what they so often are—disobedience and inattention to the work
You have given us to do.

Obedience pleases God.

Human Race

The alarm clock goes off. Too early, it seems. But you have a long day ahead. You have work to do, appointments to keep, people to care for, or all this and more. Well, you are not alone. Each day, many of us rush from one matter to another. As someone has wittily suggested, "That's why we are called the human race."

When the apostles returned from their first mission trip, they had a lot to report. But Mark did not record Jesus's evaluation of the disciples' work; rather, he focused on His concern that they rest awhile. Jesus said, "Come with me by yourselves to a quiet place and get some rest" (6:31).

> TODAY'S READING
> Mark 6:7–13, 30–32
>
> [Jesus] said to them, "Come with me by yourselves to a quiet place and get some rest."
> Mark 6:31

Ultimately, we find true rest through recognizing the presence of God and trusting Him. While we take our responsibilities seriously, we also recognize that we can relax our grip on our work and careers, our families and ministry, and give them over to God in faith. We can take time each day to tune out the distractions, put away the tense restlessness, and reflect in gratitude on the wonder of God's love and faithfulness.

So feel free to stop and take a breath. Get some real rest. 🌿

POH FANG CHIA

Lord, I thank You today for all You have given me to do.
Help me to truly rest in You—physically, emotionally, and spiritually.

We do not rest because our work is done; we rest because God commanded it and created us to have a need for it. GORDON MACDONALD

Free from Fear

ear sneaks into my heart without permission. It paints a picture of helplessness and hopelessness. It steals my peace and my concentration. What am I fearful about? I'm concerned about the safety of my family or the health of loved ones. I panic at the loss of a job or a broken relationship. Fear turns my focus inward and reveals a heart that sometimes finds it hard to trust.

When these fears and worries strike, how good it is to read David's prayer in Psalm 34: "I sought the LORD, and he answered me; he delivered me from all my fears" (v. 4). And how does God deliver us from our fears? When we "look to him" (v. 5), when we focus on Him, our fears fade; we trust Him to be in control. Then David mentions a different type of fear—not a fear that paralyzes, but a deep respect and awe of the One who surrounds us and delivers us (v. 7). We can take refuge in Him because He is good (v. 8).

> TODAY'S READING
> **Psalm 34:1–10**
>
> **I sought the LORD, and he answered me; he delivered me from all my fears.** Psalm 34:4

This awe of His goodness helps put our fears into perspective. When we remember who God is and how much He loves us, we can relax into His peace. "Those who fear him lack nothing" (v. 9), concludes David. How wonderful to discover that in the fear of the Lord we can be delivered from our fears. ✤   *KEILA OCHOA*

Lord, I'm aware of my worries and fears,
and I place them in Your hands.
Give me peace as I face the day.

Ask God to free you from your fears.

The Wrong Horseshoe

Napoleon's defeat in Russia 200 years ago was attributed to the harsh Russian winter. One specific problem was that his horses were wearing summer horseshoes. When winter came, these horses died because they slipped on icy roads as they pulled the supply wagons. The failure of Napoleon's supply chain reduced his 400,000-strong army to just 10,000. A small slip; a disastrous result!

TODAY'S READING
Psalm 34:11–18

Whoever of you loves life and desires to see many good days, keep your tongue from evil.

Psalm 34:12–13

James described how a slip of the tongue can do great damage. One wrong word can change the careers or destinies of people. So toxic is the tongue that James wrote, "No human being can tame the tongue. It is a restless evil, full of deadly poison" (JAMES 3:8). The problem has increased in our modern world as a careless email or a posting on a social media site can cause great harm. It quickly goes viral and can't always be retracted.

King David tied respect for the Lord with the way we use our words. He wrote, "I will teach you the fear of the LORD. . . . Keep your tongue from evil and your lips from telling lies" (PS. 34:11, 13). He resolved, "I will watch my ways and keep my tongue from sin; I will put a muzzle on my mouth" (39:1). Lord, help us to do the same. 🌐

C. P. HIA

What do James 3:1–12 and Proverbs 18:1–8 teach you about a slip of the tongue?

Our words have the power to build up or tear down.

Test Match

A **test match in** the game of cricket can be grueling. Competitors play from 11 a.m. to 6 p.m. with lunch and tea breaks, but the games can last up to five days. It's a test of endurance as well as skill.

The tests we face in life are sometimes intensified for a similar reason—they feel unending. The long search for a job, an unbroken season of loneliness, or a lengthy battle with cancer is made even more difficult by the fact that you wonder if it will ever end.

TODAY'S READING
Psalm 35:17–28

> **How long, Lord, will you look on? Rescue me from their ravages, my precious life from these lions.**
>
> Psalm 35:17

Perhaps that is why the psalmist cried out, "How long, Lord, will you look on? Rescue me from their ravages, my precious life from these lions" (PS. 35:17). Bible commentaries say that this was speaking of the long period in David's life when he was pursued by Saul and slandered by the king's advisors—a time of trial that lasted for years.

Yet, in the end, David sang, "The LORD be exalted, who delights in the well-being of his servant" (V. 27). His testing drove him to deeper trust in God—a trust that we can also experience in our own long seasons of testing, hardship, or loss. ❁

BILL CROWDER

As time drags on and answers seem faraway, teach me, Father,
to find my help in You and Your presence. Enable me to endure,
and empower me to trust in You.

When your burdens overwhelm you, remember that God has His arms underneath you.

God's Sandpaper

My friend's words stung. Trying to sleep, I battled to stop mulling over her pointed comments about my strong opinions. As I lay there, I asked for God's wisdom and peace. Several weeks later, still concerned about the matter, I prayed, "I hurt, Lord, but show me where I need to change. Show me where she's right."

My friend had acted as God's sandpaper in my life. My feelings felt rubbed raw, but I sensed that how I responded would lead to the building of my character—or not. My choice was to submit to the smoothing process, confessing my pride and stubborn stance. I sensed that my bumps and imperfections didn't glorify the Lord.

> TODAY'S READING
> **Proverbs 27:5–17**
>
> **As iron sharpens iron, so one person sharpens another.**
>
> Proverbs 27:17

King Solomon knew that life in community could be difficult, a theme he addressed in the book of Proverbs. In chapter 27, we see his wisdom applied to relationships. He likens the sharp words between friends as iron sharpening iron: "As iron sharpens iron, so one person sharpens another" (V. 17), shaving off the rough edges in each other's behavior. The process may bring about wounds, such as the hurt I felt from my friend's words (SEE V. 6), but ultimately the Lord can use these words to help and encourage us to make needed changes in our attitude and behavior.

How might the Lord be smoothing out your rough edges for His glory? 🌱

AMY BOUCHER PYE

Lord, this shaping process hurts, but I want to submit to the process.
Mold me and smooth me.

The Lord allows our rough edges to be smoothed over through the sandpaper of life.

Visible Vulnerability

As I ventured out several weeks after shoulder surgery, I was fearful. I had become comfortable using my arm sling, but both my surgeon and physical therapist now told me to stop wearing it. That's when I saw this statement: "At this stage, sling wear is discouraged except as a *visible sign of vulnerability* in an uncontrolled environment."

Ah, that was it! I feared the enthusiastic person who might give me a bear hug or the unaware friend who might bump me accidentally. I was hiding behind my flimsy baby-blue sling because I feared being hurt.

TODAY'S READING
Ephesians 4:2–6

Be patient, bearing with one another in love. Ephesians 4:2

Allowing ourselves to be vulnerable can be scary. We want to be loved and accepted for who we are, but we fear that if people truly knew us, they would reject us and we could get hurt. What if they found out we are not smart enough . . . kind enough . . . good enough?

But as members of God's family, we have a responsibility to *help each other* grow in faith. We're told to "encourage one another," to "build each other up" (1 THESS. 5:11), and to "be patient, bearing with one another in love" (EPH. 4:2).

When we are honest and vulnerable with other believers, we may discover we have mutual struggles battling temptation or learning how to live obediently. But most of all, we will share the wonder of God's gift of grace in our lives. 🌿 *CINDY HESS KASPER*

Dear Lord, many times my fear of being hurt keeps me from being honest about my struggles. Help me to remember how much You love me, and help me to be patient and loving with others.

Being honest about our struggles allows us to help each other.

Best Friend—Forever

One of the pieces of wisdom I have come to appreciate is my dad's often-repeated statement, "Joe, good friends are one of life's greatest treasures." How true! With good friends, you are never alone. They're attentive to your needs and gladly share life's joys and burdens.

Before Jesus came to earth, only two individuals were called friends of God. The Lord spoke to Moses "as one speaks to a friend" (EX. 33:11), and Abraham "was called God's friend" (JAMES 2:23; SEE 2 CHRON. 20:7; ISA. 41:8).

TODAY'S READING
James 2:18–26

"Abraham believed God . . . ," and he was called God's friend. James 2:23

I am amazed that Jesus calls those of us who belong to Him friends: "I have called you friends, for everything that I learned from my Father I have made known to you" (JOHN 15:15). And His friendship is so deep that He laid down His life for us. John says, "Greater love has no one than this: to lay down one's life for one's friends" (V. 13).

What a privilege and blessing to have Jesus as our friend! He is a friend who will never leave us or forsake us. He intercedes for us before the Father and supplies all our needs. He forgives all our sins, understands all our sorrows, and gives us sufficient grace in times of trouble. He is indeed our best friend! ❧

JOE STOWELL

Lord, I am thankful that You have called me Your friend.
May I ever be grateful for the privilege!

What a friend we have in Jesus.

Love Your Neighbor

An **anthropologist** was winding up several months of research in a small village, the story is told. While waiting for a ride to the airport for his return flight home, he decided to pass the time by making up a game for some children. His idea was to create a race for a basket of fruit and candy that he placed near a tree. But when he gave the signal to run, no one made a dash for the finish line. Instead the children joined hands and ran together to the tree.

When asked why they chose to run as a group rather than each racing for the prize, a little girl spoke up and said: "How could one of us be happy when all of the others are sad?" Because these children cared about each other, they wanted all to share the basket of fruit and candy.

> TODAY'S READING
> **Romans 13:8–11**
>
> **For the entire law is fulfilled in keeping this one command: "Love your neighbor as yourself."** Galatians 5:14

After years of studying the law of Moses, the apostle Paul found that all of God's laws could be summed up in one: "Love your neighbor as yourself" (GAL. 5:14; SEE ALSO ROM. 13:9). In Christ, Paul saw not only the reason to encourage, comfort, and care for one another but also the spiritual enablement to do it.

Because He cares for us, we care for each other. 🌱

MART DEHAAN

Father, thank You for the love You shower on us day by day.
Teach us, in turn, to care for others. Open our eyes to see their need and respond as You want us to.

We show our love for God when we love one another.

Embarrassing Moments

The flashing lights of the police car drew my attention to a motorist who had been pulled over for a traffic violation. As the officer, ticket book in hand, walked back to his car, I could clearly see the embarrassed driver sitting helplessly behind the wheel of her car. With her hands, she attempted to block her face from the view of passersby—hoping to hide her identity. Her actions were a reminder to me of how embarrassing it can be when we are exposed by our choices and their consequences.

TODAY'S READING
John 8:1-11

Jesus said to her, "Neither do I condemn you; go and sin no more."

John 8:11

When a guilty woman was brought before Jesus and her immorality was exposed, the crowd did more than just watch. They called for her condemnation, but Jesus showed mercy. The only One with the right to judge sin responded to her failure with compassion. After dispatching her accusers, "Jesus said to her, 'Neither do I condemn you; go and sin no more'" (JOHN 8:11). His compassion reminds us of His forgiving grace, and His command to her points to His great desire that we live in the joy of that grace. Both elements show the depth of Christ's concern for us when we stumble and fall.

Even in our most embarrassing moments of failure, we can cry out to Him and find that His grace is truly amazing. 🌐

BILL CROWDER

Amazing grace—how sweet the sound—
That saved a wretch like me!
I once was lost, but now am found;
Was blind, but now I see.

NEWTON

Our greatest comfort in sorrow is to know that God is in control.

The Price of Admission

Every year some two million people from all over the world visit St. Paul's Cathedral in London. It is well worth the admission fee to experience the magnificent structure designed and built by Sir Christopher Wren during the late 17th century. But tourism is secondary at this place of Christian worship. A primary mission of the cathedral is "to enable people in all their diversity to encounter the transforming presence of God in Jesus Christ." If you want to tour the building and admire the architecture, you must pay an admission fee. But there is no charge to enter and attend any of the daily worship services at St. Paul's.

> TODAY'S READING
> **Romans 3:21–26**
>
> **All are justified freely by his grace through the redemption that came by Christ Jesus.** Romans 3:24

How much does it cost to enter the kingdom of God? Entry is free because Jesus Christ paid the price for us by His death. "All have sinned and fall short of the glory of God, and all are justified freely by his grace through the redemption that came by Christ Jesus" (ROM. 3:23–24). When we acknowledge our spiritual need and accept by faith God's forgiveness for our sins, we have a new and everlasting life in Him.

You can enter a new life today because, by His death on the cross and His resurrection from the dead, Jesus has paid the price of admission! ❂

DAVID MCCASLAND

You can invite Jesus into your life by praying something like this:
Dear Jesus, I believe that You died for my sins and rose from the dead.
I want to accept you as my Savior and follow You. Please forgive my sins
and help me, from this moment on, to live a life that is pleasing to You.

Jesus paid the price so we can enter God's kingdom.

The Best Is Yet to Come

Are the best days of your life behind or in front of you? Our outlook on life—and our answer to that question—can change with time. When we're younger, we look ahead, wanting to grow up. And once we've grown older, we yearn for the past, wanting to be young again. But when we walk with God, whatever our age, the best is yet to come!

TODAY'S READING
Deuteronomy 34:1–12

The eternal God is your refuge, and underneath are the everlasting arms. Deuteronomy 33:27

Over the course of his long life, Moses witnessed the amazing things God did, and many of those amazing things happened when he was no longer a young man. Moses was 80 years old when he confronted Pharaoh and saw God miraculously set His people free from slavery (EX. 3–13). Moses saw the Red Sea part, saw manna fall from heaven, and even spoke with God "face to face" (14:21; 16:4; 33:11).

Throughout his life, Moses lived expectantly, looking ahead to what God would do (HEB. 11:24–27). He was 120 years old in his final year of life on this earth, and even then he understood that his life with God was just getting started and that he would never see an end to God's greatness and love.

Regardless of our age, "the eternal God is [our] refuge, and underneath are the everlasting arms" (DEUT. 33:27) that faithfully carry us into His joy each day. 🌐

JAMES BANKS

O Lord my God, I praise You for all You have done in the past.
I look forward with thankfulness for all You will do in the future.
And I thank You for today and all Your blessings.

When we walk with God, the best is yet to come.

Never Give Up!

Joop Zoetemelk is known as the Netherlands' most successful cyclist. But that's because he never gave up. He started and finished the Tour de France 16 times—placing second five times before winning in 1980. That's perseverance!

Many winners have reached success by climbing a special ladder called "never give up." However, there are also many who have lost the opportunity to achieve success because they gave up too soon. This can happen in every area of life: family, education, friends, work, service. Perseverance is a key to victory.

TODAY'S READING
2 Timothy 3:10–15

> I have fought the good fight, I have finished the race, I have kept the faith. 2 Timothy 4:7

The apostle Paul persevered despite persecution and affliction (2 TIM. 3:10–11). He viewed life with realism, recognizing that as followers of Christ we will suffer persecution (VV. 12–13), but he instructed Timothy to place his faith in God and the encouragement of the Scriptures (VV. 14–15). Doing so would help him face discouragement and endure with hope. At the end of his life, Paul said, "I have fought the good fight, I have finished the race, I have kept the faith" (4:7).

We too can allow the Scriptures to strengthen us to press on in the race marked out for us. For our God is both a promise-making and promise-keeping God and will reward those who faithfully finish the race (V. 8). 🌀

JAIME FERNÁNDEZ GARRIDO

Heavenly Father, give me strength of character and perseverance to serve you better. Help me not to get discouraged when things get tough but to rely on You to see me through.

Faith connects our weakness to God's strength.

More Than We Can Imagine

What are the five best toys of all time? Jonathan H. Liu suggested the following: A stick, a box, string, a cardboard tube, and dirt (GeekDad column at wired.com). All are readily available, versatile, appropriate for all ages, fit every budget, and are powered by imagination. No batteries required.

Imagination plays a powerful role in our lives, so it's not unusual that the apostle Paul mentioned it in his prayer for the followers of Jesus in Ephesus (EPH. 3:14–21). After asking God to strengthen them with His power through His Spirit (V. 16), Paul prayed that they would be able to grasp and experience the full dimension of the love of Christ (VV. 17–19). In closing, Paul gave glory to "him who is able to do immeasurably more than all we ask or imagine, according to his power that is at work within us" (V. 20).

> **TODAY'S READING**
> **Ephesians 3:14–21**
>
> To him who is able to do immeasurably more than all we ask or imagine, according to his power that is at work within us.
>
> Ephesians 3:20

Often our experience limits our prayers—a situation we can't picture being different; destructive habits that remain unbroken; long-held attitudes that seen to defy change. As time passes, we may begin to feel that some things cannot be changed. But Paul says that is not true.

By God's mighty power working in us, He is able to do far more than we may dare to ask or even dream of. ✎ *DAVID MCCASLAND*

Dear Father, help us today to embrace all that You have given us in Your Son—forgiveness, hope, encouragement, and power to live a new life.

Never measure God's unlimited power by your limited expectations.

Not Perfect

I n his book *Jumping through Fires*, David Nasser tells the story of his spiritual journey. Before he began a relationship with Jesus, he was befriended by a group of Christian teens. Although most of the time his buddies were generous, winsome, and nonjudgmental, David witnessed one of them lie to his girlfriend. Feeling convicted, the young man later confessed and asked for her forgiveness. Reflecting on this, David said that the incident drew him closer to his Christian friends. He realized that they needed grace, just as he did.

TODAY'S READING
Romans 7:14–25

I have the desire to do what is good, but I cannot carry it out. Romans 7:18

We don't have to act like we're perfect with the people we know. It's okay to be honest about our mistakes and struggles. The apostle Paul openly referred to himself as the worst of all sinners (1 TIM. 1:15). He also described his wrestling match with sin in Romans 7, where he said, "I have the desire to do what is good, but I cannot carry it out" (V. 18). Unfortunately, the opposite was also true: "The evil I do not want to do—this I keep on doing" (V. 19).

Being open about our struggles puts us on the same level with every other human alive—which is right where we belong! However, because of Jesus Christ, our sin will not follow us into eternity. It's like the old saying goes, "Christians aren't perfect, just forgiven." ❂

JENNIFER BENSON SCHULDT

Dear Jesus, I worship You as the only perfect human ever to live. Thank You for making it possible for me to have victory over sin.

The only difference between Christians and everyone else is forgiveness.

Who's Watching You?

No matter where you go in the city of Rio de Janeiro, you can see Jesus. Standing high above this Brazilian city and anchored to a 2,310-foot-high mountain called Corcovado is a 100-foot-tall sculpture called *Cristo Redentor* (Christ the Redeemer). With arms spread wide, this massive figure is visible day and night from almost anywhere in the sprawling city.

TODAY'S READING
Psalm 34:15–22

The eyes of the LORD are on the righteous. Psalm 34:15

As comforting as this iconic concrete and soapstone sculpture may be to all who can look up and see it, there is much greater comfort from this reality: The real Jesus sees us. In Psalm 34, David explained it like this: "The eyes of the Lord are on the righteous, and his ears are attentive to their cry" (V. 15). He noted that when the righteous call out for His help, "The Lord hears them; he delivers them from all their troubles. The Lord is close to the brokenhearted and saves those who are crushed in spirit" (VV. 17–18).

Just who are the righteous? Those of us who place our trust in Jesus Christ, who Himself is our righteousness (1 COR. 1:30). Our God oversees our lives, and He hears the cries of those who trust Him. He is near to help in our greatest times of need.

Jesus has His eyes on you. 🌼

DAVE BRANON

Sometimes, Lord, life seems out of control and I don't know exactly which direction to take. Thank You for overseeing my life and prompting me in the right way through Your Word and Your Spirit.

The Lord never lets us out of His sight.

Chin Up

Emil was a homeless man who spent a whole year looking down at the pavement as he plodded around the city day after day. He was ashamed to meet the eyes of others in case they recognized him, for his life had not always been lived out on the streets. Even more than that, he was intent on finding a coin that had been dropped or a half-smoked cigarette. His downward focus became such a habit that the bones of his spine began to become fixed in that position so that he had great difficulty in straightening up at all.

> **TODAY'S READING**
> **2 Kings 6:8–17**
>
> **Open his eyes, LORD, so that he may see.** 2 Kings 6:17

The prophet Elisha's servant was looking in the wrong direction and was terrified at the huge army the king of Aram had sent to capture his master (2 KINGS 6:15). But Elisha knew he was seeing only the danger and the size of the opposition. He needed to have his eyes opened to see the divine protection that surrounded them, which was far greater than anything Aram could bring against Elisha (V. 17).

When life is difficult and we feel we are under pressure, it's so easy to see nothing but our problems. But the author of the letter to the Hebrews suggests a better way. He reminds us that Jesus went through unimaginable suffering in our place and that if we fix our eyes on Him (12:2), He will strengthen us. ✍

MARION STROUD

Sometimes, Lord, it seems as if I can only see the knots and tangles
in the tapestry of my life. Please help me to open my eyes and
see the beautiful picture You are weaving.

Christ at the center brings life into focus.

Who Are You Defending?

When Kathleen's teacher called her to the front of the grammar class to analyze a sentence, she panicked. As a recent transfer student, she hadn't learned that aspect of grammar. The class laughed at her.

Instantly the teacher sprang to her defense. "She can out-write any of you any day of the week!" he explained. Many years later, Kathleen gratefully recalled the moment: "I started that day to try to write as well as he said I could." Eventually, Kathleen Parker would win a Pulitzer Prize for her writing.

TODAY'S READING
Mark 10:13–16

> At just the right time, when we were still powerless, Christ died for the ungodly. Romans 5:6

As did Kathleen's teacher, Jesus identified with the defenseless and vulnerable. When His disciples kept children away from Him, He grew angry. "Let the little children come to me," He said, "and do not hinder them" (MARK 10:14). He reached out to a despised ethnic group, making the Good Samaritan the hero of His parable (LUKE 10:25–37) and offering genuine hope to a searching Samaritan woman at Jacob's well (JOHN 4:1–26). He protected and forgave a woman trapped in adultery (JOHN 8:1–11). And though we were utterly helpless, Christ gave His life for all of us (ROM. 5:6).

When we defend the vulnerable and the marginalized, we give them a chance to realize their potential. We show them real love, and in a small but significant way we reflect the very heart of Jesus. 🌿

TIM GUSTAFSON

Father, help me recognize the people in my life who need someone
to stand with them. Forgive me for thinking that it's "not my problem."
Help me to love others as You do.

It is impossible to love Christ without loving others.

Because I Love Him

The day before my husband was to return home from a business trip my son said, "Mom! I want Daddy to come home." I asked him why, expecting him to say something about the presents his daddy usually brings back or that he missed playing ball with him. But with solemn seriousness he answered, "I want him to come back because I love him!"

His answer made me think about our Lord and His promise to come back. "I am coming soon," Jesus says (REV. 22:20). I long for His return, but why do I want Him to come back? Is it because I will be in His presence, away from sickness and death? Is it because I am tired of living in a difficult world? Or is it because when you've loved Him so much of your life, when He has shared your tears and your laughter, when He has been more real than anybody else, you want to be with Him forever?

I'm glad my son misses his daddy when he's away. It would be terrible if he didn't care at all about his return or if he thought it would interfere with his plans. How do we feel about our Lord's return? Let us long for that day passionately, and earnestly say, "Lord, come back! We love You." 🌐

KEILA OCHOA

> **TODAY'S READING**
> **Revelation 22:12-21**
>
> **"Yes, I am coming soon." Amen. Come, Lord Jesus.**
> Revelation 22:20

Lord, please come back soon!

Look forward eagerly for the Lord's appearing.

Who Will Tell Them?

World War II had ended. Peace had been declared. But young Lieutenant Hiroo Onoda of the Japanese Imperial Army, stationed on an island in the Philippines, didn't know the war had ended. Attempts were made to track him down. Leaflets were dropped over his location, telling him the war was over. But Onoda, whose last order in 1945 was to stay and fight, dismissed these attempts and leaflets as trickery or propaganda from the enemy. He did not surrender until March 1974—nearly 30 years after the war had ended—when his former commanding officer traveled from Japan to the Philippines, rescinded his original order, and officially relieved Onoda of duty. Onoda finally believed the war was over.

> **TODAY'S READING**
> **2 Corinthians 4:1–6**
>
> **Our Savior… has destroyed death and has brought life and immortality to light through the gospel.** 2 Timothy 1:10

When it comes to the good news about Jesus Christ, many still haven't heard or don't believe that He has "destroyed death and has brought life and immortality to light through the gospel" (2 TIM. 1:10). And some of us who have heard and believed still live defeated lives, trying to survive on our own in the jungle of life.

Someone needs to tell them the glorious news of Christ's victory over sin and death. Initially, they may respond with skepticism or doubt, but take heart. Imagine the freedom they'll find when Christ illumines their mind with the knowledge that the battle has been won. ✪

POH FANG CHIA

Lord, help me to keep an open heart to listen to others and to share about what You have done.

Will you tell someone the good news today?

Relief from the Scorching Sun

Living in Britain, I don't usually worry about sunburn. After all, the sun is often blocked by a thick cover of clouds. But recently I spent some time in Spain, and I quickly realized that with my pale skin, I could only be out in the sunshine for ten minutes before I needed to scurry back under the umbrella.

As I considered the scorching nature of the Mediterranean sun, I began to understand more deeply the meaning of the image of the Lord God as His people's shade at their right hand. Residents of the Middle East knew unrelenting heat, and they needed to find shelter from the sun's burning rays.

> **TODAY'S READING**
> **Psalm 121**
>
> **The LORD is your shade at your right hand.** Psalm 121:5

The psalmist uses this picture of the Lord as shade in Psalm 121, which can be understood as a conversation on a heart level—a dialogue with oneself about the Lord's goodness and faithfulness. When we use this psalm in prayer, we reassure ourselves that the Lord will never leave us, for He forms a protective covering over us. And just as we take shelter from the sun underneath umbrellas, so too can we find a safe place in the Lord.

We lift our eyes to the "Maker of heaven and earth" (VV. 1–2) because whether we are in times of sunshine or times of rain, we receive His gifts of protection, relief, and refreshment. ❧

AMY BOUCHER PYE

Heavenly Father, You protect me.
Shield me from anything that would take my focus
away from You.

We find refuge in the Lord.

Love We Can Trust

Perhaps the most painful statement a person can hear is, "I don't love you anymore." Those words end relationships, break hearts, and shatter dreams. Often, people who have been betrayed guard themselves against future pain by deciding not to trust anyone's love again. That settled conviction may even include the love of God.

The remarkable thing about God's love for us is His promise that it will never end. The prophet Jeremiah experienced devastating circumstances that left him emotionally depleted (LAM. 3:13–20). His own people rejected his repeated calls to respond to God's love and follow Him. At a low point, Jeremiah said, "My strength and my hope have perished from the LORD" (V. 18).

> TODAY'S READING
> **Lamentations 3:13–26**
>
> **Through the LORD's mercies we are not consumed, because His compassions fail not.** Lamentations 3:22

Yet, in his darkest hour Jeremiah considered God's unfailing love and wrote, "Through the LORD's mercies we are not consumed, because His compassions fail not. They are new every morning; great is Your faithfulness. 'The LORD is my portion,' says my soul, 'therefore I hope in Him!'" (VV. 22–24). A person may vow to love us forever yet fail to keep that promise, but God's love remains steadfast and sure. "He is the One who goes with you. He will not leave you nor forsake you" (DEUT. 31:6). That's a love we can trust. 🐟

DAVID MCCASLAND

O Love that wilt not let me go
I rest my weary soul in Thee;
I give Thee back the life I owe,
That in Thine ocean depths its flow
May richer, fuller be. *MATHESON*

God's love never fails.

Shaping Your Thoughts

When **Marshall McLuhan** coined the phrase "the medium is the message" in 1964, personal computers were unknown, mobile phones were science fiction, and the internet didn't exist. Today we understand what great foresight he had in predicting how our thinking is influenced in this digital age.

In Nicholas Carr's book *The Shallows: What the Internet Is Doing to Our Brains*, he writes, "[The media] supply the stuff of thought, but they also shape the process of thought. And what the Net seems to be doing is chipping away my capacity for concentration and contemplation. Whether I'm online or not, my mind now expects to take in information the way the Net distributes it: in a swiftly moving stream of particles."

TODAY'S READING
Romans 12:1–8

Do not conform to the pattern of this world, but be transformed by the renewing of your mind. Romans 12:2

I like J. B. Phillips's paraphrase of Paul's message to the Christians in Rome: "Don't let the world around you squeeze you into its own mould, but let God re-mould your minds from within, so that you may prove in practice that the plan of God for you is good, meets all his demands and moves towards the goal of true maturity" (ROM. 12:2). How relevant this is today as we find our thoughts and the way our minds process material affected by the world around us.

We cannot stem the tide of information that bombards us, but we can ask God each day to help us focus on Him and to shape our thinking through His presence in our lives. 🌀

DAVID MCCASLAND

Father in heaven, still and focus my mind, quiet my heart, and fill me with
Your thoughts throughout this day.

Let God's Spirit, not the world, shape your mind.

When We Don't Understand

Although I depend on technology every day to get my job done, I don't understand much about how it works. I turn my computer on, bring up a Word document, and get to work on my writing. Yet my inability to comprehend how microchips, hard drives, Wi-Fi connections, and full-color displays actually function doesn't get in the way of my benefiting from technology.

In a sense, this mirrors our relationship with God. Isaiah 55:8–9 reminds us that God is far beyond us: "'My thoughts are not your thoughts, neither are your ways my ways,' declares the LORD. 'As the heavens are higher than the earth, so are my ways higher than your ways and my thoughts than your thoughts.'"

> TODAY'S READING
> **Isaiah 55:6–13**

> **"For my thoughts are not your thoughts, neither are your ways my ways," declares the LORD.** Isaiah 55:8

Even though we don't understand everything about God, that doesn't prevent us from trusting Him. He has proven His love for us. The apostle Paul wrote, "God demonstrates his own love for us in this: While we were still sinners, Christ died for us" (ROM. 5:8). Trusting that love, we can walk with Him even when life doesn't make sense. 🌱

BILL CROWDER

Heavenly Father, thank You that although I cannot comprehend You,
I can know You. I'm grateful. Remind me that even though You and
Your ways might be beyond me, I can always count on Your love for me
and Your presence with me.

*God would not be worthy of our worship if He could be
understood by our wisdom.*

Your Father Knows

I was only four years old as I lay by my father on a floor mat on a hot summer night. (My mother, with a baby, had her own room at the time.) This was in northern Ghana where the climate is mostly dry. Sweat covered my body, and the heat parched my throat. I felt so thirsty I shook my father awake. In the middle of that dry night, he rose up and poured water from a jar for me to quench my thirst. Throughout my life, as he did that night, he exemplified the image of a caring father. He provided what I needed.

TODAY'S READING
Matthew 6:25–34

Your Father knows what you need before you ask him. Matthew 6:8

Some people may not have a good father figure in their lives. But we all have a Father who is strong and ever-present and who does not disappoint us. Jesus taught us to pray to "our Father in heaven" (MATT. 6:9). He told us that when our daily needs confront us—food, clothing, shelter, protection (V. 31)—"your Father knows what you need before you ask him" (V. 8).

We have a Father who is always there. Night or day, whenever the going gets tough, we can trust that He will never abandon us. He has promised to care for us, and He knows better than we do what we need.

LAWRENCE DARMANI

Thank You, Lord, for the privilege of coming to You as my Father.
You know my needs before I even ask.
Thank You that You will never turn me away.

Your loving heavenly Father never takes His eyes off you.

A Legacy Life

While staying in a hotel in a small town I noticed that the church across the street was having a service. People were jammed into the church with a standing-room-only crowd of both young and old flowing out onto the sidewalk. When I noticed a hearse by the curb, I realized it was a funeral. And given the crowd, I assumed that it was the celebration of the life of some local hero—perhaps a wealthy businessperson or a famous personality. Curious, I said to the desk clerk, "That's an amazing turnout for a funeral; it must be for a famous person in town."

> TODAY'S READING
> **Proverbs 22:1–16**
>
> **A good name is more desirable than great riches.**
>
> Proverbs 22:1

"No," he replied. "He wasn't rich or famous, but he was a good man."

This reminded me of the wisdom of the proverb that says, "A good name is more desirable than great riches" (PROV. 22:1). It's a good idea to think about what kind of legacy we are leaving for our family, friends, and neighbors. From God's perspective it's not our resumé or the amount of money we've accumulated that matters but rather the kind of life we have lived.

When a friend of mine passed away, his daughter wrote, "This world has lost a righteous man and in this world that is no small thing!" It's that kind of legacy that we should be seeking for the glory of God. ❧ *JOE STOWELL*

Lord, help me to pursue a life that is pleasing to You and honors Your name.

Live to leave a legacy for God's glory.

Bringing Light into Darkness

I n 1989, **Vaclav Havel** was elevated from his position as a political prisoner to become the first elected president of Czechoslovakia. Years later at his funeral in Prague in 2011, former US Secretary of State Madeleine Albright, who herself was born in Prague, described him as one who had "brought the light to places of deep darkness."

What Havel's introduction of light did in the political arena of Czechoslovakia (and later the Czech Republic), our Lord Jesus did for the whole world. He brought light into existence when He created light out of darkness at the dawn of time (JOHN 1:2-3; CF. GEN 1:2-3). Then, with His birth, He brought light to the spiritual arena. Jesus is the life and light that darkness cannot overcome (JOHN 1:5).

> TODAY'S READING
> John 1:1-8
>
> **In the same way, let your light shine before others, that they may see your good deeds and glorify your Father in heaven.** Matthew 5:16

John the Baptist came from the wilderness to bear witness to Jesus, the light of the world. We can do the same today. In fact that is what Jesus told us to do: "Let your light shine before others, that they may see your good deeds and glorify your Father in heaven" (MATT. 5:16).

In our world today—when good is often considered bad and bad is seen as good, when truth and error are switched around—people are looking for direction in life. May we be the ones who shine the light of Christ into our world. ❂   *C. P. HIA*

Father in heaven, thank You for the light of Jesus
that came into the world and for the light He has brought into my life.
Help me to remain grateful and to be Your light
in the dark world around me.

Shine the Light!

The Swagger

I n the summer of 2015, Hunter (aged 15) carried his brother Braden (8) for a fifty-seven-mile walk to raise awareness of the needs of people with cerebral palsy. Braden weighs sixty pounds, so Hunter needed frequent rest stops where others helped him stretch his muscles, and he wore special harnesses to disperse Braden's weight. Hunter says that while the harnesses helped with the physical discomfort, what helped him most were the people along the way. "If it weren't for everyone cheering and walking with us, I wouldn't have been able to do it. . . . My legs were sore, but my friends picked me up and I made it through. . . ." His mom named the arduous trek "The Cerebral Palsy Swagger."

TODAY'S READING
Rom. 16:1–3, 13, 21–23

Encourage one another and build each other up.
1 Thessalonians 5:11

The apostle Paul, who we think of as strong and courageous, also needed to be "picked up." In Romans 16 he lists a number of people who did just that for him. They served alongside him, encouraged him, met his needs, and prayed for him. He mentions Phoebe; Priscilla and Aquila, who were coworkers; Rufus's mother, who had been like a mother to him as well; Gaius, who showed him hospitality; and many more.

We all need friends who pick us up, and we all know of others who need our encouragement. As Jesus helps and carries us, let us help one another. ❁   ANNE CETAS

Lord, in Your wisdom You established Your church as a place for us
to love and care for each other. Help me to extend
the grace I've received to others.

Encouragers pick others up when troubles weigh them down.

That Thing You Do

As the convoy waited to roll out, a young marine rapped urgently on the window of his team leader's vehicle. Irritated, the sergeant rolled down his window. "What?" "You gotta do that thing," the marine said. "What thing?" asked the sergeant. "You know, that thing you do," replied the marine.

Then it dawned on the sergeant. He always prayed for the convoy's safety, but this time he hadn't. So he dutifully climbed out of the Humvee and prayed for his marines. The marine understood the value of his praying leader.

In ancient Judah, Abijah doesn't stand out as a great king. First Kings 15:3 tells us, "His heart was not fully devoted to the LORD his God." But as Judah prepared for war against Israel, outnumbered two to one, Abijah knew this much: Faithful people in his kingdom of Judah had continued worshiping God (2 CHRON. 13:10–12), while the ten tribes of Israel had driven out the priests of God and worshiped pagan gods instead (VV. 8–9). So Abijah turned confidently to the one true God.

Surely Abijah's checkered history had caused grave damage. But he knew where to turn in the crisis, and his army won soundly "because they relied on the LORD, the God of their ancestors" (V. 18). Our God welcomes whoever comes to Him and relies on Him. ✿

TIM GUSTAFSON

> TODAY'S READING
> **2 Chronicles 13:10–18**
>
> **The people of Judah were victorious because they relied on the LORD, the God of their ancestors.**
>
> 2 Chronicles 13:18

I know that prayer isn't a good-luck charm.
But I come to You now, Lord, because there's no one better to talk to.
I trust You with all of my circumstances today.

God will never turn away whoever turns to Him in faith.

Comparison Obsession

Thomas J. DeLong, a professor at Harvard Business School, has noted a disturbing trend among his students and colleagues—a "comparison obsession." He writes: "More so than ever before, . . . business executives, Wall Street analysts, lawyers, doctors, and other professionals are obsessed with comparing their own achievements against those of others. . . . This is bad for individuals and bad for companies. When you define success based on external rather than internal criteria, you diminish your satisfaction and commitment."

> **TODAY'S READING**
> **Matthew 20:1–16**
>
> Don't I have the right to do what I want with my own money? Or are you envious because I am generous?
>
> Matthew 20:15

Comparison obsession isn't new. The Scriptures warn us of the dangers of comparing ourselves to others. When we do so, we become proud and look down on them (LUKE 18:9–14). Or we become jealous and want to be like them or have what they have (JAMES 4:1). We fail to focus on what God has given us to do. Jesus intimated that comparison obsession comes from believing that God is unfair and that He doesn't have a right to be more generous to others than He is to us (MATT. 20:1–16).

By God's grace we can learn to overcome comparison obsession by focusing on the life God has given to us. As we take moments to thank God for everyday blessings, we change our thinking and begin to believe deep down that God is good. ❧

MARVIN WILLIAMS

I need a better focus, Lord. Help me to keep my eyes off others and instead on You and Your good heart for all of us.

God expresses His goodness to His children in His own way.

Giants in the Land

After being encamped near Mt. Sinai for two years, the people of Israel were on the verge of entering Canaan—the land God had promised them. God told them to send twelve spies to assess the land and the people living there. When the spies saw the strength of the Canaanites and the size of their cities, ten of them said, "We can't!" Two said, "We can!"

TODAY'S READING
Numbers 13:25–14:9

We should go up and take possession of the land, for we can certainly do it.

Numbers 13:30

What made the difference?

When the ten compared the giants with themselves and the giants loomed large, the two—Caleb and Joshua—compared the giants with God, and the giants were cut down to size. "The LORD is with us," they said. "Do not be afraid of them" (NUM. 14:9).

Unbelief never lets us get beyond the difficulties—the impregnable cities and the impossible giants. It preoccupies itself with them, brooding over them, pitting them against mere human resources.

Faith, on the other hand, though it never minimizes the dangers and difficulties of any circumstance, looks away from them to God and counts on His invisible presence and power.

What are your "giants"? A habit you cannot break? A temptation you cannot resist? A difficult marriage? A drug-abusing son or daughter? If we compare ourselves with our difficulties, we will always be overwhelmed. Faith looks away from the greatness of the undertaking to the greatness of an ever-present, allpowerful God. ✎

DAVID ROPER

Dear Lord, when the "giants" in my life begin to overwhelm me with fear, help me to trust in You.

When fear knocks, answer it with faith.

Let Us

While standing in line for a popular attraction at Disneyland, I noticed that most people were talking and smiling instead of complaining about the long wait. It made me ponder what made waiting in that line an enjoyable experience. The key seemed to be that very few people were there by themselves. Instead, friends, families, groups, and couples were sharing the experience, which was far different than standing in line alone.

The Christian life is meant to be lived in company with others, not alone. Hebrews 10:19–25 urges us to live in community with other followers of Jesus. "Let us draw near to God with a sincere heart and with the full assurance that faith brings.... Let us hold unswervingly to the hope we profess, for he who promised is faithful. And let us consider how we may spur one another on toward love and good deeds, not giving up meeting together" (VV. 22–25). In community we reassure and reinforce each other, "encouraging one another" (V. 25).

> TODAY'S READING
> **Hebrews 10:19–25**
>
> **Let us consider how we may spur one another on toward love and good deeds.**
>
> Hebrews 10:24

Even our most difficult days can become a meaningful part of our journey of faith when others share them with us. Don't face life alone. Let us travel together. 🌱 *DAVID MCCASLAND*

Lord, may we fulfill Your calling today by walking the road of faith and encouragement with others.

Life in Christ is meant to be a shared experience.

At Risk of Falling

When my friend Elaine was recovering after a bad fall, a hospital worker placed a bright yellow bracelet on her wrist. It read "Fall Risk." That phrase meant: Watch this person carefully. She may be unsteady on her feet. Help her get from place to place.

First Corinthians 10 contains something like a "Fall Risk" warning for believers. With a glance back at his ancestors, Paul noted the human potential to fall into sin. The Israelites complained, worshiped idols, and had immoral relationships. God grew unhappy with them and allowed them to experience consequences for their wrongdoing. However, Paul said,

> TODAY'S READING
> **1 Corinthians 10:1–13**
>
> **If you think you are standing firm, be careful that you don't fall!**
>
> 1 Corinthians 10:12

"These things happened to them as examples and were written down as warnings for us. . . . So, if you think you are standing firm, be careful that you don't fall!" (VV. 11–12).

It's easy to trick ourselves into believing that we're done with a particular sort of sin. Even when we've struggled through the worst of it—admitting our problem, repenting, and recommitting ourselves to following God's ways—temptation may come calling. God makes it possible for us to avoid falling back into the same patterns. He does this by providing a way out of the sinful act we're considering. Our part is to respond to His offer of escape. ✦   *JENNIFER BENSON SCHULDT*

Lord, let me see the way of escape You offer when I am tempted.
Give me the strength to accept Your help so I can stay faithful to You.
I know this is Your desire for me, and I thank You that You are
at work in me.

Great blessings are often followed by great temptations.

God Talk

Recently, my son-in-law was explaining to my grand-daughter Maggie that we can talk with God and that He communicates with us. When Ewing told Maggie that God sometimes speaks to us through the Bible, she responded without hesitation: "Well, He's never said anything to me. I've never heard God talk to me."

Most of us would probably agree with Maggie, if hearing an audible voice telling us, "Sell your house, and go take care of orphans in a faraway land," is what we mean by God communicating with us. But when we talk about hearing God "speak," we usually mean something quite different.

We "hear" God through reading Scripture. The Bible tells us about Jesus and says that God "has spoken to us by his Son" who is "the radiance of God's glory and the exact representation of his being" (HEB. 1:2–3). Scripture tells us how to find salvation in Jesus and how to live in ways that please Him (2 TIM. 3:14–17). In addition to Scripture itself, we have the Holy Spirit.

> **TODAY'S READING**
> **Hebrews 1:1–12**
>
> **What we have received is … the Spirit who is from God, so that we may understand what God has freely given us.**
>
> 1 Corinthians 2:12

First Corinthians 2:12 says that we are given the Spirit "so that we may understand what God has freely given us."

Has it been a while since you've heard from God? Talk to Him and listen to the Spirit, who reveals Jesus to us through His Word. Tune in to the wonderful things God has to say to you. 🌿

DAVE BRANON

Speak to me, Lord. Help me to understand the message of Scripture,
the lessons of Jesus, and the urgings of the Holy Spirit.

God speaks through His Word when we take time to listen.

Watch and Pray

From my window I can see a 1,700-meter hill called the *Cerro del Borrego*, or "Hill of the Sheep." In 1862, the French army invaded Mexico. While the enemy camped in the central park of Orizaba, the Mexican army established its position at the top of the hill. However, the Mexican general neglected to guard access to the top. While the Mexican troops were sleeping, the French attacked and killed 2,000 of them.

> TODAY'S READING
> **Mark 14:32–42**
>
> **Watch and pray so that you will not fall into temptation.** Mark 14:38

This reminds me of another hill, the Mount of Olives, and the garden at its foot where a group of disciples fell asleep. Jesus rebuked them, saying, "Watch and pray so that you will not fall into temptation. The spirit is willing, but the flesh is weak" (MARK 14:38).

How easy it is to sleep or become careless in our Christian walk. Temptation strikes when we are most vulnerable. When we neglect certain areas of our spiritual lives—such as prayer and Bible study—we become drowsy and let our guard down, making us easy targets for our enemy, Satan, to strike (1 PETER 5:8).

We need to be alert to the possibilities of an attack and pray to maintain vigilance. If we remain watchful and pray—for ourselves and for others—the Spirit will enable us to resist temptation. ❧

KEILA OCHOA

> Lord Jesus, I know my spirit is willing, but my body is weak.
> Help me to watch and pray today for myself and for others.

Satan is powerless against the power of Christ.

Remembering...

One difficult part of growing older is the fear of dementia and the loss of short-term memory. But Dr. Benjamin Mast, an expert on the topic of Alzheimer's disease, offers some encouragement. He says that patients' brains are often so "well worn" and "habitual" that they can hear an old hymn and sing along to every word. He suggests that spiritual disciplines such as reading Scripture, praying, and singing hymns cause truth to become "embedded" in our brains, ready to be accessed when prompted.

> **TODAY'S READING**
> **Ps. 119:17–19, 130–134**
>
> **I have hidden your word in my heart.**
>
> Psalm 119:11

In Psalm 119:11, we read how the power of hiding God's words in our heart can keep us from sinning. It can strengthen us, teach us obedience, and direct our footsteps (vv. 28, 67, 133). This in turn gives us hope and understanding (vv. 49, 130). Even when we begin to notice memory slips in ourselves or in the life of a loved one, God's Word, memorized years earlier, is still there, "stored up" or "treasured" in the heart (v. 11 ESV, NASB). Even as our minds lose the keen edge of youth, we know that God's words, hidden in our hearts, will continue to speak to us.

Nothing—not even failing memories—can separate us from His love and care. We have His word on it. 🌱 *CINDY HESS KASPER*

Lord, You are such an amazing comfort to us.
Thank You that our salvation and spiritual well-being
does not depend on our failing minds and bodies,
but on You and Your faithfulness to Your Word.

God's promises never fail.

Honorable Living

While delivering a well-publicized speech, a respected leader and statesman got the attention of his nation by declaring that most of his country's honorable Members of Parliament (MPs) were quite *dishonorable*. Citing lifestyles of corruption, pompous attitudes, unsavory language, and other vices, he rebuked the MPs and urged them to reform. As expected, his comments didn't go well with them and they dispatched counter-criticisms his way.

We may not be public officials in positions of leadership, but we who follow Christ are a "chosen people, a royal priesthood, a holy nation, God's special possession" (1 PETER 2:9). As such, our Lord calls us to lifestyles that honor Him.

TODAY'S READING
1 Peter 2:9–12

You are a chosen people, a royal priesthood, a holy nation, God's special possession.
1 Peter 2:9

The disciple Peter had some practical advice on how to do this. He urged us to "abstain from sinful desires, which wage war against your soul" (V. 11). Although he didn't use the word *honorable*, he was calling us to behavior worthy of Christ.

As the apostle Paul phrased it in his letter to the Philippians, "Whatever is pure, whatever is lovely, whatever is admirable—if anything is excellent or praiseworthy—think about such things" (PHIL. 4:8). Indeed, these are the characteristics of behavior that honor our Lord. 🌱

LAWRENCE DARMANI

Lord, when we are honest with You, we understand how often we fall far short of honorable behavior. We know how much we need You. By Your Spirit, help us replace any selfish thoughts, words, and actions with things that please You and draw others to You.

We honor God's name when we call Him our Father and live like His children.

God's Mouthpiece

My nerves fluttering, I waited for the phone to ring and the radio interview to start. I wondered what questions the host would ask and how I would respond. "Lord, I'm much better on paper," I prayed. "But I suppose it's the same as Moses—I need to trust that you will give me the words to speak."

Of course I'm not comparing myself with Moses, the leader of God's people who helped them escape slavery in Egypt to life in the Promised Land. A reluctant leader, Moses needed the Lord to reassure him that the Israelites would listen to him. The Lord revealed several signs to him, such as turning his shepherd's staff into a snake (EX. 4:3), but Moses hesitated to accept the mantle of leadership, saying he was slow of speech (V. 10). So God reminded him that He is the Lord and that He would help him speak. He would "be with his mouth" (as the original language translates, according to biblical scholars).

> TODAY'S READING
> **Exodus 4:1–12**
>
> **Who gave human beings their mouths? . . . Is it not I, the LORD? Now go; I will help you speak.**
>
> Exodus 4:11–12

We know that since the coming of the Holy Spirit at Pentecost, God's Spirit lives within His children and that however inadequate we may feel, He will enable us to carry out the assignments He gives to us. The Lord will "be with our mouths." ✷

AMY BOUCHER PYE

Lord Jesus, You dwell with me.
May my words today build up someone for Your glory.

As God's people we are His mouthpiece to spread His good news.

Naming God

n his book *The God I Don't Understand*, Christopher Wright observes that an unlikely person is one of the first to give God a name. It's Hagar!

Hagar's story provides a disturbingly honest look at human history. It's been years since God told Abram and Sarai they would have a son, and Sarai has only grown older and more impatient. In order to "help" God, she resorts to a custom of the day. She gives her slave, Hagar, to her husband, and Hagar becomes pregnant.

TODAY'S READING
Genesis 16:1-13

I have now seen the One who sees me. Genesis 16:13

Predictably, dissension arises. Sarai mistreats Hagar, who runs away. Alone in the desert, she meets the angel of the Lord, who makes a promise strikingly similar to one God had made earlier—to Abram (SEE GEN. 15:5). "I will increase your descendants so much that they will be too numerous to count" (16:10). The angel names Hagar's son Ishmael, which means "God hears" (V. 11). In response, this slave from a culture with multiple gods that could neither see nor hear gives God the name "You are the God who sees me" (V. 13).

"The God who sees us" is the God of impatient heroes and powerless runaways. He's the God of the wealthy and well-connected as well as the destitute and lonely. He hears and sees and cares, achingly and deeply, for each of us. 🌿 *TIM GUSTAFSON*

Lord, You didn't sugarcoat the story of Your people in the Bible and yet You loved them—as You love us—in spite of all the dirt and drama. You are the God who sees us, and yet we can still run to You.

God sees us with eyes of compassion.

The Ultimate Road Trip

Madagascar's National Road 5 offers the beauty of a white sand coastline, palm forests, and the Indian Ocean. Its 125 miles of two-track road, bare rock, sand, and mud, however, have given it a reputation for being one of the worst roads in the world. Tourists looking for breathtaking views are advised to have a four-wheel-drive vehicle, an experienced driver, and an onboard mechanic.

John the Baptist came to announce the good news of the coming Messiah to those traveling on rough roads and through barren landscape. Repeating the words of the prophet Isaiah written centuries earlier, he urged curious crowds to "prepare the way for the Lord" and to "make straight paths for him" (LUKE 3:4–5; ISA. 40:3)

TODAY'S READING
Isaiah 40:1–11

In the wilderness prepare the way for the LORD; make straight in the desert a highway for our God. Isaiah 40:3

John knew that if the people of Jerusalem were going to be ready to welcome their long-awaited Messiah, their hearts needed to change. Mountains of religious pride would need to come down. Those in the valley of despair because of their broken lives would need to be lifted up.

Neither could be done by human effort alone. Those who refused to respond to the Spirit of God by accepting John's baptism of repentance failed to recognize their Messiah when He came (LUKE 7:29–30). Yet those who saw their need for change discovered in Jesus the goodness and wonder of God. ✒ *MART DEHAAN*

Father in heaven, we need You to do in us what we cannot do for ourselves. Please remove any mountain of pride or valley of despair that would keep us from welcoming You into our lives.

Repentance clears the way for our walk with God.

Gentle Influence

A **few years before** he became the 26th U.S. president (1901–1909), Theodore Roosevelt got word that his oldest son, Theodore Jr., was ill. While his son would recover, the cause of Ted's illness hit Roosevelt hard. Doctors told him that *he* was the cause of his son's illness. Ted was suffering from "nervous exhaustion," having been pressed unmercifully by Theodore to become the "fighter" hero-type he himself had not been during his own frail childhood. Upon hearing this, the elder Roosevelt made a promise to relent: "Hereafter I shall never press Ted either in body or mind."

The father was true to his word. From then on he paid close attention to how he treated his son—the very same son who would one day bravely lead the landing of Allied soldiers on Utah Beach in World War II.

> TODAY'S READING
> **Colossians 3:12–17**
>
> **Clothe yourselves with compassion, kindness, humility, gentleness and patience.** Colossians 3:12

God has entrusted each of us with influence in the lives of others. We have a deep responsibility in those relationships, not only to spouses and children, but to friends, employees, and customers. The temptation to press too hard, to demand too much, to force progress, or to orchestrate success can lead us to harm others even when we don't realize it. For this very reason, followers of Christ are urged to be patient and gentle with one another (COL. 3:12). Since Jesus, the Son of God, came in humility, how can we withhold such kindness from one another? ❧

RANDY KILGORE

What kind of expectations do you have of the people in your life—at home and at work? Think about the influence you might have on others. How can you reflect more of the character of Jesus?

What God does for us we should do for others.

Free Indeed

Olaudah Equiano (C. 1745–1796) was only 11 years old when he was kidnapped and sold into slavery. He made the harrowing journey from West Africa to the West Indies, then to the colony of Virgina, and then to England. By the age of 20 he purchased his own freedom, still bearing the emotional and physical scars of the inhumane treatment he had experienced.

Unable to enjoy his own freedom while others were still enslaved, Equiano became active in the movement to abolish slavery in England. He wrote his autobiography (an unheard of achievement for a former slave in that era) in which he described the horrific treatment of the enslaved.

When Jesus came, He fought a battle for all of us who are enslaved and unable to fight for ourselves. Our slavery is not one of outward chains. We are held by our own brokenness and sin. Jesus said, "Everyone who sins is a slave to sin. Now a slave has no permanent place in the family, but a son belongs to it forever. So if the Son sets you free, you will be free indeed" (JOHN 8:34–36).

Wherever such a freedom seems unheard of, His words need to be declared. We can be liberated from our guilt, shame, and hopelessness. By trusting Jesus, we can be free indeed! 🍂

> **TODAY'S READING**
> **John 8:31–37**
>
> **If the Son sets you free, you will be free indeed.** John 8:36

BILL CROWDER

Thank You, Lord Jesus, for making the sacrifice that has secured my freedom and eternal life. May I learn to love You in a way that honors the love You have shown me.

The price of our freedom from sin was paid by Jesus's blood.

"Because You Prayed"

What do you do with your worries? Do you turn them inward, or turn them upward?

When the brutal Assyrian King Sennacherib was preparing to destroy Jerusalem, he sent a message to King Hezekiah saying that Judah would be no different from all the other nations he had conquered. Hezekiah took this message to the temple in Jerusalem, and "spread it out before the LORD" (ISA. 37:14). He then prayed and asked for help from Almighty God.

Soon afterward Isaiah the prophet delivered this message to Hezekiah from the Lord: "Because you prayed about King Sennacherib of Assyria, the LORD has spoken" (ISA. 37:21–22 NLT). Scripture tells us that Hezekiah's prayer was answered that very night. God intervened miraculously, conquering the enemy forces outside the city gates. The Assyrian army didn't even "shoot an arrow" (V. 33). Sennacherib would leave Jerusalem, never to return.

> TODAY'S READING
> **Isaiah 37:9–22, 33**
>
> **Do not be anxious about anything, but in every situation, by prayer and petition, with thanksgiving, present your requests to God.**
>
> Philippians 4:6

Three words in God's message to Hezekiah—"Because you prayed"—show us the best place to go with our worries. Because Hezekiah turned to God, He rescued him and his people. When we turn our worries into prayer, we discover that God is faithful in unexpected ways! ❧ *JAMES BANKS*

Father, please help me to turn my worries into prayer.
My problems are better in Your hands than in my own.

Prayer moves the hand that moves the world. E.M. BOUNDS

How to Carve a Duck

My wife, Carolyn, and I met Phipps Festus Bourne in 1995 in his shop in Mabry Hill, Virginia. Bourne, who died in 2002, was a master wood carver whose carvings are almost exact replicas of real objects. "Carving a duck is simple," he said. "You just look at a piece of wood, get in your head what a duck looks like, and then cut off everything that doesn't look like it."

So it is with God. He looks at you and me—blocks of rough wood—envisions the Christlike woman or man hidden beneath the bark, knots, and twigs and then begins to carve away everything that does not fit that image. We would be amazed if we could see how beautiful we are as finished "ducks."

TODAY'S READING
Ps. 138:7–8; Eph. 2:6–10

For those God foreknew he also predestined to be conformed to the image of his Son.

Romans 8:29

But first we must accept that we are a block of wood and allow the Artist to cut, shape, and sand us where He will. This means viewing our circumstances—pleasant or unpleasant—as God's tools that shape us. He forms us, one part at a time, into the beautiful creature He envisioned in our ungainly lump of wood.

Sometimes the process is wonderful; sometimes it is painful. But in the end, all of God's tools conform us "to the image of his Son" (ROM. 8:29).

Do you long for that likeness? Put yourself in the Master Carver's hands. 🌿

DAVID ROPER

Father, You are the craftsman who shapes me. You are the one who knows what shape my life should take. Thank You for carving me into the image You have planned. Help me to trust that the pieces and parts that You shave from me are the right ones.

Growing in Christ comes from a deepening relationship with Him.

Good Imitation

"**T**oday we're going to play a game called *Imitation*," our children's minister told the kids gathered around him for the children's sermon. "I'll name something and you act out what it does. Ready? *Chicken!*" The kids flapped their arms, cackled, and crowed. Next it was *elephant*, then *football player*, and then *ballerina*. The last one was *Jesus*. While many of the children hesitated, one six-year-old with a big smile on his face immediately threw his arms wide open in welcome. The congregation applauded.

> TODAY'S READING
> **1 Thessalonians 1:1–10**
>
> **You became imitators of us and of the Lord.**
> 1 Thessalonians 1:6

How easily we forget that our calling is to be like Jesus in the everyday situations of life. "Follow God's example, therefore, as dearly loved children and walk in the way of love, just as Christ loved us and gave himself up for us as a fragrant offering and sacrifice to God" (EPH. 5:1–2).

The apostle Paul commended the followers of Jesus in Thessalonica for the outward demonstration of their faith in difficult circumstances. "You became imitators of us and of the Lord," Paul wrote. "And so you became a model to all the believers in Macedonia and Achaia" (1 THESS. 1:6–7).

It is the life of Jesus in us that encourages and enables us to walk through this world as He did—with the good news of God's love and with arms open wide in welcome to all. 🌿

DAVID MCCASLAND

Lord Jesus, may Your words of invitation and welcome,
"Come to Me," be lived out through our lives today.

Jesus's arms of welcome are always open.

Doing What He Says

needed an underground water tank and knew precisely how I wanted it constructed, so I gave clear instructions to the builder. The next day when I inspected the project, I was annoyed when I realized that he had failed to carry out my instructions. He had changed the plan and therefore the effect. The excuse he gave was as irritating as his failure to follow my directives.

As I watched him redo the concrete work, and as my frustration diminished, a guilty conviction swept over me: How many times have I needed to redo things in my life in obedience to the Lord?

Like the ancient Israelites who frequently failed to do what God asked them to do, we too often go our own way. Yet obedience is a desired result of our deepening relationship with God. Moses told the people, "Be careful to do what the LORD your God has commanded you .... Walk in obedience to all that [he] has commanded you" (DEUT. 5:32–33). Long after Moses, Jesus urged His disciples to trust Him and to love one another.

This is still the kind of surrender of our hearts that leads to our well-being. As the Spirit helps us to obey, it is good to remember that He "works in [us] to will and to act in order to fulfill his good purpose" (PHIL. 2:13). 🌿

LAWRENCE DARMANI

> **TODAY'S READING**
> **Deuteronomy 5:28–33**
>
> **Walk in obedience to all that the LORD your God has commanded you.**
>
> Deuteronomy 5:33

Lord, thank You for second and third chances.
Please help us to want to follow Your ways and to follow through in obedience.

The closer we walk with God, the clearer we see His guidance.

A Bubble Break

A **young boy** showered my husband, Carl, and me with bubbles as he came running by us on the Atlantic City boardwalk. It was a light and fun moment on a difficult day. We had come to the city to visit our brother-in-law in the hospital and to help Carl's sister who was struggling and having trouble getting to her doctors' appointments. So as we took a break and walked along the seaside boardwalk we were feeling a bit overwhelmed by the needs of our family.

Then came the bubbles. Just bubbles blown at us whimsically by a little boy in the ocean breeze—but they had a special significance to me. I love bubbles and keep a bottle in my office to use whenever I need the smile of a bubble break. Those

> TODAY'S READING
> **2 Corinthians 4:7–18**
>
> **We fix our eyes not on what is seen, but on what is unseen.**
>
> 2 Corinthians 4:18

bubbles and the vast Atlantic Ocean reminded me of what I can count on: God is always close. He is powerful. He always cares. And He can use even the smallest experiences, and briefest moments, to help us remember that His presence is like an ocean of grace in the middle of our heavy moments.

Maybe one day our troubles will seem like bubbles—momentary in light of eternity for "what is seen is temporary, but what is unseen is eternal" (2 COR. 4:18). 🕊

ANNE CETAS

What gifts of grace has God given to you in a difficult time?
How might you be a blessing to others?

Jesus provides an oasis of grace in the desert of trials.

Graded with Grace

My son's blue eyes sparkled with excitement as he showed me a paper he had brought home from school. It was a math test, marked with a red star and a grade of 100 percent. As we looked at the exam, he said he had three questions left to answer when the teacher said time was up. Puzzled, I asked how he could have received a perfect score. He replied, "My teacher gave me grace. She let me finish the test although I had run out of time."

TODAY'S READING
Romans 5:6–15

While we were still sinners, Christ died for us. Romans 5:8

As my son and I discussed the meaning of grace, I pointed out that God has given us more than we deserve through Christ. We deserve death because of our sin (ROM. 3:23). Yet, "while we were still sinners, Christ died for us" (5:8). We were unworthy, yet Jesus—sinless and holy—gave up His life so we could escape the penalty for our sin and one day live forever in heaven.

Eternal life is a gift from God. It's not something we earn by working for it. We are saved by God's grace, through faith in Christ (EPH. 2:8–9). 🍂

JENNIFER BENSON SCHULDT

Dear God, Your undeserved favor has made it possible for us to be saved from our sin. You have shown us amazing grace. Thank You for the gift You gave. Use me to tell others about You and what You have done.

Grace and mercy are unearned blessings.

She Did What She Could

When her friends say thoughtless or outrageous things on social media, Charlotte chimes in with gentle but firm dissent. She respects the dignity of everyone, and her words are unfailingly positive.

A few years ago she became Facebook friends with a man who harbored anger toward Christians. He appreciated Charlotte's rare honesty and grace. Over time his hostility melted. Then Charlotte suffered a bad fall. Now housebound, she fretted over what she could do. About that time her Facebook

TODAY'S READING
Mark 14:3–9

She did what she could. Mark 14:8

friend died and then this message arrived from his sister: "[Because of your witness] I know he's now experiencing God's complete and abiding love for him."

During the week in which Christ would be killed, Mary of Bethany anointed Him with expensive perfume (JOHN 12:3; MARK 14:3). Some of those present were appalled, but Jesus applauded her. "She has done a beautiful thing to me," He said. "She did what she could. She poured perfume on my body beforehand to prepare for my burial" (MARK 14:6–8).

"She did what she could." Christ's words take the pressure off. Our world is full of broken, hurting people. But we don't have to worry about what we can't do. Charlotte did what she could. So can we. The rest is in His capable hands. ❧   *TIM GUSTAFSON*

Lord, help us not to define our self-worth by what we do for You,
but by what You have done for us. Show us how we can
show Your love to others.

Do thy duty, that is best; leave unto the Lord the rest.

HENRY WADSWORTH LONGFELLOW

Everything Comes from God

was 18 years old when I got my first fulltime job, and I learned an important lesson about the discipline of saving money. I worked and saved until I had enough money for a year of school. Then my mom had emergency surgery, and I realized I had the money in the bank to pay for her operation.

My love for my mother suddenly took precedence over my plans for the future. These words in the book *Passion and Purity* by Elisabeth Elliot took on new meaning: "If we hold tightly to anything given to us, unwilling to let it go when the time comes

TODAY'S READING
1 Chronicles 29:14–19

All of it belongs to you. 1 Chronicles 29:16

to let it go or unwilling to allow it to be used as the Giver means it to be used, we stunt the growth of the soul. It is easy to make a mistake here, 'If God gave it to me', we say, 'it's mine. I can do what I want with it.' No. The truth is that it is ours to thank Him for and ours to offer back to Him, . . . ours to let go of."

I realized that the job I had received and the discipline of saving were gifts from God! I could give generously to my family because I was sure God was capable of seeing me through school another way, and He did.

Today, how might God want us to apply David's prayer from 1 Chronicles 29:14, "Everything we have has come from you, and we give you only what you first gave us" (NLT). 🌐

KEILA OCHOA

Lord, we know there is nothing that we have that we obtained
on our own. It's all Yours. Help us to have open hands for You
to give and take as You please. Increase our faith.

Everything belongs to God.

What Matters Most

As Jesus's beloved disciple John grew older, his teaching became increasingly narrowed, focusing entirely on the love of God in his three letters. In the book *Knowing the Truth of God's Love*, Peter Kreeft cites an old legend which says that one of John's young disciples once came to him complaining, "Why don't you talk about anything else?" John replied, "Because there isn't anything else."

TODAY'S READING
1 John 4:7–19

He sent his one and only Son into the world that we might live through him. 1 John 4:9

God's love is certainly at the heart of the mission and message of Jesus. In his earlier gospel account, John recorded the words, "For God so loved the world that he gave his one and only Son, that whoever believes in him shall not perish but have eternal life" (JOHN 3:16).

The apostle Paul tells us that God's love is at the core of how we live, and he reminds us that "neither death nor life, neither angels nor demons, neither the present nor the future, nor any powers, neither height nor depth, nor anything else in all creation, will be able to separate us from the love of God that is in Christ Jesus our Lord" (ROM. 8:38–39).

God's love is so strong, available, and stabilizing that we can confidently step into each day knowing that the good things are gifts from His hand and the challenges can be faced in His strength. For all of life, His love is what matters most. ✒

BILL CROWDER

Thank You, O Lord, that Your love is rich and pure,
measureless and strong!

God's love stands when all else has fallen.

Evie's Decision

Evie was one of 25 American teenagers in a high school choir who traveled to Jamaica to sing, witness, and show God's love to people of a different culture and generation. And for Evie, one day of that trip was particularly memorable and joy-filled.

That day, the choir went to a nursing home to sing and visit with the residents. After they sang, Evie sat down with a young woman who lived at the home, a woman in her early 30s. As they began to chat, Evie felt that she should talk about Jesus—who He was and what He did for us. She showed her verses in the Bible

> **TODAY'S READING**
> **Acts 1:1–8**
>
> **Go into all the world and preach the gospel to all creation.** Mark 16:15

that explained salvation. Soon the woman said she wanted to trust Jesus as her Savior. And that's just what she did.

Because of Evie's decision to start a conversation about Jesus, our group celebrated a new birth into God's family that day.

Mark 16:15 tells us that what Evie did is what is expected of all believers. Here's how *The Message* paraphrases that verse: "Go everywhere and announce the Message of God's good news to one and all."

May we never underestimate the wonder of what it means for anyone, anywhere to hear the good news and to say yes to our Savior. ✿

DAVE BRANON

Lord, it's not easy to strike up a conversation about the gospel.
Please allow the Holy Spirit to work in me so I will be willing and able to mention the good news to anyone who needs You.

Effective witnesses not only know their faith but show their faith.

Emergency Prayer

On **September 11, 2001,** Stanley Praimnath was working on the 81st floor of the World Trade Center South Tower when he saw an airplane flying directly toward him. Stanley prayed a quick prayer as he dove under a desk for protection: "Lord, I can't do this! You take over!"

The terrible impact of the plane crash trapped Stanley behind a wall of debris. But as he prayed and cried for help, Brian Clark, a worker from another office, heard and responded. Making their way through rubble and darkness, the two found their way down 80 flights of stairs to the ground floor and out.

> **TODAY'S READING**
> **Psalm 71:1–12**
>
> **Be my rock of refuge, to which I can always go.**
>
> Psalm 71:3

When encountering terrible threats, David asked God for help. He wanted to be assured of God's nearness as he faced enemies in battle. In a heartfelt petition David said, "Be my rock of refuge, to which I can always go.... Do not be far from me, my God; come quickly, God, to help me" (PS. 71:3, 12).

We aren't promised deliverance from every difficult situation we face. But we can be confident that God hears our prayers and will walk alongside us through everything. 🌿 *DENNIS FISHER*

Whatever comes my way, please come near to me, Lord, to help.
I cannot make it through anything without You.
Thank You.

Nearness to God is our conscious security. A child in the dark is comforted by grasping its father's hand. CHARLES HADDON SPURGEON

Ready for the Wedding

I'm hungry," said my eight-year-old daughter. "I'm sorry," I said, "I don't have anything for you. Let's play tic-tac-toe." We had been waiting over an hour for the bride to arrive at the church for what was supposed to be a noon wedding. As I wondered how much longer it would be, I hoped I could occupy my daughter until the wedding started.

As we waited, I felt like we were enacting a parable. Although the vicarage where we live is a stone's throw from the church, I knew if I went to fetch some crackers, the bride could come at any moment and I would miss her entrance. As I employed many distraction techniques with my hungry daughter, I also thought about Jesus's parable about the ten virgins (MATT. 25:1-13). Five came prepared with enough oil for their lamps to stay lit as they waited for the bridegroom, but five did not. Just as it was too late for me to dash back to the vicarage, so it was too late for the young women to go and buy more oil for their lamps.

> TODAY'S READING
> **Matthew 25:1–13**
>
> **Therefore keep watch, because you do not know the day or the hour.** Matthew 25:13

Jesus told this parable to emphasize that we need to be prepared, for when He comes again we will give an account over the state of our hearts. Are we waiting and ready? ❧

AMY BOUCHER PYE

What does waiting for Jesus's return look like in your life?
Have you left something undone that you could attend to today?

We need to be ready for Christ to come again.

Ready for a Change?

Self-control is probably one of the hardest things to master. How often have we been defeated by a bad habit, a lousy attitude, or a wrong mindset? We make promises to improve. We ask someone to hold us accountable. But deep inside, we know that we don't have the will or the ability to change. We can talk, we can plan, we can read self-help books, but we still find it difficult to overcome and control many of the things that are inside us!

> TODAY'S READING
> **Galatians 5:16–25**
>
> **But the fruit of the Spirit is ... self-control.** Galatians 5:22–23

Thankfully, God knows our weakness, and He also knows the remedy! The Bible says, "The fruit of the Spirit is love, joy, peace, forbearance, kindness, goodness, faithfulness, gentleness and self-control" (GAL. 5:22–23). The only way to gain self-control is by allowing the Holy Spirit to control us.

In other words, our key focus is not *effort* but *surrender*—to live moment by moment submissively trusting in the Lord rather than in self. Paul says this is what it means to "walk by the Spirit" (V. 16).

Are you ready for a change? You can change, for God is in you. As you surrender control to Him, He will help you bear the fruit of His likeness. 🌱

JAIME FERNÁNDEZ GARRIDO

I am in need, Lord, of Your power so that I might change and grow.
I surrender myself to You. Please help me to understand
how to be submissive to You that I might be filled with Your Spirit.

God is not nearly as concerned with our ability as He is with our surrender.

Beyond Time

During 2016, theater companies in Britain and around the world staged special productions to mark the 400th anniversary of the death of William Shakespeare. Concerts, lectures, and festivals drew crowds who celebrated the enduring work of the man widely considered to be the greatest playwright in the English language. Ben Jonson, one of Shakespeare's contemporaries, wrote of him, "He was not of an age, but for all time."

While the influence of some artists, writers, and thinkers may last for centuries, Jesus Christ is the only person whose life and work will endure beyond time. He claimed to be "the bread that came down from heaven . . . whoever feeds on this bread will live forever" (V. 58).

When many people who heard Jesus's teaching were offended by His words and stopped following Him (JOHN 6:61–66), the Lord asked His disciples if they also wanted to leave (V. 67). Peter replied, "Lord, to whom shall we go? You have the words of eternal life. We have come to believe and to know that you are the Holy One of God" (VV. 68–69).

When we invite Jesus to come into our lives as our Lord and Savior, we join His first disciples and all those who have followed Him in a new life that will last forever—beyond time. 🕊

> **TODAY'S READING**
> **John 6:53–69**
>
> **"Lord, to whom shall we go? You have the words of eternal life. We have come to believe and to know that you are the Holy One of God."** John 6:68–69

DAVID McCASLAND

Lord Jesus, thank You for the gift of eternal life in fellowship with You today and forever.

Jesus is the Son of God, the Man beyond time, who gives us eternal life.

Two Mites

Jesus sat in the temple near the treasury and watched as people walked by and deposited their gifts for the temple (MARK 12). Some made a show of it, perhaps so others could see how much they had given. Just then a poor woman came by and threw in two "mites."

A mite was the least valuable coin in circulation. Thus, the widow's gift was very small, amounting to nothing in most folks' eyes. But our Lord saw what others did not see. She had given "all that she had" (MARK 12:44). The widow wasn't trying to draw attention to herself. She was simply doing what she was able to do. And Jesus noticed!

We mustn't forget that our Lord sees all that we do, though it may seem very small. It may be nothing more than showing a cheerful countenance in difficult times or an unnoticed act of love and kindness to someone who happens to pass by. It may be a brief, silent prayer for a neighbor in need.

> TODAY'S READING
> **Mark 12:41–44**
>
> **She out of her poverty put in all that she had, her whole livelihood.**
>
> Mark 12:44

Jesus said, "Take heed that you do not do your charitable deeds before men, to be seen by them. Otherwise you have no reward from your Father in heaven.…But when you do a charitable deed,…may [it] be in secret; and your Father who sees in secret will Himself reward you openly" (MATT. 6:1–4). *DAVID ROPER*

May our gifts be sacrificial,
From our hearts, and full of love;
Secretive and never showy,
Pleasing our great God above. *SPER*

God looks at the heart, not the hand; the giver, not the gift.

A Pleasing Aroma

A perfumer who works in New York declares that she can recognize certain combinations of scents and guess the perfumer behind a fragrance. With just a sniff she can say, "This is Jenny's work."

When writing to the followers of Christ in the city of Corinth, Paul at one point used an example that would have reminded them of a victorious Roman army in a conquered city burning incense (2 COR. 2:14). The general would come through first, followed by his troops and then the defeated army. For the Romans, the aroma of the incense meant victory; for the prisoners, it meant death.

> **TODAY'S READING**
> **2 Corinthians 2:12–17**
>
> **We are to God the pleasing aroma of Christ.** 2 Corinthians 2:15

Paul said we are to God the pleasing aroma of Christ's victory over sin. God has given us the fragrance of Christ Himself so we can become a sweet-smelling sacrifice of praise. But how can we live so we spread this pleasing fragrance to others? We can show generosity and love, and we can share the gospel with others so they can find the way to salvation. We can allow the Spirit to display through us His gifts of love, joy, and kindness (GAL. 5:22–23).

Do others observe us and say, "This is Jesus's work"? Are we allowing Him to spread His fragrance through us and then telling others about Him? He is the Ultimate Perfumer—the most exquisite fragrance there will ever be. ❧   *KEILA OCHOA*

Do others recognize the work of God in my life?
Am I spreading the fragrance of Christ? How?

A godly life is a fragrance that draws others to Christ.

The Survival Float

Sunlight glittered on the swimming pool in front of me. I overheard an instructor speaking to a student who had been in the water for quite a while. He said, "It looks like you're getting tired. When you're exhausted and in deep water, try the survival float."

Certain situations in life require us to spend our mental, physical, or emotional energy in a way that we can't sustain. David described a time when his enemies were threatening him and he felt the emotional weight of their anger. He needed to escape the distress he was experiencing.

> **TODAY'S READING**
> **Psalm 55:4–23**
>
> **Cast your cares on the LORD and he will sustain you.**
>
> Psalm 55:22

As he processed his feelings, he found a way to rest in his troubled thoughts. He said, "Cast your cares on the LORD and he will sustain you" (PS. 55:22). He recognized that God supports us if we dare to release our problems to Him. We don't have to take charge of every situation and try to craft the outcome—that's exhausting! God is in control of every aspect of our life.

Instead of trying to do everything in our own effort, we can find rest in God. Sometimes it's as simple as asking Him to handle our problems. Then we can pause, relax, and enjoy the knowledge that He is sustaining us. 🌿 *JENNIFER BENSON SCHULDT*

God, today I give my problems to You. I know that You are
in control of everything and I believe You are willing to help me.
Please help me to find peace in You.

God is a safe resting place.

Making Preparations

As we viewed my father-in-law's body in his casket at the funeral home, one of his sons took his dad's hammer and tucked it alongside his folded hands. Years later, when my mother-in-law died, one of the children slipped a set of knitting needles under her fingers. Those sweet gestures brought comfort to us as we remembered how often they had used those tools during their lives.

Of course, we knew that they wouldn't actually need those items in eternity. We had no illusions, as the ancient Egyptians did, that tools or money or weapons buried with someone would better prepare them for the next life. You can't take it with you! (PS. 49:16–17; 1 TIM. 6:7).

TODAY'S READING
John 14:1–6

> If I go and prepare a place for you, I will come back and take you to be with me that you also may be where I am. John 14:3

But some preparation for eternity had been necessary for my in-laws. That preparation had come years before when they trusted Jesus as their Savior.

Planning for the life to come can't begin at the time of our death. Each of us must prepare our heart by accepting the gift of salvation made possible by Jesus's sacrifice on the cross.

At the same time, God has made preparations as well: "If I go and prepare a place for you, I will come back and take you to be with me that you also may be where I am" (JOHN 14:3). He has promised to prepare a place for us to spend eternity with Him. ❧

CINDY HESS KASPER

Father, we're grateful that we will have a place with You one day.
Thank You that you will fill us with joy in Your Presence.

God gives us time—to prepare for eternity.

Worth the Calories?

love egg *roti prata*, a popular pancake in my country of Singapore. So I was intrigued to read that a 125-pound (57 kg) person must run 5 miles (8 km) per hour for 30 minutes to burn 240 calories. That's equivalent to only one egg *roti prata*.

Ever since I started working out in the gym, those numbers have taken on a new significance for me. I find myself asking: Is this food worth the calories?

TODAY'S READING
Philippians 4:4–9

While it is wise to watch our food consumption, it is even more important to watch our media consumption. Research shows that what we see can stay in our minds for a long time and influence our behavior. It has a "clingy effect," sticking to us like that stubborn fat we find so hard to lose.

If anything is excellent or praiseworthy— think about such things. Philippians 4:8

With the wide variety of media content surrounding us today, we need to be discerning consumers. That doesn't mean we read only Christian literature or watch only faith-related movies, but we are careful about what we allow our eyes to see. We might ask ourselves: Is this worth my time?

In Philippians 4:8, the apostle Paul tells us in essence, "Feed your eyes and minds on things that are true, noble, just, pure, lovely, of good report, virtuous and praiseworthy." This is a "diet" worthy of what Christ has done and is doing in us. ✪

POH FANG CHIA

Are my viewing habits enhancing my life
or are they drawing me away from things that really matter?
Help me, Lord, to make wise choices.

The mind is formed by what it takes in. WILL DURANT

Connecting the Dots

n the 1880s French artist Georges Seurat introduced an art form known as pointillism. As the name suggests, Seurat used small dots of color, rather than brush strokes of blended pigments, to create an artistic image. Up close, his work looks like groupings of individual dots. Yet as the observer steps back, the human eye blends the dots into brightly colored portraits or landscapes.

The big picture of the Bible is similar. Up close, its complexity can leave us with the impression of dots on a canvas. As we read it, we might feel like Cleopas and his friend on the road to Emmaus. They couldn't understand the tragic "dotlike" events of the Passover weekend. They had hoped that Jesus "was the one who was going to redeem Israel" (LUKE 24:21), but they had just witnessed His death.

TODAY'S READING
Luke 24:13–32

Beginning with Moses and all the Prophets, he explained to them what was said in all the Scriptures concerning himself.
Luke 24:27

Suddenly a man they did not recognize was walking alongside them. After showing an interest in their conversation, He helped them connect the dots of the suffering and death of their long-awaited Messiah. Later, while eating a meal with them, Jesus let them recognize Him—and then He left as mysteriously as He came.

Was it the scarred dots of the nail wounds in His hands that caught their attention? We don't know. What we do know is that when we connect the dots of Scripture and Jesus's suffering (VV. 27, 44), we see a God who loves us more than we can imagine. ❧

MART DEHAAN

Jesus laid down His life to show His love for us.

Fiery Trials

Fire can be one of the worst enemies of trees. But it can also be helpful. Experts say that small, frequent fires called "cool" fires clean the forest floor of dead leaves and branches but don't destroy the trees. They leave behind ashes, which are perfect for seeds to grow in. Surprisingly, low-intensity fires are necessary for healthy growth of trees.

Similarly, trials—pictured as fire in the Bible—are necessary for our spiritual health and growth (1 PETER 1:7; 4:12). James wrote, "Consider it pure joy, my brothers and sisters, whenever you face trials of many kinds, because you know that the testing of your faith produces perseverance. Let perseverance finish its work so that you may be mature and complete, not lacking anything" (JAMES 1:2–4).

> TODAY'S READING
> **James 1:2–12**
>
> **Consider it pure joy, my brothers and sisters, whenever you face trials of many kinds.** James 1:2

It is in the season of trial that God's purposes are often realized, for there the conditions are right for us to grow into spiritual maturity. This growth not only equips us for living, but it also enables us to more accurately reflect Jesus to a world that desperately needs Him.

In the hands of our Father, our trials can achieve His purposes for our good and for His honor. They can shape us into the likeness of His Son. ✿

BILL CROWDER

Father, teach me to trust You for the strength to endure difficulties and
the faith to wait for Your good purposes to be accomplished in me.

Faith is seeing God in the dark and in the light.

The Gates of Worship

When you enter some of the greatest cities in the world, you can encounter famous gates such as the Brandenburg Gate (Berlin), the Jaffa Gate (Jerusalem), and the gates at Downing Street (London). Whether the gates were built for defensive or ceremonial purposes, they all represent the difference between being outside or inside certain areas of the city. Some are open; some are closed to all but a few.

The gates into the presence of God are always open. The familiar song of Psalm 100 is an invitation for the Israelites to enter into the presence of God through the temple gates. They were told to "shout for joy" and "come before him with joyful songs" (vv. 1–2).

> **TODAY'S READING**
> **Psalm 100**
>
> Enter his gates with thanksgiving and his courts with praise; give thanks to him and praise his name. Psalm 100:4

Shouting for joy was an appropriate expression when greeting a monarch in the ancient world. All the earth was to sing joyfully about God! The reason for this joyful noise was that God had given them their identity (v. 3). They entered the gates with praise and thanksgiving because of God's goodness and His steadfast and enduring love which continues through all generations (vv. 4–5). Even when they forgot their identity and wandered away from Him, God remained faithful and still invited them to enter His presence.

The gates into God's presence are still open, inviting us to come and worship. 🌱

MARVIN WILLIAMS

What should motivate us to worship God?
What statement of praise could you give to God today?

The gates into the presence of God are always open.

Words for the Weary

A **few days after** his father died, 30-year-old C. S. Lewis received a letter from a woman who had cared for his mother during her illness and death more than two decades earlier. The woman offered her sympathy for his loss and wondered if he remembered her. "My dear Nurse Davison," Lewis replied. "Remember you? I should think I do."

Lewis recalled how much her presence in their home had meant to him as well as to his brother and father during a difficult time. He thanked her for her words of sympathy and said, "It is *really* comforting to be taken back to those old days. The time during which you were with my mother seemed very long to a child and you became part of home."

TODAY'S READING
Isaiah 50:4–10

> The Sovereign LORD has given me a well-instructed tongue, to know the word that sustains the weary.
>
> Isaiah 50:4

When we struggle in the circumstances of life, an encouraging word from others can lift our spirits and our eyes to the Lord. The Old Testament prophet Isaiah wrote, "The Sovereign LORD has given me a well-instructed tongue, to know the word that sustains the weary" (50:4). And when we look to the Lord, He offers words of hope and light in the darkness. ✱ *DAVID MCCASLAND*

Heavenly Father, help me to hear Your word of hope today.
And help me to speak words of hope and encouragement to others,
pointing them to You.

Kind words can lift a heavy heart.

Pass It On

enjoy watching relay races. The physical strength, speed, skill, and endurance required of the athletes amaze me. But one crucial point of the race always gets my special attention and makes me anxious. It is the moment the baton is passed to the next athlete. One moment of delay, one slip, and the race could be lost.

TODAY'S READING
Psalm 78:1–8

We will tell the next generation the praiseworthy deeds of the LORD.

Psalm 78:4

In a sense, Christians are in a relay race, carrying the baton of faith and the knowledge of the Lord and of His Word. And the Bible tells us about our need to pass this baton from one generation to another. In Psalm 78, Asaph declares: "I will utter… things from of old—things we have heard and known, things our ancestors have told us…. We will tell the next generation the praiseworthy deeds of the LORD, his power, and the wonders he has done" (VV. 2–4).

Moses said something similar to the Israelites: "Do not forget the things your eyes have seen or let them fade from your heart as long as you live. Teach them to your children and to their children after them" (DEUT. 4:9).

For generations to come, we are called to lovingly and courageously do whatever we can to pass along "the praises of him who called [us] out of darkness into his wonderful light" (1 PETER 2:9). 🕯️

LAWRENCE DARMANI

Father, help me to be faithful in passing my faith along to someone else.

We influence future generations by living for Christ today.

Words that Matter

Early in my days of working as an editor for *Our Daily Bread*, I selected the cover verse for each month's devotional. After a while, I began to wonder if it made a difference.

Not long after that, a reader wrote and described how she had prayed for her son for more than twenty years, yet he wanted nothing to do with Jesus. Then one day he stopped by to visit her, and he read the verse on the cover of the booklet that sat on her table. The Spirit used those words to convict him, and he gave his life to Jesus at that very moment.

I don't recall the verse or the woman's name. But I'll never forget the clarity of God's message to me that day. He had chosen to answer a woman's prayers through a verse selected nearly a year earlier. From a place beyond time, He brought the wonder of His presence to my work and His words.

TODAY'S READING
1 John 1:1–4

> **That which was from the beginning, which we have heard, which we have seen with our eyes . . . this we proclaim concerning the Word of life.** 1 John 1:1

John the disciple called Jesus "the Word of life" (1 JOHN 1:1). He wanted everyone to know what that meant. "We proclaim to you the eternal life, which was with the Father and has appeared to us," he wrote of Jesus (V. 2). "We proclaim to you what we have seen and heard, so that you also may have fellowship with us" (V. 3).

There is nothing magical in putting words on a page. But there is life-changing power in the words of Scripture because they point us to the Word of life—Jesus. 🌱   *TIM GUSTAFSON*

Thank You, Father, that Your Word is living and powerful!

Words that point us to Christ are always words that matter.

Calming Your Soul

While attending a concert, my mind detoured to a troublesome issue that insisted on my attention. Thankfully, the distraction was short-lived as the words of a beautiful hymn began to reach deep into my being. A men's a capella group was singing "Be Still, My Soul." Tears welled up as I listened to the words and contemplated the restful peace that only God can give:

Be still, my soul: the Lord is on thy side! Bear patiently the cross of grief or pain; leave to thy God to order and provide; in every change He faithful will remain.

> **TODAY'S READING**
> **Matthew 11:25–30**
>
> **Be still, and know that I am God.**
> Psalm 46:10

When Jesus was denouncing the unrepentant towns where He had done most of His miracles (MATT. 11:20-24), He still had words of comfort for those who would come to Him. He said, "Come to me, all you who are weary and burdened…learn from me, for I am gentle and humble in heart, and you will find rest for your souls" (VV. 28–29).

This statement is striking! Immediately following His strong words for those who were rejecting Him, Jesus extended an invitation to all to draw near to Him to find the peace we all yearn for. Jesus is the only one who can calm our restless, weary souls. ❧

JOE STOWELL

I come to You now, Lord, in need of rest for my heart. Help me to trust You and be confident in Your love.

When we keep our minds on Jesus, He keeps our minds at peace.

True Riches

At the memorial service for my friend's dad, someone said to her, "Until I met your father, I didn't know a person could have fun while helping others." Her dad contributed his part in helping to build the kingdom of God through serving people, laughing and loving, and meeting strangers who became friends. When he died, he left a legacy of love. In contrast, my friend's aunt—her father's older sister—viewed her possessions as her legacy, spending her latter years worrying about who would protect her heirlooms and rare books.

TODAY'S READING
Luke 12:22–34

For where your treasure is, there your heart will be also. Luke 12:34

In His teaching and by His example, Jesus warned His followers to avoid hoarding possessions, to give to the poor, and to value what will not rust or decay. "For where your treasure is," Jesus said, "there your heart will be also" (LUKE 12:34).

We might think our things give meaning to our life. But when the latest gadget breaks or we misplace or lose something valuable, we begin to realize that it is our relationship with the Lord that satisfies and endures. It is our love and care for others that does not wither and fade away.

Let's ask the Lord to help us see clearly what we value, to show us where our heart is, and to help us seek His kingdom above all (12:31). 🌱   *AMY BOUCHER PYE*

What do you value? Read the story about the manna in the wilderness in Exodus 16. Consider how this story relates to Jesus's words to the crowds in Luke 12.

What we value reveals the state of our heart.

Praying for You Today

When we face a perplexing situation or a tough problem, we often ask our brothers and sisters in Christ to pray for us. It's a great encouragement to know that others who care are holding us up to God in prayer. But what if you don't have close Christian friends? Perhaps you live where the gospel of Christ is opposed. Who will pray for you?

Romans 8, one of the great, triumphant chapters of the Bible, declares, "We do not know what we ought to pray for, but the Spirit himself intercedes for us through wordless groans. . . . The Spirit intercedes for God's people in accordance with the will of God" (ROM. 8:26–27). The Holy Spirit is praying for you today.

> TODAY'S READING
> **Romans 8:22–34**
>
> **The Spirit himself intercedes for us.... [Christ Jesus] is also interceding for us.** Romans 8:26, 34

In addition, "Christ Jesus who died—more than that, who was raised to life—is at the right hand of God and is also interceding for us" (V. 34). The living Lord Jesus Christ is praying for you today.

Think of it! The Holy Spirit and the Lord Jesus Christ mention your name and your needs to God the Father, who hears and acts on your behalf.

No matter where you are or how confusing your situation, you do not face life alone. The Spirit and the Son are praying for you today! ✿ *DAVID MCCASLAND*

Dear God, I bow in humble thanks for the prayers spoken by the Holy Spirit and by Your Son today—for me. What an amazing truth!

The Holy Spirit and Jesus are always praying for you.

Within a Stone's Throw

As a group of religious leaders herded an adulterous woman toward Jesus, they couldn't know they were carrying her within a stone's throw of grace. Their hope was to discredit Him. If He told them to let the woman go, they could claim He was breaking Mosaic law. But if He condemned her to death, the crowds following Him would have dismissed His words of mercy and grace.

TODAY'S READING
John 7:53–8:11

Let any one of you who is without sin be the first to throw a stone at her. John 8:7

But Jesus turned the tables on the accusers. Scripture says that rather than answering them directly, He started writing on the ground. When the leaders continued to question Him, He invited any of them who had never sinned to throw the first stone, and then He started writing on the ground again. The next time He looked up, all the accusers were gone.

Now the only person who could have thrown a stone—the only sinless one—looked at the woman and gave her mercy. " 'Then neither do I condemn you,' Jesus declared. 'Go now and leave your life of sin' " (JOHN 8:11).

Whether today finds you needing forgiveness for judging others or desiring assurance that no sin is beyond His grace, be encouraged by this: No one is throwing stones today; go and be changed by God's mercy. ❧   *RANDY KILGORE*

Father, cleanse me of my judging nature and free me from the bonds of sin. Let me taste Your mercy and then help me to live a changed life.

We serve a Savior who is eager to forgive.

Bad Faith, Good Faith

"Y**ou gotta have** faith," people say. But what does that mean? Is *any* faith good faith?

"Believe in yourself and all that you are," wrote one positive thinker a century ago. "Know that there is something inside you that is greater than any obstacle." As nice as that may sound, it falls to pieces when it crashes into reality. We need a faith in something bigger than ourselves.

God promised Abram he would have a multitude of descendants (GEN. 15:4-5), so he faced a huge obstacle—he was old and childless. When he and Sarah got tired of waiting for God to make good on His promise, they tried to overcome that obstacle on their own. As a result, they fractured their family and created a lot of unnecessary dissension (SEE GEN. 16 AND 21:8-21).

> **TODAY'S READING**
> Romans 4:18–25
>
> [Abraham] did not waver through unbelief regarding the promise of God, but was strengthened in his faith and gave glory to God.
>
> Romans 4:20

Nothing Abraham did in his own strength worked. But ultimately he became known as a man of tremendous faith. Paul wrote of him, "Against all hope, Abraham in hope believed and so became the father of many nations, just as it had been said to him, 'So shall your offspring be'" (ROM. 4:18). This faith, said Paul, "was credited to him as righteousness" (V. 22).

Abraham's faith was in something far bigger than himself—the one and only God. It's the object of our faith that makes all the difference. 🌿

TIM GUSTAFSON

Lord, I want a strong faith in You, not just faith in myself
or my abilities or in others. I am nothing without You.

Our faith is good if it's in the right Person.

Hold On

Tianmen Mountain in Zhangjiajie, China, is considered one of the most beautiful mountains in the world. To view its towering cliffs in all their glorious splendor, you must take the Tianmen Shan cable car, which covers a distance of 7,455 meters (4.5 miles). It's amazing how this cable car can travel such long distances and scale such steep mountains without any motor on the car itself. Yet it moves safely up these spectacular heights by keeping a strong grip on a cable that is moved by a powerful motor.

TODAY'S READING
Philippians 3:12–4:1

Stand firm in the Lord. Philippians 4:1

In our journey of faith, how can we finish the race well and "press on toward the goal to win the prize for which God has called [us] heavenward in Christ Jesus"? (PHIL. 3:14). Like the cable car, we keep a strong grip on Christ, which is what Paul meant when he said "stand firm in the Lord" (4:1). We have no resources of our own. We depend fully on Christ to keep us moving forward. He will take us through the greatest challenges and lead us safely home.

Toward the end of his earthly life, the apostle Paul declared, "I have fought the good fight, I have finished the race, I have kept the faith" (2 TIM. 4:7). You can too. Simply keep a strong grip on Christ. 🌐

ALBERT LEE

We're grateful, Lord, that while we aim to keep a strong grip on You, You always keep a strong grip on us! You are working in us and giving us what we need to continue trusting You on our faith journey.

Keeping the faith means trusting God to faithfully keep you.

God's Reminders

My friend **Bob Horner** refers to Jesus as "the Master Reminder." And that is good, because we are so doubting and forgetful. No matter how often Jesus met the needs of the people who came to Him when He was here on earth, His first disciples feared they would somehow be left in need. After witnessing miracles, they failed to understand the greater meaning the Lord wanted them to remember.

> **TODAY'S READING**
> **Mark 8:11–21**
>
> **He said to them, "Do you still not understand?"**
> Mark 8:21

On a journey across the Sea of Galilee, the disciples realized they had forgotten to bring bread and were talking about it. Jesus asked them, "Do you still not see or understand? Are your hearts hardened? Do you have eyes but fail to see, and ears but fail to hear? And don't you remember?" (MARK 8:17–18). Then He reminded them that when He fed five thousand people with five loaves, the disciples had collected twelve basketfuls of leftover pieces. And when He fed four thousand with seven loaves, they filled seven baskets with leftovers. Then "He said to them, 'Do you still not understand?'" (V. 21).

The Lord's miraculous provision for people's physical needs pointed to the greater truth—that He was the Bread of Life and that His body would be "broken" for them and for us.

Every time we eat the bread and drink the cup during the Lord's Supper, we are reminded of our Lord's great love and provision for us. ❤   *DAVID MCCASLAND*

In the Lord's Supper, Jesus left us a great reminder of His sacrifice.
Read about it in Matthew 26:17–30; Luke 22:14–20; 1 Corinthians 11:23–26.

Communion is the Lord's reminder to us of His love and provision.

No Outsiders

I n the remote region of Ghana where I lived as a boy, "Chop time, no friend" was a common proverb. It was a humorous way of acknowledging the fact that food in certain areas was scarce, and Ghanaians are by nature very giving people. Were you to walk in, they might well give you the last of their food.

In the Philippines, where I also lived for a time, if you visit unannounced at mealtime, your hosts will insist on sharing with you regardless of whether they have enough for themselves.

TODAY'S READING
Deuteronomy 10:12–22

What does the LORD your God ask of you but to fear the LORD your God, to walk in obedience to him, to love him.

Deuteronomy 10:12

As the Israelites left Egypt, God provided specific instructions to govern their culture. But rules—even God's rules—can never change hearts. So Moses said, "Change your hearts and stop being stubborn" (DEUT. 10:16 NLT). Interestingly, right after issuing that challenge Moses took up the topic of Israel's treatment of outsiders. God "loves the foreigner residing among you," he said, "giving them food and clothing. And you are to love those who are foreigners, for you yourselves were foreigners in Egypt" (VV. 18–19).

Israel served the "God of gods and Lord of lords, the great God, mighty and awesome" (V. 17). One powerful way they were to show their identification with God was by loving foreigners—those from outside their culture.

What might this small picture of God's character mean for us today? How can we show His love to the marginalized and the needy in our world? 🔶

TIM GUSTAFSON

Heavenly Father, help us bless others today by showing Your love in some small way.

In Christ, there are no outsiders.

Setting Prisoners Free

When my wife and I visited the National Museum of the Mighty Eighth Air Force near Savannah, Georgia, we were especially moved by the prisoner-of-war exhibit, with its re-creation of a German prisoner-of-war camp's barracks.

Marlene's dad, Jim, served in the Eighth Air Force, the "Mighty Eighth," as they flew missions over Europe during World War II. During the war, the Eighth Air Force suffered over 47,000 injuries and more than 26,000 deaths. Jim was one of those shot down and held as a prisoner of war. As we walked through the exhibit, we recalled Jim telling about the absolute joy he and his fellow prisoners felt the day they were set free.

> TODAY'S READING
> **Psalm 146**
>
> **The LORD sets prisoners free.**
> Psalm 146:7

God's care for the oppressed and liberation of the imprisoned are declared in Psalm 146. The psalmist describes the one who "upholds the cause of the oppressed and gives food to the hungry," who "sets prisoners free" (V. 7). All of this is cause for celebration and praise. But the greatest freedom of all is freedom from our guilt and shame. No wonder Jesus said, "So if the Son sets you free, you will be free indeed" (JOHN 8:36).

Through Christ's sacrifice, we are set free from the prison of sin to know His joy and love and the freedom that only forgiveness can bring. ❧

BILL CROWDER

The prison of sin cannot withstand the power of Christ's forgiveness.

Good Medicine

Careless driving, rising tempers, and use of foul language among some taxi and minibus drivers are a constant source of traffic fights in our city of Accra, Ghana. But one traffic incident I witnessed took a different turn. A bus was almost hit by a careless taxi driver. I expected the bus driver to get angry and yell at the other driver, but he didn't. Instead, the bus driver relaxed his stern face and smiled broadly at the guilty-looking taxi driver. And the smile worked wonders. With a raised hand, the taxi driver apologized, smiled back, and moved away—the tension diffused.

> TODAY'S READING
> **Ephesians 4:25–32**
>
> **A cheerful heart is good medicine.**
> Proverbs 17:22

A smile has a fascinating effect on our brain chemistry. Researchers have found that "when we smile it releases brain chemicals called endorphins which have an actual physiological relaxing effect." Not only can a smile diffuse a tense situation, but it can also diffuse tension within us. Our emotions affect us as well as others. The Bible teaches us to "get rid of all bitterness, rage and anger, brawling and slander, along with every form of malice. Be kind and compassionate to one another" (EPH. 4:31–32).

When anger or tension or bitterness threatens our relationship with the Lord and with others, it helps to remember that "a cheerful heart is good medicine" for our own joy and well-being. ❧

LAWRENCE DARMANI

Think about a time when you were angry with someone
or when you had an argument. How did you feel inside?
What parts of your life did it affect?

We find joy when we learn to live in Jesus's love.

Praising and Asking

Teen Challenge, a ministry to at-risk youth that started in New York City, was born from an unusual commitment to prayer. Its founder, David Wilkerson, sold his television set and spent his TV-watching time (two hours each night) praying. In the months that followed, he not only gained clarity about his new endeavor but he also learned about the balance between praising God and asking Him for help.

TODAY'S READING
2 Chronicles 6:12–21

The highest heavens . . . cannot contain you. How much less this temple I have built! 2 Chronicles 6:18

King Solomon's temple dedication prayer shows this balance. Solomon began by highlighting God's holiness and faithfulness. Then he gave God credit for the success of the project and emphasized God's greatness, declaring, "The heavens, even the highest heavens, cannot contain you. How much less this temple I have built!" (2 CHRON. 6:18).

After exalting God, Solomon asked Him to pay special attention to everything that happened inside the temple. He asked God to show mercy to the Israelites and to provide for them when they confessed their sin.

Immediately after Solomon's prayer, "fire came down from heaven and consumed the burnt offering and the sacrifices, and the glory of the LORD filled the temple" (7:1). This incredible response reminds us that the mighty One we praise and speak to when we pray is the same One who listens to and cares about our requests. 🌿 *JENNIFER BENSON SCHULDT*

How would you describe your conversations with God? What might help you grow closer to Him as you pray?

Prayer helps us see things as God sees them.

Grasping the Cross

n 1856, Charles Spurgeon, the great London preacher, founded the Pastors' College to train men for the Christian ministry. It was renamed Spurgeon's College in 1923. Today's college crest shows a hand grasping a cross and the Latin words, *Et Teneo, Et Teneor*, which means, "I hold and am held."

In his autobiography, Spurgeon wrote, "This is our College motto. We . . . hold forth the Cross of Christ with a bold hand . . . because that Cross holds us fast by its attractive power. Our desire is that every man may both hold the Truth, and be held by it; especially the truth of Christ crucified."

In Paul's letter to the Philippians, he expressed this truth as the bedrock of his life. "Not that I have . . . already arrived at my goal, but I press on to take hold of that for which Christ Jesus took hold of me" (PHIL. 3:12). As followers of Jesus, we extend the message of the cross to others as Jesus holds us fast in His grace and power. "I have been crucified with Christ; and I no longer live, but Christ lives in me" (GAL. 2:20).

> **TODAY'S READING**
> **Philippians 3:7–12**
>
> **Not that I have . . . already arrived at my goal, but I press on to take hold of that for which Christ Jesus took hold of me.**
>
> Philippians 3:12

Our Lord holds us in His grip of love each day—and we hold out His message of love to others. ❧

DAVID MCCASLAND

Lord Jesus, Your cross is the focal point of history
and the turning point of our lives. Hold us tightly as we
cling to Your cross and extend Your love to others.

We hold to the cross of Christ and are held by it.

The Drinkable Book

Because it is so difficult in parts of the world to find clean drinking water, an organization called Water Is Life developed a wonderful resource called "The Drinkable Book." The paper in the book is coated in silver nanoparticles that filter out almost 99.9 percent of harmful bacteria! Each tear-out page can be used and reused to filter up to 100 liters of water at the cost of only four pennies per page.

TODAY'S READING
John 4:7–15

The water I give them will become in them a spring of water welling up to eternal life.

John 4:14

The Bible is also an unusually "drinkable" Book. In John 4, we read of a particular kind of thirst and a special kind of water. The woman at the well needed much more than to quench her physical thirst with clean, clear liquid. She was desperate to know the source of "living water." She needed the grace and forgiveness that comes from God alone.

God's Word is the ultimate "drinkable" Book that points to God's Son as the sole source of "living water." And those who accept the water that Jesus gives will experience "a spring of water welling up to eternal life" (V. 14). 🌱   *CINDY HESS KASPER*

Father, we yearn for the satisfaction that only You can give. Help us discard the things that leave us empty and thirsting, and exchange them for the satisfaction of the living water You offer.

Jesus is the sole source of living water.

United in Christ

When we come across a list of names in the Bible, we might be tempted to skip over it. But we can find treasures there, such as in the list of the twelve apostles whom Jesus called to serve in His name. Many are familiar—Simon whom Jesus called Peter, the rock. Brothers James and John, fishermen. Judas Iscariot, the betrayer. But we could easily overlook that Matthew the tax collector and Simon the Zealot must once have been enemies.

Matthew collected taxes for Rome, and therefore, in the eyes of his fellow Jews, collaborated with the enemy. Tax collectors were despised for their corrupt practices and for requiring the Jewish people to give money to an authority other than God. On the other hand, before Jesus's call, Simon the Zealot was devoted to a group of Jewish nationalists who hated Rome and sought to overturn it, often through aggressive and violent means.

> TODAY'S READING
> **Mark 3:13–19**
>
> **He appointed twelve that they might be with him and that he might send them out to preach.** Mark 3:14

Although Matthew and Simon held opposing political beliefs, the gospels don't document them bickering or fighting about them. They must have had at least some success in leaving their previous allegiances behind as they followed Christ.

When we too fix our eyes on Jesus, the God who became Man, we can find increasing unity with our fellow believers through the bond of the Holy Spirit. 🌱　　　*AMY BOUCHER PYE*

Father, Son, and Holy Spirit, You exist in perfect harmony.
May Your Spirit dwell in us that the world might see You, and believe.

Our strongest allegiance is to Christ, who gives us unity with each other.

Doing the Opposite

A wilderness excursion can seem daunting, but for outdoor enthusiasts this only adds to the appeal. Because hikers need more water than they can carry, they purchase bottles with built-in filters so they can use water sources along the way. But the process of drinking from such a container is counterintuitive. Tipping the bottle does nothing. A thirsty hiker has to blow into it to force the water through the filter. Reality is contrary to what seems natural.

TODAY'S READING
Colossians 2:20–3:4

For you died, and your life is now hidden with Christ in God. Colossians 3:3

As we follow Jesus, we find much that is counterintuitive. Paul pointed out one example: Keeping rules won't draw us closer to God. He asked, "Why, as though you still belonged to the world, do you submit to its rules: 'Do not handle! Do not taste! Do not touch!'? These rules . . . are based on merely human commands and teachings" (COL. 2:20–22).

So what are we to do? Paul gave the answer. "Since, then, you have been raised with Christ, set your hearts on things above" (3:1). "You died," he told people who were still very much alive, "and your life is now hidden with Christ in God" (V. 3).

We are to consider ourselves "dead" to the values of this world and alive to Christ. We now aspire to a way of life demonstrated by the One who said, "Whoever wants to become great among you must be your servant" (MATT. 20:26). ✿   *TIM GUSTAFSON*

Consider what these counterintuitive principles from the Bible might mean for you: "Whoever loses their life for me will find it" (MATT. 16:25). "The last will be first, and the first will be last" (MATT. 20:16). "When I am weak, then I am strong" (2 COR. 12:10).

God chose the foolish things of the world to shame the wise. 1 CORINTHIANS 1:27

Changing Hearts

On the last day of the US Civil War, officer Joshua Chamberlain was in command of the Union army. His soldiers lined up on both sides of the road that the Confederate army had to march down in surrender. One wrong word or one belligerent act and the longed-for peace could be turned to slaughter. In an act as brilliant as it was moving, Chamberlain ordered his troops to salute their foe! No taunting here, no vicious words—only guns in salute and swords raised to honor.

When Jesus offered His words about forgiveness in Luke 6, He was helping us understand the difference between people of grace and people without grace. Those who know His forgiveness are to be strikingly unlike everyone else. We must do what others think impossible: Forgive and love our enemies. Jesus said, "Be merciful, just as your Father is merciful" (V. 36).

Imagine the impact in our workplaces and on our families if we were to embrace this principle. If a salute can make armies whole again, what power there must be in Christ's grace reflected through us! Scripture gives evidence of this in Esau's embrace of his deceitful brother (GEN. 33:4), in Zacchaeus's joyful penance (LUKE 19:1–10), and in the picture of a father racing to greet his prodigal son (LUKE 15).

With the grace of Christ, may we let this be the final day of bitterness and dispute between our enemies and us. 🍂

RANDY KILGORE

Lord, we know how the gentle power of forgiveness can bring healing in relationships. Grant us the courage to end our conflicts by Your grace.

Anger almost always vanishes in the face of grace.

Warning!

The following warnings have been found on consumer products:

"Remove child before folding." (baby stroller)

"Does not supply oxygen." (dust mask)

"Never operate your speakerphone while driving." (hands-free cell phone product called the "Drive 'n' Talk")

"This product moves when used." (scooter)

An appropriate warning label that Nabal could have worn would have been: "Expect folly from a fool" (SEE 1 SAM. 25). He certainly was irrational as he addressed David. On the run from Saul, David had provided security detail for the sheep of a wealthy man named Nabal. When David learned that Nabal was shearing those sheep and celebrating with a feast, he sent ten of his men to politely ask for food as remuneration for these duties (VV. 4-8).

TODAY'S READING
1 Samuel 25:1–12

His name means Fool, and folly goes with him!
1 Samuel 25:25

Nabal's response to David's request was beyond rude. He said, "Who is this David? . . . Why should I take my bread and water, and the meat . . . , and give it to men coming from who knows where?" (VV. 10-11). He broke the hospitality code of the day by not inviting David to the feast, disrespected him by calling out insults, and essentially stole from him by not paying him for his work.

The truth is, we all have a little bit of Nabal in us. We act foolishly at times. The only cure for this is to acknowledge our sin to God. He will step in to forgive us, instruct us, and give us His wisdom. ✿

MARVIN WILLIAMS

I'm selfish sometimes, Lord. I get more concerned with what I need than what others need. Give me a heart of integrity and compassion.

God's wisdom overshadows our self-centeredness.

All Welcome!

The much-prayed-for film night at the church youth club had finally arrived. Posters had been displayed all around the village and pizzas were warming in the oven. Steve, the youth pastor, hoped that the film—about gang members in New York who were brought face-to-face with the claims of Jesus by a young pastor—would bring new recruits to the club.

TODAY'S READING
Luke 5:27–32

I have not come to call the righteous, but sinners to repentance. Luke 5:32

But he hadn't realized that a key football match was being shown on television that evening, so attendance was much smaller than he had hoped for. Sighing inwardly, he was about to dim the lights and begin the film when five leather-clad members of the local motorbike club came in. Steve went pale.

The leader of the group, who was known as TDog, nodded in Steve's direction. "It's free and for everyone, right?" he said. Steve opened his mouth to say, "Youth club members only" when TDog bent down and picked up a bracelet with the letters WWJD (What Would Jesus Do) stamped on it. "This yours, mate?" he asked. Steve nodded, hot with embarrassment, and waited while the new guests found a seat.

Have you ever been in Steve's situation? You long to share the good news about Jesus, but you have a mental list of the "right" people who would be acceptable? Jesus was often criticized by the religious authorities for the company He kept. But He welcomed those everyone else avoided, because He knew they needed Him most (LUKE 5:31–32). 🌿   *MARION STROUD*

Lord, please help me to see people through Your eyes of love and to welcome all those You bring into my life.

A heart that is open to Christ will be open to those He loves.

Dying for Others

love birds, which is why I bought six caged birds and carried them home to our daughter Alice, who began to care for them daily. Then one of the birds fell ill and died. We wondered if the birds would be more likely to thrive if they were not caged. So we freed the surviving five and observed them fly away in jubilation.

Alice then pointed out, "Do you realize, Daddy, that it was the death of one bird that caused us to free the rest?"

Isn't that what the Lord Jesus did for us? Just as one man's sin (Adam's) brought condemnation to the world, so one Man's righteousness (Jesus's) brought salvation to those who believe (ROM. 5:12–19). Jesus said, "I am the good shepherd. The good shepherd lays down his life for the sheep" (JOHN 10:11).

> TODAY'S READING
> **1 John 3:16–17**
>
> **I am the good shepherd. The good shepherd lays down his life for the sheep.** John 10:11

John makes it more practical when he says, "Jesus Christ laid down his life for us. And we ought to lay down our lives for our brothers and sisters" (1 JOHN 3:16). This won't likely mean literal death, but as we align our lives with Jesus's example of sacrificial love, we find that we are "laying down our lives." For instance, we might choose to deprive ourselves of material goods in order to share them with others (V. 17) or make time to be with someone who needs comfort and companionship.

Who do you need to sacrifice for today? 🌐   *LAWRENCE DARMANI*

In what ways have others sacrificed for your well-being?

Christ's ultimate sacrifice for us motivates us to sacrifice ourselves for others.

A Fan for Life

Cade Pope, a 12-year-old boy from Oklahoma, mailed out 32 handwritten letters—one to each executive in charge of a National Football League (NFL) team in the US. Cade wrote, "My family and I love football. We play fantasy football and watch [the] games every weekend.... I am ready to pick an NFL team to cheer on for a lifetime!"

> **TODAY'S READING**
> Psalm 86:1–13
>
> **I call to you, because you answer me.** Psalm 86:7

Jerry Richardson, owner of the Carolina Panthers football team, responded with a handwritten note of his own. The first line read: "We would be honored if our [team] became your team. We would make you proud." Richardson went on to commend some of his players. His letter was not only personal and kindhearted—it was the *only* response that Cade received. Not surprisingly, Cade became a loyal fan of the Carolina Panthers.

In Psalm 86, David spoke about his allegiance to the one true God. He said, "When I am in distress, I call to you, because you answer me. Among the gods there is none like you, Lord" (VV. 7–8). Our devotion to God is born from His character and His care for us. He is the one who answers our prayers, guides us by His Spirit, and saves us through the death and resurrection of His Son, Jesus Christ. He deserves our lifelong loyalty. ❧

JENNIFER BENSON SCHULDT

Dear God, there is no one like You.
Help me to consider Your holiness and let it lead me into
deeper devotion to You.

Only God is worthy of our adoration and devotion.

Keep Up the Good Work

My son loves to read. If he reads more books than what is required at school, he receives an award certificate. That bit of encouragement motivates him to keep up the good work.

When Paul wrote to the Thessalonians he motivated them not with an award but with words of encouragement. He said, "Brothers and sisters, we instructed you how to live in order to please God, as in fact you are living. Now we ask you and urge you in the Lord Jesus to do this more and more" (1 THESS. 4:1). These Christians were pleasing God through their lives, and Paul encouraged them to continue to live more and more for Him.

> TODAY'S READING
> **1 Thessalonians 4:1–12**
>
> **We . . . urge you . . . to do this more and more.**
> 1 Thessalonians 4:1

Maybe today you and I are giving our best to know and love and please our Father. Let's take Paul's words as an incentive to continue on in our faith.

But let's go one step further. Who might we encourage today with Paul's words? Does someone come to mind who is diligent in following the Lord and seeking to please Him? Write a note or make a phone call and urge this person to keep on in their faith journey with Him. What you say may be just what they need to continue following and serving Jesus. ❧

KEILA OCHOA

Dear Lord, thank You for encouraging me through Your Word to keep living for You.

Encourage someone today to keep living for God.

Do We Have To?

Joie started the children's program with prayer, then sang with the kids. Six-year-old Emmanuel squirmed in his seat when she prayed again after introducing Aaron, the teacher. Then Aaron began and ended his talk with prayer. Emmanuel complained: "That's *four* prayers! I can't sit still that long!"

If you think Emmanuel's challenge is difficult, look at 1 Thessalonians 5:17: "Pray continually" or always be in a spirit of prayer. Even some of us adults can find prayer to be boring. Maybe that's because we don't know what to say or don't understand that prayer is a conversation with our Father.

TODAY'S READING
1 Thessalonians 5:12–28

Jesus often withdrew to lonely places and prayed.
Luke 5:16

Back in the seventeenth century, François Fénelon wrote some words about prayer that have helped me: "Tell God all that is in your heart, as one unloads one's heart, its pleasures and its pains, to a dear friend. Tell Him your troubles, that He may comfort you; tell Him your joys, that He may sober them; tell Him your longings, that He may purify them." He continued, "Talk to Him of your temptations, that He may shield you from them: show Him the wounds of your heart, that He may heal them .... If you thus pour out all your weaknesses, needs, troubles, there will be no lack of what to say."

May we grow in our intimacy with God so that we will want to spend more time with Him. ❂

ANNE CETAS

For further study, read about Jesus's example of prayer
in John 17 and Luke 5:16.

Prayer is an intimate conversation with our God.

From the Heart

In many cultures, loud weeping, wailing, and the tearing of clothing are accepted ways of lamenting personal sorrow or a great national calamity. For the people of Old Testament Israel, similar outward actions expressed deep mourning and repentance for turning away from the Lord.

An outward demonstration of repentance can be a powerful process when it comes from our heart. But without a sincere inward response to God, we may simply be going through the motions, even in our communities of faith.

After a plague of locusts devastated the land of Judah, God, through the prophet Joel, called the people to sincere repentance to avoid His further judgment. "'Even now,' declares the LORD, 'return to me with all your heart, with fasting and weeping and mourning'" (JOEL 2:12).

> **TODAY'S READING**
> **Joel 2:12–17**
>
> **Rend your heart and not your garments. Return to the LORD your God, for he is gracious and compassionate.**
>
> Joel 2:13

Then Joel called for a response from deep inside: "Rend your heart and not your garments. Return to the LORD your God, for he is gracious and compassionate, slow to anger and abounding in love, and he relents from sending calamity" (V. 13). True repentance comes from the heart.

The Lord longs for us to confess our sins to Him and receive His forgiveness so we can love and serve Him with all our heart, soul, mind, and strength.

Whatever you need to tell the Lord today, just say it—from the heart. 🍂 *DAVID MCCASLAND*

Lord, please give me a heart of repentance to see myself as You do.
Give me the grace to respond to Your merciful call for change.

God wants to hear your heart.

Desert Solitaire

Desert Solitaire is Edward Abbey's personal history of his summers as a park ranger in what is now called Arches National Park in Utah. The book is worth reading if only for Abbey's bright language and vivid descriptions of the US Southwest.

But Abbey, for all his artistry, was an atheist who could see nothing beyond the surface of the beauty he enjoyed. How sad! He lived his entire life in praise of beauty and missed the point of it all.

> **TODAY'S READING**
> **Psalm 136:1–9**
>
> **And God saw that it was good.**
> Genesis 1:12

Most ancient peoples had theories of origins enshrouded in legend, myth, and song. But Israel's story of creation was unique: It told of a God who created beauty for our enjoyment and childlike delight. God thought up the cosmos, spoke it into being and pronounced it "beautiful." (The Hebrew word for *good* also signifies beauty.) Then, having created a paradise, God in love spoke *us* into being, placed us in Eden, and told us, "Enjoy!"

Some see and enjoy the beauty of the Creator's good gifts all around them, but don't "worship him as God or even give him thanks." They "think up foolish ideas of what God [is] like. As a result, their minds become dark and confused" (ROM. 1:21 NLT).

Others see beauty, say "Thank You, God," and step into His light. 🌿

DAVID ROPER

Loving Father, we praise You because You are good.
Thank You for infusing Your creation with beauty and purpose
and for placing us here to enjoy it as we discover You.
Your love endures forever!

All of creation reflects the beauty of God.

Your Journey

I grew up in the rebellious 1960s and turned my back on religion. I had attended church all my life but didn't come to faith until my early twenties after a terrible accident. Since that time, I have spent my adult years telling others of Jesus's love for us. It has been a journey.

TODAY'S READING
John 14:15–21

I will not leave you as orphans; I will come to you.

John 14:18

Certainly "a journey" describes life in this broken world. On the way we encounter mountains and valleys, rivers and plains, crowded highways and lonely roads—highs and lows, joys and sorrows, conflict and loss, heartache and solitude. We can't see the road ahead, so we must take it as it comes, not as we wish it would be.

The follower of Christ, however, never faces this journey alone. The Scriptures remind us of the constant presence of God. There is nowhere we can go that He is not there (PS. 139:7–12). He will never leave us or forsake us (DEUT. 31:6; HEB. 13:5). Jesus, after promising to send the Holy Spirit, told His disciples, "I will not leave you as orphans; I will come to you" (JOHN 14:18).

The challenges and opportunities we face on our journey can be met confidently, for God has promised us His never-failing presence. ❂

BILL CROWDER

Loving Lord, thank You that You not only know the path I take,
You walk it with me. Help me to rely on Your presence,
help, and wisdom every day of my journey through life.

Faith never knows where it is being led, but it loves and knows the One who is leading. OSWALD CHAMBERS, MY UTMOST FOR HIS HIGHEST

Unfailing Love

On a recent airline flight the landing was a little rough, jostling us left and right down the runway. Some of the passengers were visibly nervous, but the tension broke when two little girls sitting behind me cheered, "Yeah! Let's do that again!"

Children are open to new adventures and see life with humble, wide-eyed wonder. Perhaps this is part of what Jesus had in mind when He said that we have to "receive the kingdom of God like a little child" (MARK 10:15).

TODAY'S READING
Lamentations 3:21–26

Your unfailing love is better than life itself; how I praise you! Psalm 63:3 NLT

Life has its challenges and heartaches. Few knew this better than Jeremiah, who is also called "the weeping prophet." But in the middle of Jeremiah's troubles, God encouraged him with an amazing truth: "The faithful love of the LORD never ends! His mercies never cease. Great is his faithfulness; his mercies begin afresh each morning" (LAM. 3:22–23 NLT).

God's fresh mercies can break into our lives at any moment. They are always there, and we see them when we live with childlike expectation—watching and waiting for what only He can do. Jeremiah knew that God's goodness is not defined only by our immediate circumstances and that His faithfulness is greater than life's rough places. Look for God's fresh mercies today. ❧   *JAMES BANKS*

Lord, please help me to have the faith of a child so that I can live with
expectation, always looking forward to what You will do next.

God is greater than anything that happens to us.

My Brothers and Sisters

Several years ago when the Southern California economy took a downturn, Pastor Bob Johnson saw not only difficulty but also opportunity. So he scheduled a meeting with the mayor of his city and asked, "What can our church do to help you?" The mayor was astonished. People usually came to him for help. Here was a minister offering him the services of an entire congregation.

> **TODAY'S READING**
> **Matthew 25:31–40**
>
> **Whatever you did for one of the least of these brothers and sisters of mine, you did for me.** Matthew 25:40

Together the mayor and pastor came up with a plan to address several pressing needs. In their county alone, more than 20,000 seniors had gone the previous year without a single visitor. Hundreds of foster children needed families. And many other kids needed tutoring to help them succeed in school.

Some of those needs could be addressed without much financial investment, but they all required time and interest. And that's what the church had to give.

Jesus told His disciples about a future day in which He would say to His faithful followers, "Come, you who are blessed by my Father; take your inheritance" (MATT. 25:34). He also said they would express surprise at their reward. Then He would tell them, "Whatever you did for one of the least of these brothers and sisters of mine, you did for me" (V. 40).

God's kingdom work gets done when we give generously of the time, love, and resources He has provided us. ✤ *TIM GUSTAFSON*

What lonely person is the Spirit bringing to your mind right now? Can you visit them, call, or write? What young person in your life could use some of your time and attention?

Giving isn't just for the wealthy; it's for all of us.

I Am With You

When I served as an intern for a Christian magazine, I wrote a story about a person who had become a Christian. In a dramatic change, he said goodbye to his former life and embraced his new Master: Jesus. A few days after the magazine hit the street, an anonymous caller threatened, "Be careful, Darmani. We are watching you! Your life is in danger in this country if you write such stories."

TODAY'S READING
Jeremiah 1:1–10

Do not be afraid of them, for I am with you. Jeremiah 1:8

That was not the only time I have been threatened for pointing people to Christ. On one occasion a man told me to vanish with the tract I was giving him or else! In both cases, I cowered. But these were only verbal threats. Many Christians have had threats carried out against them. In some cases simply living a godly lifestyle attracts mistreatment from people.

The Lord told Jeremiah, "You must go to everyone I send you to and say whatever I command you" (JER. 1:7), and Jesus told His disciples, "I am sending you out like sheep among wolves" (MATT. 10:16). Yes, we may encounter threats, hardships, and even pain. But God assures us of His presence. "I am with you," He told Jeremiah (JER. 1:8), and Jesus assured His followers, "I am with you always" (MATT. 28:20).

Whatever struggles we face in our attempt to live for the Lord, we can trust in the Lord's presence. ❀ *LAWRENCE DARMANI*

Lord, we're grateful that You are near to us in everything we face.
Please protect Your people around the world.

*Blessed are those who are persecuted because of righteousness,
for theirs is the kingdom of heaven. MATTHEW 5:10*

Choosing to Change

When my son acquired a small robot, he had fun programming it to perform simple tasks. He could make it move forward, stop, and then retrace its steps. He could even get it to beep and replay recorded noises. The robot did exactly what my son told it to do. It never laughed spontaneously or veered off in an unplanned direction. It had no choice.

When God created humans, He didn't make robots. God made us in His image, and this means we can think, reason, and make decisions. We're able to choose between right and wrong. Even if we have made a habit of disobeying God, we can decide to redirect our lives.

When the ancient Israelites found themselves in trouble with God, He spoke to them through the prophet Ezekiel.

> **TODAY'S READING**
> **Ezekiel 18:25–32**
>
> **Rid yourselves of all the offenses you have committed, and get a new heart and a new spirit.**
> Ezekiel 18:31

Ezekiel said, "Repent! Turn away from all your offenses; then sin will not be your downfall. . . . Get a new heart and a new spirit" (EZEK. 18:30–31).

This kind of change can begin with just one choice, empowered by the Holy Spirit (ROM. 8:13). It might mean saying no at a critical moment. No more gossip. No more greed. No more jealousy. No more _____. (*You fill in the blank.*) If you know Jesus, you're not a slave to sin. You can choose to change, and with God's help, this personal revolution can start today. 🌺

JENNIFER BENSON SCHULDT

Dear God, all things are possible with You.
Through the power of Jesus's resurrection help me to take the first step toward a life of greater devotion to You.
For a new start, ask God for a new heart.

This Gift

A number of years ago I wrote an essay about my collection of canes, staffs, and walking sticks and mused that I might someday graduate to a walker. Well, the day has come. A combination of back issues and peripheral neuropathy has left me pushing a three-wheel walker. I can't hike; I can't fish; I can't do many of the things that used to bring me great joy.

I'm trying to learn, however, that my limitation, whatever it may be, is a gift from God, and it is with this gift that I am to serve Him. *This* gift and not another. This is true of all of us, whether our limits are emotional, physical, or intellectual. Paul was so bold as to say that he boasted in his weakness for it was in weakness that God's power was revealed in him (2 COR. 12:9).

> **TODAY'S READING**
> **2 Corinthians 12:6–10**
>
> **Therefore I will boast all the more gladly about my weaknesses, so that Christ's power may rest on me.**
>
> 2 Corinthians 12:9

Seeing our so-called liabilities this way enables us to go about our business with confidence and courage. Rather than complain, feel sorry for ourselves, or opt out, we make ourselves available to God for His intended purposes.

I have no idea what He has in mind for you and me, but we shouldn't worry about that. Our task today is just to accept things as they are and to be content, knowing that in the love, wisdom, and providence of God this moment is as good as it can possibly be. ❧
DAVID ROPER

Dear Lord, I know that You are good and You love me.
I trust You to give me everything I need for today.

Contentment enables you to grow where God has planted you.

Mending Hearts

Not long ago I went to a seamstress to have some clothing altered. As I entered her shop I was encouraged by what I saw on the walls. One sign read, "We can mend your clothes but only God can mend your heart." Near it was a painting of Mary Magdalene weeping in anguish as the risen Christ was about to reveal Himself to her. Another sign asked, "Need prayer? Let us pray with you."

TODAY'S READING
Matthew 5:1–16

You are the light of the world. Matthew 5:14

The owner told me that she had been running this small business for fifteen years. "We've been surprised how the Lord has worked here through the statements of faith we have posted in different places. A while back someone trusted Christ as their Savior right here. It is amazing to watch God work." I told her I too was a Christian and commended her for telling others about Christ in her workplace.

Not all of us are able to be so bold in our workplace, but we can find many creative and practical ways of showing others unexpected love, patience, and kindness wherever we are. Since leaving that shop, I've been thinking about how many ways there are to live out our Lord's statement: "You are the light of the world" (MATT. 5:14). 🌿　　　　　*DENNIS FISHER*

Dear Father, use me to be a light today to the world around me.
I love You and want others to know and love You too.

God pours His love into our hearts to flow out to others' lives.

Stage by Stage

Numbers 33 is a chapter in the Bible we might pass by without reflection. It appears to be nothing more than a long list of places tracing Israel's pilgrimage from Rameses in Egypt to their arrival in the plains of Moab. But it must be important because it's the only section in Numbers that follows with the words: "At the LORD's command Moses recorded . . ." (V. 2).

Why keep a record of this? Could it be that this list provides a framework upon which the Israelites emerging from the wilderness could retrace that forty-year journey in their thoughts and recall God's faithfulness at each location?

I envision an Israelite father, sitting near a campfire, reminiscing with his son: "I will never forget Rephidim! I was dying of thirst, nothing but sand and sage for hundreds of miles. Then God directed Moses to take his staff and strike a rock—actually a hard slab of flint. I thought, *What a futile gesture; he'll never get anything out of that stone.* But to my amazement water gushed out of that rock! A generous flow that satisfied the thirst of the thousands of Israelites. I'll never forget that day!" (SEE PS. 114:8; EX. 17:1–7; NUM. 33:14).

So why not give it a try? Reflect on your life—stage by stage—and remember all the ways God has shown you His faithful, covenant love. 🖉　　　　　　　*DAVID ROPER*

> **TODAY'S READING**
> **Numbers 33:1–15, 36–37**
>
> **At the LORD's command Moses recorded the stages in their journey.**
> Numbers 33:2

Count your many blessings, name them one by one.
JOHNSON OATMAN JR.

God's faithfulness extends to all generations.

Learning to Count

My son is learning to count from one to ten. He counts everything from toys to trees. He counts things I tend to overlook, like the wildflowers on his way to school or the toes on my feet.

My son is also teaching me to count again. Often I become so immersed in things I haven't finished or things I don't have that I fail to see all the good things around me. I have forgotten to count the new friends made this year and the answered prayers received, the tears of joy shed and the times of laughter with good friends.

> **TODAY'S READING**
> **Psalm 139:14–18**
>
> **How precious to me are your thoughts, God!**
> Psalm 139:17

My ten fingers are not enough to count all that God gives me day by day. "Many, LORD my God, are the wonders you have done, the things you planned for us. None can compare with you; were I to speak and tell of your deeds, they would be too many to declare" (PS. 40:5). How can we even begin to count all the blessings of salvation, reconciliation, and eternal life?

Let us join David as he praises God for all His precious thoughts about us and all He has done for us, when he says, "How precious to me are your thoughts, God! How vast is the sum of them! Were I to count them, they would outnumber the grains of sand" (139:17–18).

Let's learn to count again! ❧

KEILA OCHOA

Lord, Your works are so many and good I can't count them all.
But I thank You for each one.

Let's thank God for His countless blessings.

The Praying Patient

The obituary for **Alan Nanninga**, a man in my city, identified him as "foremost, a dedicated witness for Christ." After a description of his family life and career, the article mentioned nearly a decade of declining health. It concluded by saying, "His hospital stays . . . earned him the honorary title of 'The Praying Patient'" because of his ministry to other patients. Here was a man who, in his times of distress, reached out to pray for and with the people in need around him.

Hours before Judas betrayed Him, Jesus prayed for His disciples. "I will remain in the world no longer, but they are still in the world, and I am coming to you. Holy Father, protect them by the power of your name, the name you gave me, so that they may be one as we are one" (JOHN 17:11). Knowing what was about to happen, Jesus looked beyond Himself to focus on His followers and friends.

During our times of illness and distress, we long for and need the prayers of others. How those prayers help and encourage us! But may we also, like our Lord, lift our eyes to pray for those around us who are in great need. ❧ *DAVID MCCASLAND*

> **TODAY'S READING**
> **John 17:6–19**
>
> Holy Father, protect them by the power of your name, the name you gave me, so that they may be one as we are one.
> John 17:11

Lord, even in our difficult times, may we honor You and
encourage others by praying for those who are suffering today.

Our troubles can fill our prayers with love and empathy for others.

Hearing God

felt like I was underwater, sounds muffled and muted by a cold and allergies. For weeks I struggled to hear clearly. My condition made me realize how much I take my hearing for granted.

Young Samuel in the temple must have wondered what he was hearing as he struggled out of sleep at the summons of his name (1 SAM. 3:4). Three times he presented himself before Eli, the high priest. Only the third time did Eli realize it was the Lord speaking to Samuel. The word of the Lord had been rare at that time (V. 1), and the people were not in tune with His voice. But Eli instructed Samuel how to respond (V. 9).

> **TODAY'S READING**
> **1 Samuel 3:1–10**
>
> Samuel said, "Speak, for your servant is listening." 1 Samuel 3:10

The Lord speaks much more now than in the days of Samuel. The letter to the Hebrews tells us, "In the past God spoke to our ancestors through the prophets . . . but in these last days he has spoken to us by his Son" (1:1–2). And in Acts 2 we read of the coming of the Holy Spirit at Pentecost (VV. 1–4), who guides us in the things Christ taught us (JOHN 16:13). But we need to learn to hear His voice and respond in obedience.

Like me with my cold, we may hear as if underwater. We need to test what we think is the Lord's guidance with the Bible and with other mature Christians. As God's beloved children, we *do* hear His voice. He loves to speak life into us. 🕮 *AMY BOUCHER PYE*

Open our eyes, Lord, that we might see You.
Open our ears, that we may hear You.
Open our mouths, that we might speak Your praise.

The Lord speaks to His children, but we need to discern His voice.

It Never Runs Out

When I asked a friend who is about to retire what she feared about her next stage of life, she said, "I want to make sure I don't run out of money." The next day as I was talking to my financial counselor he gave me advice on how I might avoid running out of money. Indeed, we all want the security of knowing we'll have the resources we need for the rest of our lives.

No financial plan can provide an absolute guarantee of earthly security. But there is a plan that extends far beyond this life and indefinitely into the future. The apostle Peter describes it like this: "In his great mercy he has given us new birth into a living hope through the resurrection of Jesus Christ from the dead, and into an inheritance that can never perish, spoil or fade" (1 PETER 1:3–4).

> **TODAY'S READING**
> **1 Peter 1:3–9**
>
> He has given us new birth into . . . an inheritance that can never perish.
> 1 Peter 1:3–4

When we place our faith in Jesus to forgive our sins we receive an eternal inheritance through God's power. Because of this inheritance, we'll live forever and never run short of what we need.

Planning for retirement is a good idea if we're able to do so. But more important is having an eternal inheritance that never runs out—and that is available only through faith in Jesus Christ. ❧

DAVE BRANON

Dear God, I want that assurance of an eternal inheritance—
the certainty of everlasting life with You. I put my faith in Jesus to
forgive my sins and make me His child. Thank You for saving me and
reserving a place for me in Your eternal kingdom.

The promise of heaven is our eternal hope.

Run to Me

During a walk at a local park, my children and I encountered a couple of unleashed dogs. Their owner didn't seem to notice that one of them had begun to intimidate my son. My son tried to shoo the dog away, but the animal only became more intent on bothering him.

Eventually, my son panicked. He bolted several yards into the distance, but the dog pursued him. The chase continued until I yelled, "Run to me!" My son doubled back, calmed down, and the dog finally decided to make mischief somewhere else.

There are moments in our lives when God calls to us and says, "Run to Me!" Something troubling is on our heels. The faster and farther we go, the more closely it pursues us. We can't shake it. We're too afraid to turn and confront the trouble on our own. But the reality is that we aren't on our own. God is there, ready to help and comfort us. All we have to do is turn away from whatever scares us, and move in His direction. His Word says, "The name of the LORD is a fortified tower; the righteous run to it and are safe" (PROV. 18:10). 🖋 *JENNIFER BENSON SCHULDT*

> **TODAY'S READING**
> **Proverbs 18:4–12**
>
> **The name of the LORD is a fortified tower; the righteous run to it and are safe.**
>
> Proverbs 18:10

Dear Jesus, You are the Prince of Peace. I need the kind of peace that only You can give. Help me to turn to You when I am troubled.

God is our refuge in times of trouble.

Watchful and Alert

My desk sits close to a window that opens into our neighborhood. From that vantage point I'm privileged to watch birds perch on the trees nearby. Some come to the window to eat insects trapped in the screen.

The birds check their immediate surroundings for any danger, listening attentively as they look about them. Only when they are satisfied that there is no danger do they settle down to feed. Even then, they pause every few seconds to scan the area.

TODAY'S READING
Genesis 3:1–7

Be on your guard; stand firm in the faith. 1 Corinthians 16:13

The vigilance these birds demonstrate reminds me that the Bible teaches us to practice vigilance as Christians. Our world is full of temptations, and we need to remain constantly alert and not forget about the dangers. Like Adam and Eve, we easily get entangled in attractions that make the things of this world seem "good for food and pleasing to the eye, and also desirable for gaining wisdom" (GEN. 3:6).

"Be on your guard," Paul admonished, "stand firm in the faith" (1 COR. 16:13). And Peter cautioned, "Be alert and of sober mind. Your enemy the devil prowls around like a roaring lion looking for someone to devour" (1 PETER 5:8).

As we work for our own daily bread, are we alert to what could start consuming us? Are we watching for any hint of self-confidence or willfulness that could leave us wishing we had trusted our God? ❦

LAWRENCE DARMANI

Lord, keep us from the secret sins and selfish reactions we're so naturally inclined toward. By Your grace, turn our temptations into moments of growth in Christlikeness.

The best way to escape temptation is to run to God.

Leading with Love

I n his book *Spiritual Leadership*, J. Oswald Sanders explores the qualities and the importance of *tact* and *diplomacy*. "Combining these two words," Sanders says, "the idea emerges of skill in reconciling opposing viewpoints without giving offense and without compromising principle."

During Paul's imprisonment in Rome, he became the spiritual mentor and close friend of a runaway slave named Onesimus, whose owner was Philemon. When Paul wrote to Philemon, a leader of the church in Colossae, asking him to receive Onesimus as a brother in Christ, he exemplified tact and diplomacy. "Although in Christ I could be bold and order you to do what you ought to do, yet I prefer to appeal to you on the basis of love.... [Onesimus] is very dear to me but even dearer to you, both as a fellow man and as a brother in the Lord" (PHILEM. 8–9, 16).

> **TODAY'S READING**
> **Philemon 8–18**
>
> **I prefer to appeal to you on the basis of love.** Philemon 9

Paul, a respected leader of the early church, often gave clear commands to the followers of Jesus. In this case, though, he appealed to Philemon on the basis of equality, friendship, and love. "I did not want to do anything without your consent, so that any favor you do would not seem forced but would be voluntary" (V. 14).

In all our relationships, may we seek to preserve harmony and principle in the spirit of love. 🍂 *DAVID MCCASLAND*

Father in heaven, in all our relationships,
give us grace and wisdom to be wise leaders, parents, and friends.

Leaders who serve will serve as good leaders.

Strong Conqueror

Most of us hope for good government. We vote, we serve, and we speak out for causes we believe are fair and just. But political solutions remain powerless to change the condition of our hearts.

Many of Jesus's followers anticipated a Messiah who would bring a vigorous political response to Rome and its heavy-handed oppression. Peter was no exception. When Roman soldiers came to arrest Christ, Peter drew his sword and took a swing at the head of the high priest's servant, lopping off his ear in the process.

TODAY'S READING
John 18:10–14, 36–37

My kingdom is from another place. John 18:36

Jesus halted Peter's one-man war, saying, "Put your sword away! Shall I not drink the cup the Father has given me?" (JOHN 18:11). Hours later, Jesus would tell Pilate, "My kingdom is not of this world. If it were, my servants would fight to prevent my arrest by the Jewish leaders" (V. 36).

The Lord's restraint in that moment, as His life hung in the balance, astonishes us when we ponder the scope of His mission. On a future day, He will lead the armies of heaven into battle. John wrote, "With justice he judges and wages war" (REV. 19:11).

But as He endured the ordeal of His arrest, trial, and crucifixion, Jesus kept His Father's will in view. By embracing death on the cross, He set in motion a chain of events that truly transforms hearts. And in the process, our Strong Conqueror defeated death itself. ❧

TIM GUSTAFSON

Father, how prone I am to reacting quickly rather than wisely.
Show me Your will for my life so that I will purposefully choose the path
You have for me.

Real restraint is not weakness, for it arises out of genuine strength.

Love in Action

"Do you have** a few items you'd like me to wash?" I asked a visitor to our home in London. His face lit up, and as his daughter walked by, he said, "Get your dirty clothes—Amy's doing our laundry!" I smiled, realizing that my offer had been extended from a few items to a few loads.

Later as I hung clothes outside on the line, a phrase from my morning's Bible reading floated through my mind: "In humility value others above your-selves" (PHIL. 2:3). I had been reading Paul's letter to the people of Philippi, in which he exhorts them to live worthy of Christ's calling through serving and being united with others. They were facing persecu-tion, but Paul wanted them to be of one mind. He knew that their unity, birthed through their union with Christ and expressed through serving each other, would enable them to keep strong in their faith.

> **TODAY'S READING**
> **Philippians 1:27–2:4**
>
> **Do nothing out of selfish ambition or vain conceit. Rather, in humility value others above yourselves.**
>
> Philippians 2:3

We might claim to love others without selfish ambition or vain conceit, but the true state of our hearts isn't revealed until we put our love into action. Though I felt tempted to grumble, I knew that as a follower of Christ, my call was to put my love for my friends into practice—with a clean heart.

May we find ways to serve our family, friends, and neigh-bors for God's glory. ❧

AMY BOUCHER PYE

Read Luke 22:22–27 and consider how you can pattern yourself after Jesus the servant, looking especially at the words, "But I am among you as one who serves."

The gift of unity can result from serving each other.

A Safe Place

A young Japanese man had a problem—he was afraid of leaving his house. To avoid other people, he slept through the day and stayed up all night watching TV. He was a *hikikomori*, or a modern-day hermit. The problem began when he stopped going to school because of poor grades. The longer he remained apart from society, the more he felt like a social misfit. Eventually he broke off all communication with his friends and family. He was helped on his journey to recovery, though, by visiting a youth club in Tokyo known as an *ibasho*—a safe place where broken people could start reintroducing themselves to society.

What if we thought of the church as an *ibasho*—and far more? Without a doubt, we are a community of broken people. When the apostle Paul wrote to the church in Corinth he described their former way of life as anti-social, harmful, and dangerous to themselves and others (1 COR. 6:9–10). But in Jesus they were being transformed and made whole. And Paul encouraged these rescued people to love one another, to be patient and kind, not to be jealous or proud or rude (13:4–7).

> **TODAY'S READING**
> **1 Cor. 6:9–11; 13:4–7**
>
> **That is what some of you were. But you were washed, you were sanctified, you were justified in the name of the Lord Jesus Christ and by the Spirit of our God.**
>
> 1 Corinthians 6:11

The church is to be an *ibasho* where all of us, no matter what struggles or brokenness we face, can know and experience God's love. May the hurting world experience the compassion of Christ from all who follow Him. ❀ *POH FANG CHIA*

Only God can transform a sin-stained soul into a masterpiece of grace.

A Difficult Hill

High in a fold of **Jughandle Peak** in the mountains north of our home in Idaho lies a glacial lake. The route to the lake goes up a steep, exposed ridge through boulders and loose stones. It's a strenuous ascent.

At the beginning of the climb, however, there is a brook—a spring that seeps out of soft, mossy earth and flows through a lush meadow. It's a quiet place to drink deeply and prepare for the hard climb ahead.

In John Bunyan's classic allegory of the Christian life, *The Pilgrim's Progress*, Christian arrives at the foot of a steep ascent called the Hill Difficulty, "at the bottom of which was a spring.…Christian now went to the spring and drank to refresh himself, and then began to go up the hill."

> **TODAY'S READING**
> **Psalm 110**
>
> **He will drink from a brook along the way, and so he will lift his head high.**
> Psalm 110:7

Perhaps the difficult mountain you face is a rebellious child or a serious medical diagnosis. The challenge seems more than you can endure.

Before you face your next major task, visit the spring of refreshment that is God Himself. Come to Him with all your weakness, weariness, helplessness, fear, and doubt. Then drink deeply of His power, strength, and wisdom. God knows all your circumstances and will supply a store of comfort, of spiritual strengthening and consolation. He will lift up your head and give you strength to go on. ❧   *DAVID ROPER*

Father, at this moment I turn to You for strength in my weakness,
energy for my weariness, and faith in my doubt.

He who overrules all things…enabled Christian to…continue on his way.
JOHN BUNYAN, THE PILGRIM'S PROGRESS

We Had No Idea

Volunteers from a local church spent a frigid evening distributing food to people in a low-income apartment complex. One woman who received the food was overjoyed. She showed them her bare cupboard and told them they were an answer to her prayers.

As the volunteers returned to the church, one woman began to cry. "When I was a little girl," she said, "that lady was my Sunday school teacher. She's in church every Sunday. We had no idea she was almost starving!"

TODAY'S READING
Galatians 6:2–10

Carry each other's burdens. Galatians 6:2

Clearly, these were caring people who were seeking ways to carry the burdens of others, as Paul suggests in Galatians 6:2. Yet somehow they hadn't noticed the needs of this woman—someone they saw every Sunday—and she hadn't shared her needs. This can be a gentle reminder for all of us to be more aware of those around us and, as Paul said, to "do good to all people, especially to those who belong to the family of believers" (6:10).

People who worship together have the privilege of assisting one another so no one in the body of Christ goes without help. As we get to know each other and care for each other, perhaps we won't ever have to say, "We had no idea." ❧

DAVE BRANON

Dear Lord, help me to notice the needs of those around me
and to do what I can to meet those needs in Your name.

Nothing costs as much as caring—except not caring.

Signs and Feelings

Ayoung man I know has a habit of asking God for signs. That's not necessarily bad, but his prayers tend to seek confirmation of his *feelings*. For instance, he'll pray, "God, if You want me to do X, then You please do Y, and I'll know it's okay."

This has created a dilemma. Because of the way he prays and the way he thinks God is answering, he feels that he should get back with his ex-girlfriend. Perhaps unsurprisingly, she feels strongly that God doesn't want that.

TODAY'S READING
Matthew 16:1–4

Your word is a lamp for my feet, a light on my path.

Psalm 119:105

The religious leaders of Jesus's day demanded a sign from Him to prove the validity of His claims (MATT. 16:1). They weren't seeking God's guidance; they were challenging His divine authority. Jesus replied, "A wicked and adulterous generation looks for a sign" (V. 4). The Lord's strong response wasn't a blanket statement to prevent anyone from seeking God's guidance. Rather, Jesus was accusing them of ignoring the clear prophecies in Scripture that indicated He was the Messiah.

God wants us to seek His guidance in prayer (JAMES 1:5). He also gives us the guidance of the Spirit (JOHN 14:26) and His Word (PS. 119:105). He provides us with mentors and wise leaders. And He's given us the example of Jesus Himself.

It's wise to ask God for clear direction, but He may not always give it in ways that we expect or want. Perhaps the larger point of prayer is that we learn more about God's nature and develop a relationship with our Father. ❧ *TIM GUSTAFSON*

The best way to know God's will is to say, "I will" to God.

A New Purpose

Jacob Davis was a tailor with a problem. It was the height of the Gold Rush in the 1800s American West and the gold miners' work pants kept wearing out. His solution? Davis went to a local dry goods company owned by Levi Strauss, purchased tent cloth, and made work pants from that heavy, sturdy material—and blue jeans were born. Today, denim jeans in a variety of forms (including Levi's) are among the most popular clothing items in the world, and all because tent material was given a new purpose.

TODAY'S READING
Mark 1:16–22

"Come, follow me," Jesus said, "and I will send you out to fish for people." Mark 1:17

Simon and his friends were fishermen on the Sea of Galilee. Then Jesus arrived and called them to follow Him. He gave them a new purpose. No longer would they fish for fish. As Jesus told them, "Come, follow me, . . . and I will send you out to fish for people" (MARK 1:17).

With this new purpose set for their lives, these men were taught and trained by Jesus so that, after His ascension, they could be used by God to capture the hearts of people with the message of the cross and resurrection of Christ. Today, we follow in their steps as we share the good news of Christ's love and salvation.

May our lives both declare and exhibit this love that can change the lives, purposes, and eternal destinies of others. ✪

BILL CROWDER

Help me, Lord, to represent You well so that others might be drawn to
Your love and salvation.

With our new life in Christ we have been given a new purpose.

Sacrificial Faith

I t's Sunday afternoon, and I'm sitting in the garden of our home, which is near the church where my husband is the minister. I hear wafts of praise and worship music floating through the air in the Farsi language. Our church in London hosts a vibrant Iranian congregation, and we feel humbled by their passion for Christ as they share some of their stories of persecution and tell of those, such as the senior pastor's brother, who have been martyred for their faith. These faithful believers are following in the footsteps of the first Christian martyr, Stephen.

> **TODAY'S READING**
> Acts 6:8–15; 7:59–60
>
> Blessed are those who are persecuted because of righteousness, for theirs is the kingdom of heaven.
> Matthew 5:10

Stephen, one of the first appointed leaders in the early church, garnered attention in Jerusalem when he performed "great wonders and signs" (ACTS 6:8) and was brought before the Jewish authorities to defend his actions. He gave an impassioned defense of the faith before describing the hard-heartedness of his accusers. But instead of repenting, they were "furious and gnashed their teeth at him" (7:54). They dragged him from the city and stoned him to death—even as he prayed for their forgiveness.

The stories of Stephen and modern martyrs remind us that the message of Christ can be met with brutality. If we have never faced persecution for our faith, let's pray for the persecuted church around the world. And may we, if and when tested, find grace to be found faithful to the One who suffered so much more for us. ❧

AMY BOUCHER PYE

May we find grace to walk in the Master's steps.

Bread!

I live in a small Mexican city where every morning and evening you can hear a distinctive cry: "Bread!" A man with a huge basket on his bike offers a great variety of fresh sweet and salty breads for sale. I used to live in a bigger city, where I had to go to the bakery to buy bread. So I enjoy having fresh bread brought to my door.

TODAY'S READING
John 6:34–51

I am the bread of life. John 6:48

Moving from the thought of feeding physical hunger to spiritual hunger, I think of Jesus's words: "I am the living bread that came down from heaven. Whoever eats this bread will live forever" (JOHN 6:51).

Someone has said that evangelism is really one beggar telling another beggar where he found bread. Many of us can say, "Once I was spiritually hungry, spiritually starving because of my sins. Then I heard the good news. Someone told me where to find bread: in Jesus. And my life changed!"

Now we have the privilege and the responsibility of pointing others to this Bread of Life. We can share Jesus in our neighborhood, in our workplace, in our school, in our places of recreation. We can talk about Jesus in the waiting room, on the bus, or on the train. We can take the good news to others through doors of friendship.

Jesus is the Bread of Life. Let's tell everybody the great news. ❧

KEILA OCHOA

Lord Jesus, I want to be Your witness everywhere I go.

Share the Bread of Life wherever you are.

Pay Close Attention

As I sat in the auditorium, I faced the pastor with my eyes fixed on him. My posture suggested I was absorbing everything he was saying. Suddenly I heard everybody laughing and clapping. Surprised, I looked about. The preacher had apparently said something humorous, but I had no clue what it might have been. From all appearances I had been listening carefully, but in reality my mind was far away.

It's possible to hear what is being said but not listen, to watch but not see, to be present and yet absent. In such a condition, we may miss important messages meant for us.

TODAY'S READING
Neh. 8:2–6; Acts 8:4–8

All the people listened attentively to the Book of the Law. Nehemiah 8:3

As Ezra read God's instructions to the people of Judah, "All the people listened attentively to the Book of the Law" (NEH. 8:3). Their attention to the explanation produced understanding (V. 8), which resulted in their repentance and revival. In another situation in Samaria, Philip, after persecution of the believers broke out in Jerusalem (ACTS 8:1), reached out to the Samaritan people. The crowd not only observed the miraculous signs he did, but they also "paid close attention to what he said" (V. 6). "So there was great joy in that city" (V. 8).

The mind can be like a wandering adventurer that misses a lot of excitement close by. Nothing deserves more attention than words that help us discover the joy and wonder of our Father in heaven. ✒ *LAWRENCE DARMANI*

Lord, our minds are so prone to distraction. Help us to be present in the moment, especially when listening to those who instruct us in Your ways.

The receiving of the Word consists in two parts: attention of the mind and intention of the will. WILLIAM AMES

All Together Now

While **Andy Taylor** was boarding a train in Perth, Australia, his leg became wedged in the gap between the platform and a commuter car. When safety officials could not free him, they coordinated the efforts of nearly 50 passengers who lined up and, on the count of three, pushed against the train. Working in unison, they shifted the weight just enough to free Taylor's leg.

TODAY'S READING
Romans 15:1–7

> **With one mind and one voice . . . glorify the God and Father of our Lord Jesus Christ.** Romans 15:6

The apostle Paul recognized the power of Christians working together in many of his letters to the early churches. He urged the Roman believers to accept each other the way Christ had accepted them and said, "[May God] give you the same attitude of mind toward each other that Christ Jesus had, so that with one mind and one voice you may glorify the God and Father of our Lord Jesus Christ" (ROM. 15:5-6).

Unity with other believers enables us to broadcast God's greatness and also helps us to endure persecution. Knowing that the Philippians would pay a price for their faith, Paul encouraged them to strive "together as one for the faith of the gospel without being frightened in any way by those who oppose you" (PHIL. 1:27-28).

Satan loves to divide and conquer, but his efforts fail when, with God's help, we "make every effort to keep the unity of the Spirit through the bond of peace" (EPH. 4:3). ✒

JENNIFER BENSON SCHULDT

Dear God, please let Christians everywhere experience the blessing of unity in You. Remind us of what we have in common: one hope, one faith, and one Lord—Jesus Christ.

Our unity comes from our union with Christ.

Costume or Uniform?

Eunice McGarrahan gave an inspiring talk on Christian discipleship in which she said, "A costume is something you put on and pretend that you are what you are wearing. A uniform, on the other hand, reminds you that you are, in fact, what you wear."

Her comment sparked memories of my first day in US Army basic training when we were each given a box and ordered to put all our civilian clothes in it. The box was mailed to our home address. Every day after that, the uniform we put on reminded us that we had entered a period of disciplined training designed to change our attitudes and actions.

> **TODAY'S READING**
> **Romans 13:11-14**
>
> **Put on the Lord Jesus Christ, and make no provision for the flesh, to fulfill its lusts.**
> Romans 13:14

"Cast off the works of darkness," the apostle Paul told the followers of Jesus living in Rome, "and . . . put on the armor of light" (ROM. 13:12). He followed this with the command to "put on the Lord Jesus Christ, and make no provision for the flesh, to fulfill its lusts" (V. 14). The goal of this "casting off" and "putting on" was a new identity and transformed living (V. 13).

When we choose to follow Christ as our Lord, He begins the process of making us more like Him each day. It is not a matter of pretending to be what we aren't but of becoming more and more what we are in Christ. ✪   *DAVID McCASLAND*

O to be like Thee, O to be like Thee,
Blessed Redeemer, pure as Thou art!
Come in Thy sweetness, come in Thy fullness;
Stamp Thine own image deep on my heart. *CHISHOLM*

Salvation is free, but discipleship will cost you your life. DIETRICH BONHOEFFER

The Twelfth Man

A large sign at the Texas A&M University football stadium says "HOME OF THE 12TH MAN." While each team is allowed eleven players on the field, the 12th Man is the presence of thousands of A&M students who remain standing during the entire game to cheer their team on.

TODAY'S READING
Hebrews 11:32–12:3

Let us run with perseverance the race marked out for us. Hebrews 12:1

The tradition traces its roots to 1922 when the coach called a student from the stands to suit up and be ready to replace an injured player. Although he never entered the game, his willing presence on the sideline greatly encouraged the team.

Hebrews 11 describes heroes of the faith who faced great trials and remained loyal to God. Chapter 12 begins, "Therefore, since we are surrounded by such a great cloud of witnesses, let us throw off everything that hinders and the sin that so easily entangles. And let us run with perseverance the race marked out for us" (v. 1).

We are not alone on our journey of faith. The great saints and ordinary people who have been faithful to the Lord encourage us by their example and also by their presence in heaven. They are a spiritual 12th Man standing with us while we are still on the field.

As we fix our eyes on Jesus, "the pioneer and perfecter of faith" (12:2), we are spurred on by all those who followed Him. 🌿

DAVID MCCASLAND

Lord, may we be aware of those in heaven who are cheering us on.
Give us strength to run our race of faith today.

Faithful Christians from the past encourage us today.

A Façade

Kerri tries hard to get people to admire her. She acts happy most of the time so that others will notice and compliment her on her joyful attitude. Some affirm her because they see her helping people in the community. But in a transparent moment Kerri will admit, "I love the Lord, but in some ways I feel like my life is a façade." Her own sense of insecurity is behind much of her effort of trying to look good to others, and she says she's running out of energy to keep it up.

TODAY'S READING
Matthew 6:1–6

Give your gifts in private, and your Father, who sees everything, will reward you.

Matthew 6:4 NLT

We can probably all relate in some way because it's not possible to have perfect motives. We love the Lord and others, but our motives for how we live the Christian life are sometimes mixed with our desire to be valued or praised.

Jesus talked about those who give, pray, and fast in order to be seen (MATT. 6:1–18). He taught in the Sermon on the Mount to "give your gifts in private," to "pray to your Father in private," and "when you fast, don't make it obvious" (VV. 4, 6, 16 NLT).

Serving is most often done publicly, but maybe a little anonymous service could help us learn to rest in God's opinion of us. He who created us in His image values us so much that He gave us His Son and shows us His love each day. 🌼 *ANNE CETAS*

Dear Lord, please forgive me for desiring praise from others
more than from You. Please help me as I struggle to keep my
motives pure.

Our desire to please God should be our highest motive for obeying God.

Love without Borders

During the Boxer Rebellion in China in 1900, missionaries trapped in a home in T'ai Yüan Fu decided their only hope for survival rested on running through the crowd that was calling for their deaths. Aided by weapons they held, they escaped the immediate threat. However, Edith Coombs, noticing that two of her injured Chinese students had not escaped, raced back into danger. She rescued one, but stumbled on her return trip for the second student and was killed.

TODAY'S READING
Luke 22:39–46

Greater love has no one than this: to lay down one's life for one's friends. John 15:13

Meanwhile, missionaries in Hsin Chou district had escaped and were hiding in the countryside, accompanied by their Chinese friend Ho Tsuen Kwei. But he was captured while scouting an escape route for his friends in hiding and was martyred for refusing to reveal their location.

In the lives of Edith Coombs and Tsuen Kwei we see a love that rises above cultural or national character. Their sacrifice reminds us of the greater grace and love of our Savior.

As Jesus awaited His arrest and subsequent execution, He prayed earnestly, "Father, if you are willing, take this cup from me." But He concluded that request with this resolute example of courage, love, and sacrifice: "Yet not my will, but yours be done" (LUKE 22:42). His death and resurrection made our eternal lives possible. ❧

RANDY KILGORE

Lord, may the world see our love for each other—and the deeds that come from it—as a great testimony to the bond of unity we have in You. May they want to know You too.

Only the light of Christ's love can eliminate the darkness of hatred.

Skywatcher

Unsettled by issues at work and at home, Matt decided to take a walk. The evening spring air beckoned. As the infinite sky deepened from blue to black, a thickening fog spilled slowly over the marsh. Stars began to glimmer, heralding the full moon rising in the east. The moment, for Matt, was deeply spiritual. *He's there,* he thought. *God is there, and He's got this.*

Some people look at the night sky and see nothing but nature. Others see a god as distant and cold as Jupiter. But the same God who "sits enthroned above the circle of the earth" also "brings out the starry host one by one and calls forth each of them by name" (ISA. 40:22, 26). He knows His creation intimately.

TODAY'S READING
Isaiah 40:21–31

He . . . brings out the starry host one by one and calls forth each of them by name. Isaiah 40:26

It is this personal God who asked His people, "Why do you say, Israel, 'My way is hidden from the LORD; my cause is disregarded by my God'?" Aching for them, God reminded them of the wisdom in seeking Him. "Do you not know? Have you not heard? . . . He gives strength to the weary and increases the power of the weak" (VV. 27–29).

We are easily tempted to forget God. Our problems won't disappear with an evening stroll, but we can find rest and certainty that God is always working toward His good purposes. "I'm here," He says. "I've got you." ◕

TIM GUSTAFSON

Thank You, Lord, for a night sky that helps us glimpse eternity.
We can't begin to understand it fully, but we know it is there, and we
know You are there. Help us trust You for what we don't know.

*We should give God the same place in our hearts
that He holds in the universe.*

Seeing Well

Raleigh looks like a powerful dog—he is large and muscular and has a thick coat of fur. And he weighs over 100 pounds! Despite his appearance, Raleigh connects well with people. His owner takes him to nursing homes and hospitals to bring people a smile.

Once, a four-year-old girl spotted Raleigh across a room. She wanted to pet him, but was afraid to get close. Eventually, her curiosity overcame her sense of caution and she spent several minutes talking to him and petting him. She discovered that he is a gentle creature, even though he is powerful.

TODAY'S READING
John 15:12–17

You are my friends if you do what I command. John 15:14

The combination of these qualities reminds me of what we read about Jesus in the New Testament. Jesus was approachable—He welcomed little children (MATT. 19:13–15). He was kind to an adulterous woman in a desperate situation (JOHN 8:1–11). Compassion motivated Him to teach crowds (MARK 6:34). At the same time, Jesus's power was astounding. Heads turned and jaws dropped as He subdued demons, calmed violent storms, and resurrected dead people! (MARK 1:21–34; 4:35–41; JOHN 11).

The way we see Jesus determines how we relate to Him. If we focus only on His power, we may treat Him with the detached worship we'd give a comic book superhero. Yet, if we overemphasize His kindness, we risk treating Him too casually. The truth is that Jesus is both at once—great enough to deserve our obedience yet humble enough to call us friends. ✿

JENNIFER BENSON SCHULDT

Jesus, thank You for the privilege of knowing You. I acknowledge Your gentle power. I worship You as the Son of God—full of grace and glory.

What we think of Jesus shows in how we relate with Him.

What about You?

Emily listened as a group of friends talked about their Thanksgiving traditions with family. "We go around the room and each one tells what he or she is thankful to God for," Gary said.

TODAY'S READING
Ephesians 4:25–32

The tongue has the power of life and death. Proverbs 18:21

Another friend mentioned his family's Thanksgiving meal and prayertime. He recalled time with his dad before he had died: "Even though Dad had dementia, his prayer of thanks to the Lord was clear." Randy shared, "My family has a special time of singing together on the holiday. My grandma goes on and on and on!" Emily's sadness and jealousy grew as she thought of her own family, and she complained: "Our traditions are to eat turkey, watch television, and never mention anything about God or giving thanks."

Right away Emily felt uneasy with her attitude. *You are part of that family. What would you like to do differently to change the day?* she asked herself. She decided she wanted to privately tell each person she was thankful to the Lord that they were her sister, niece, brother, or great-niece. When the day arrived, she expressed her thankfulness for them one by one, and they all felt loved. It wasn't easy because it wasn't normal conversation in her family, but she experienced joy as she shared her love for each of them.

"Let everything you say be good and helpful," wrote the apostle Paul, "so that your words will be an encouragement to those who hear them" (EPH. 4:29 NLT). Our words of thanks can remind others of their value to us and to God. 🕊 *ANNE CETAS*

Dear Lord, show me how I can be an encouragement to others
with my words.

The human spirit fills with hope at the sound of an encouraging word.

Game of Thanks

Every autumn we throw a scrumptious Thanksgiving feast on campus at Cornerstone University. Our students love it! Last year a group of students played a game at their table. They challenged each other to name something they were thankful for—in three seconds or less—without repeating what someone else had said. Anyone who hesitated was out of the game.

There are all kinds of things that students might gripe about—tests, deadlines, rules, and a host of other college-type complaints. But these students had chosen to be thankful. And my guess is that they all felt a lot better after the game than they would have if they had chosen to complain.

While there will always be things to complain about, if we look carefully there are always blessings to be thankful for. When Paul describes our newness in Christ, "thankfulness" is the only characteristic mentioned more than once. In fact it is mentioned three times. "Be thankful," he says in Colossians 3:15. Sing to God "with gratitude in your hearts" (V. 16). And whatever you do, be sure to be "giving thanks to God the Father" (V. 17). Paul's instruction to be thankful is astonishing when we consider that he wrote this letter from prison!

Today, let's make the choice to have an attitude of thankfulness. ✒

JOE STOWELL

Lord, teach me the liberating joy of being thankful! Help me to find the blessings that are locked up in the things I complain about and to regularly express my gratitude to You and others.

Choose the attitude of gratitude.

Best Deal Ever!

How much is enough? We might ask this simple question on a day that many developed countries increasingly devote to shopping. I speak of Black Friday, the day after the US Thanksgiving holiday, in which many stores open early and offer cut-price deals; a day that has spread from the States to other nations. Some shoppers have limited resources and are trying to purchase something at a price they can afford. But sadly, for others greed is the motivation, and violence erupts as they fight for bargains.

The wisdom of the Old Testament writer known as "the Teacher" (ECCL. 1:1) provides an antidote to the frenzy of consumerism we may face in the shops—and in our hearts. He points out that those who love money never will have enough and will be ruled by their possessions. And yet, they will die with nothing: "As everyone comes, so they depart" (5:15). The apostle Paul echoes the Teacher in his letter to Timothy, when he says that the love of money is a root of all kinds of evil, and that we should strive for "godliness with contentment" (1 TIM. 6:6–10).

Whether we live in a place of plenty or not, we all can seek unhealthy ways of filling the God-shaped hole in our hearts. But when we look to the Lord for our sense of peace and well-being, He will fill us with His goodness and love. 🌀   *AMY BOUCHER PYE*

You have formed us for Yourself, and our hearts are restless
till they find rest in You. *AUGUSTINE,* THE CONFESSIONS

True contentment does not depend on anything in this world.

Longing for Home

My wife walked into the room and found me poking my head inside the cabinet of our grandfather clock. "What are you doing?" she asked. "This clock smells just like my parents' house," I answered sheepishly, closing the door. "I guess you could say I was going home for a moment."

The sense of smell can evoke powerful memories. We had moved the clock across the country from my parents' house nearly twenty years ago, but the aroma of the wood inside it still takes me back to my childhood.

> **TODAY'S READING**
> **Hebrews 11:8–16**
>
> **They were longing for a better country—a heavenly one.**
>
> Hebrews 11:16

The writer of Hebrews tells of others who were longing for home in a different way. Instead of looking backward, they were looking ahead with faith to their home in heaven. Even though what they hoped for seemed a long way off, they trusted that God was faithful to keep His promise to bring them to a place where they would be with Him forever (HEB. 11:13–16).

Philippians 3:20 reminds us that "our citizenship is in heaven," and we are to "eagerly await a Savior from there, the Lord Jesus Christ." Looking forward to seeing Jesus and receiving everything God has promised us through Him help us keep our focus. The past or the present can never compare with what's ahead of us! 🌱

JAMES BANKS

Jesus, thank You that You are faithful to keep Your promises.
Please help me to always look forward to You.

The best home of all is our home in heaven.

Fame and Humility

Many of us are obsessed with fame—either with being famous ourselves or with following every detail of famous people's lives. International book or film tours. Late-night show appearances. Millions of followers on Twitter.

In a recent study in the US, researchers ranked the names of famous individuals using a specially developed algorithm that scoured the internet. Jesus topped the list as the most famous person in history.

Wherever Jesus went, crowds soon gathered. The miracles He performed drew people to Him. But when they tried to make Him a king by force, He slipped away by Himself (JOHN 6:15). United in purpose with His Father, He repeatedly deferred to the Father's will and timing (4:34; 8:29; 12:23). "He humbled himself by becoming obedient to death—even death on a cross" (PHIL. 2:8).

Fame was never Jesus's goal. His purpose was simple. As the Son of God, He humbly, obediently, and voluntarily offered Himself as the sacrifice for our sins. ❧

> TODAY'S READING
> **Philippians 2:1–11**
>
> **He humbled himself by becoming obedient to death—even death on a cross!**
> Philippians 2:8

CINDY HESS KASPER

You are to be celebrated, Lord, above all others. You have been highly exalted and given a name that is above every name. One day every knee will bow and every tongue confess that You are Lord.

Jesus came not to be famous, but to humbly offer Himself as the sacrifice for our sins.

Unsend

Have you ever sent an email and suddenly realized it went to the wrong person or it contained harmful, harsh words? If only you could press a key and stop it. Well, now you can. Several companies offer a feature that gives you a brief time after sending an email to stop it from leaving your computer. After that, the email is like a spoken word that cannot be unsaid. Rather than being seen as a cure-all, an "unsend" feature should remind us that it's extremely important to guard what we say.

TODAY'S READING
1 Peter 3:8–12

> **Whoever would love life and see good days must keep their tongue from evil and their lips from deceitful speech.** 1 Peter 3:10

In the apostle Peter's first letter, he told the followers of Jesus, "Do not repay evil with evil or insult with insult. On the contrary, repay evil with blessing.... For, 'whoever would love life and see good days must keep their tongue from evil and their lips from deceitful speech. They must turn from evil and do good; they must seek peace and pursue it'" (1 PETER 3:9–11).

The psalmist David wrote, "Set a guard over my mouth, LORD; keep watch over the door of my lips" (PS. 141:3). That's a great prayer for the beginning of each day and in every situation when we want to strike back with words.

Lord, guard our words today so we may not harm others by what we say. ✸

DAVID MCCASLAND

Father, teach us first to guard our hearts so that we may
guard our tongues. And help us, when we do say things we regret,
to humbly apologize and seek forgiveness.

The tongue has the power of life and death. PROVERBS 18:21

The Red Hackle

Several years ago I stumbled across a bit of fishing lore in a second-century AD work by the Greek writer Aelian. "Between Boroca and Thessalonica runs a river called the Astracus, and in it there are fish with spotted skins [trout]." He then describes a "snare for the fish, by which they get the better of them. They fastened crimson red wool round a hook and attached two feathers. Then they would throw their snare, and the fish, attracted by the color, comes up, thinking to get a mouthful" *(On the Nature of Animals)*.

> **TODAY'S READING**
> **Psalm 92:12–15**
>
> **They will still bear fruit in old age.**
> Psalm 92:14

Fishermen still use this lure today. It is called the Red Hackle. First used over 2,200 years ago, it remains a snare for trout by which we "get the better of them."

When I read that ancient work I thought: *Not all old things are passé—especially people.* If through contented and cheerful old age we show others the fullness and deepness of God, we'll be useful to the end of our days. Old age does not have to focus on declining health, pining over what once was. It can also be full of tranquility and mirth and courage and kindness, the fruit of those who have grown old with God.

"Those who are planted in the house of the LORD . . . shall still bear fruit in old age; they shall be fresh and flourishing" (PS. 92:13–14 NKJV). 🍃

DAVID ROPER

Lord, thank You for Your faithfulness throughout our lives.
Help us finish our lives well in service to You and to remember that
old age does not mean uselessness.

As the years add up, God's faithfulness keeps multiplying.

Beautiful

Picture two teenage girls. The first girl is strong and healthy. The other girl has never known the freedom of getting around on her own. From her wheelchair she faces not only the emotional challenges common to life, but also a stream of physical pains and struggles.

But both girls are smiling cheerfully as they enjoy each other's company. Two beautiful teenagers—each seeing in the other the treasure of friendship.

TODAY'S READING
Luke 7:36–50

She has done a beautiful thing to me. Mark 14:6

Jesus devoted much of His time and attention to people like the girl in the wheelchair. People with lifelong disabilities or physical deformities as well as those who were looked down on by others for various reasons. In fact, Jesus let one of "those people" anoint Him with oil, to the disdain of the religious leaders (LUKE 7:39). On another occasion, when a woman demonstrated her love with a similar act, Jesus told her critics, "Leave her alone.... She has done a beautiful thing to me" (MARK 14:6).

God values everyone equally; there are no distinctions in His eyes. In reality, we are all in desperate need of Christ's love and forgiveness. His love compelled Him to die on the cross for us.

May we see each person as Jesus did: made in God's image and worthy of His love. Let's treat everyone we meet with Christlike equality and learn to see beauty as He does. ✸ *DAVE BRANON*

> Dear Lord, help me to see people as You see them—not important because of what they can do or how they look, but because they are made in God's image and You loved them enough to die for them.

Everyone we meet bears the image of God.

I'm Rich!

Perhaps you've seen the TV ad in which a person answers the door and finds someone who hands over a check for an enormous amount of money. Then the amazed recipient begins shouting, dancing, jumping, and hugging everyone in sight. "I won! I'm rich! I can't believe it! My problems are solved!" Striking it rich evokes a great emotional response.

TODAY'S READING
Psalm 119:9–16

I rejoice in following your statutes as one rejoices in great riches. Psalm 119:14

In Psalm 119, the longest chapter in the Bible, we find this remarkable statement: "I rejoice in following your statutes as one rejoices in great riches" (V. 14). What a comparison! Obeying God's instructions for living can be just as exhilarating as receiving a fortune! Verse 16 repeats this refrain as the psalmist expresses grateful gladness for the Lord's commands. "I delight in your decrees; I will not neglect your word."

But what if we don't feel that way? How can delighting in God's instructions for living be just as exhilarating as receiving a fortune? It all begins with gratitude, which is both an attitude and a choice. We pay attention to what we value, so we begin by expressing our gratitude for those gifts of God that nourish our souls. We ask Him to open our eyes to see the storehouse of wisdom, knowledge, and peace He has given us in His Word.

As our love for Jesus grows each day, we indeed strike it rich! ❧

DAVID MCCASLAND

Dear Father, open our eyes that we may see wonderful things in Your law.
Thank You that Your instructions give wise advice.

Rich treasures of God's truth are waiting to be discovered in His Word.

What Are You Worth?

There is a story that in 75 BC a young Roman nobleman named Julius Caesar was kidnapped by pirates and held for ransom. When they demanded 20 talents of silver in ransom (about $600,000 today), Caesar laughed and said they obviously had no idea who he was. He insisted they raise the ransom to 50 talents! Why? Because he believed he was worth far more than 20 talents.

What a difference we see between Caesar's arrogant measure of his own worth and the value God places on each of us. Our worth is not measured in terms of monetary value but by what our heavenly Father has done on our behalf.

What ransom did He pay to save us? Through the death of His only Son on the cross, the Father paid the price to rescue us from our sin. "It was not with perishable things such as silver or gold that you were redeemed from the empty way of life handed down to you from your ancestors, but with the precious blood of Christ" (1 PETER 1:18–19).

God loved us so much that He gave up His Son to die on the cross and rise from the dead to ransom and rescue us. That is what you are worth to Him. 🌱

BILL CROWDER

> **TODAY'S READING**
> **1 Peter 1:17–23**
>
> It was not with perishable things such as silver or gold that you were redeemed . . . but with the precious blood of Christ.
>
> 1 Peter 1:18–19

Father, thank You for the love You have shown to me and for
the price You paid for my forgiveness. Help my life to be an
ongoing expression of gratitude, for You are the One whose worth is
beyond measure.

Our worth is measured by what God paid to rescue us.

The View from 400 Miles

"**M**y perspective on earth** changed dramatically the very first time I went into space," says Space Shuttle astronaut Charles Frank Bolden Jr. From four hundred miles above the earth, all looked peaceful and beautiful to him. Yet Bolden recalled later that as he passed over the Middle East, he was "shaken into reality" when he considered the ongoing conflict there. During an interview with film producer Jared Leto, Bolden spoke of that moment as a time when he saw the earth with a sense of how it ought to be—and then sensed a challenge to do all he could to make it better.

TODAY'S READING
John 1:1–14

The true light that gives light to everyone was coming into the world. John 1:9

When Jesus was born in Bethlehem, the world was not the way God intended it. Into this moral and spiritual darkness Jesus came bringing life and light to all (JOHN 1:4). Even though the world didn't recognize Him, "to all who did receive him, to those who believed in his name, he gave the right to become children of God" (V. 12).

When life is not the way it ought to be we are deeply saddened—when families break up, children go hungry, and the world wages war. But God promises that through faith in Christ anyone can begin to move in a new direction.

The Christmas season reminds us that Jesus, the Savior, gives the gift of life and light to everyone who will receive and follow Him. ❡

DAVID MCCASLAND

Father in heaven, may we share the light and life of Jesus
with others today.

God is at work to make us who He intends us to be.

Quiet Conversations

Do you ever talk to yourself? Sometimes when I'm working on a project—usually under the hood of a car—I find it helpful to think aloud, working through my options on the best way to make the repair. If someone catches me in my "conversation" it can be a little embarrassing—even though talking to ourselves is something most of us do every day.

The psalmists often talked to themselves in the Psalms. The author of Psalm 116 is no exception. In verse 7 he writes, "Return to your rest, my soul, for the LORD has been good to you." Reminding himself of God's kindness and faithfulness in the past is a practical comfort and help to him in the present. We see "conversations" like this frequently in the Psalms. In Psalm 103:1 David tells himself, "Praise the LORD, my soul; all my inmost being, praise his holy name." And in Psalm 62:5 he affirms, "Yes, my soul, find rest in God; my hope comes from him."

> **TODAY'S READING**
> **Psalm 116:5–9**
>
> **Praise the LORD, my soul, and forget not all his benefits.** Psalm 103:2

It's good to remind ourselves of God's faithfulness and the hope we have in Him. We can follow the example of the psalmist and spend some time naming the many ways God has been good to us. As we do, we'll be encouraged. The same God who has been faithful in the past will continue His love for us in the future. ❀

JAMES BANKS

Dear Lord, please help me to stay in touch with Your heart today by reminding myself of Your faithfulness and love.

Reminding ourselves about God's goodness can keep us filled with His peace.

Listeners and Doers

The phone rang in the night for my husband, a minister. One of the prayer warriors in our church, a woman in her seventies who lived alone, was being taken to the hospital. She was so ill that she was no longer eating or drinking, nor could she see or walk. Not knowing if she would live or die, we asked God for His help and mercy, feeling particularly concerned for her welfare. The church sprang into action with a round-the-clock schedule of visitors who not only ministered to her but showed Christian love to the other patients, visitors, and medical staff.

James's letter to the early Jewish Christians encouraged the church to care for the needy. James wanted the believers to go beyond just listening to the Word of God and to put their beliefs into action (1:22–25). By citing the need to care for orphans and widows (v. 27), he named a vulnerable group, for in the ancient world the family would have been responsible for their care.

How do we respond to those who are at risk in our church and community? Do we see caring for the widows and orphans as a vital part of the exercise of our faith? May God open our eyes to the opportunities to serve people in need everywhere. ❧

AMY BOUCHER PYE

Father God, Your heart beats for the vulnerable
and for those who are alone. Help us to love Your people as You love
them, for we are made in Your image.

True faith demands not only our words, but our actions.

The Treasure in Tomb 7

In 1932, Mexican archaeologist Alfonso Caso discovered Tomb 7 at Monte Albán, Oaxaca. He found more than four hundred artifacts, including hundreds of pieces of pre-Hispanic jewelry he called "The Treasure of Monte Albán." It is one of the major finds of Mexican archaeology. One can only imagine Caso's excitement as he held a jade cup in its purest form.

TODAY'S READING
Psalm 119:161–168

> **I rejoice in your promise like one who finds great spoil.** Psalm 119:162

Centuries earlier, the psalmist wrote of a treasure more valuable than gold or rock crystal. He said, "I rejoice in your promise like one who finds great spoil" (PS. 119:162). In Psalm 119, the writer knew how valuable God's instructions and promises are to our lives, so he compared them to the great treasure that comes in hand with the victory of a conqueror.

Caso's name is remembered today because of his discovery in Tomb 7. We can enjoy it if we visit a museum in Oaxaca. However, the psalmist's treasure is at our fingertips. Day by day we can dig into the Scriptures and find diamonds of promises, rubies of hope, and emeralds of wisdom. But by far the greatest thing we find is the person whom the book points to: Jesus Himself. After all, He is the Author of the book.

Let us seek diligently with the confidence that this is the treasure that will enrich us. As the psalmist said, "Your laws are my treasure; they are my heart's delight" (V. 111 NLT). 🌐

KEILA OCHOA

Father, I want to value the Scriptures as a treasure.
Help me enjoy Your Word every day.

God's Word is a valuable possession and a guide to life.

Christmas Lights

Each year for several weeks around Christmas, Singapore's tourist belt, Orchard Road, is transformed into a wonderland of lights and colors. This light-up is designed to attract tourists to spend their money at the many stores along the street during this "golden month of business." Shoppers come to enjoy the festivities, listen to choirs sing familiar Christmas carols, and watch performers entertain.

TODAY'S READING
John 8:12–20

I am the light of the world. Whoever follows me will never walk in darkness, but will have the light of life. John 8:12

The first Christmas "light-up" ever was not created by electrical cables, glitter, and neon lights but by "the glory of the Lord [that] shone around" (LUKE 2:9). No tourists saw it, just a few simple shepherds out in their field. And it was followed by an unexpected rendition of "Glory to God in the Highest" by an angelic choir (V. 14).

The shepherds went to Bethlehem to see if what the angels said was true (V. 15). After they had confirmed it, they could not keep to themselves what they had heard and seen. "When they had seen him, they spread the word concerning what had been told them about this child" (V. 17).

Many of us have heard the Christmas story often. This Christmas, why not share the good news with others that Christ—"the light of the world"—has come (JOHN 8:12). 🌱   *C. P. HIA*

Lord, help me this Christmas to reflect the light of Your presence and goodness to others.

The gift of God's love in us can bring light to any darkness.

Constant Kindness

When I was a child I was an ardent reader of L. Frank Baum's Land of Oz books. I recently came across *Rinkitink in Oz* with all the original artwork. I laughed again at the antics of Baum's irrepressible, good-hearted King Rinkitink with his down-to-earth goodness. Young Prince Inga described him best: "His heart is kind and gentle and that is far better than being wise."

How simple and how sensible! Yet who has not wounded the heart of someone dear to us by a harsh word? By doing so, we disturb the peace and quiet of the hour and we can undo much of the good we have done toward those we love. "A small unkindness is a great offense," said Hannah More, an 18th-century English writer.

> **TODAY'S READING**
> **Psalm 141:1–3**
>
> **Be kind and compassionate to one another.**
> Ephesians 4:32

Here's the good news: Anyone can become kind. We may be incapable of preaching an inspiring sermon, fielding hard questions, or evangelizing vast numbers, but we can all be kind.

How? Through prayer. It is the only way to soften our hearts. "Set a guard over my mouth, LORD; keep watch over the door of my lips. Do not let my heart be drawn to what is evil [or harsh]" (PS. 141:3–4).

In a world in which love has grown cold, a kindness that comes from the heart of God is one of the most helpful and healing things we can offer to others. 🍃   *DAVID ROPER*

Forgive me, Lord, when I bring anger into a situation. Soften my heart and help me use my words to encourage others.

The knowledge that God has loved me beyond all limits will compel me to go into the world to love others in the same way. OSWALD CHAMBERS

Beautiful Unity

Seeing three large predatory animals cuddle and play to-gether is extremely unusual. Yet this is precisely what happens daily in an animal sanctuary in Georgia. In 2001, after months of neglect and abuse, a lion, a Bengal tiger, and a black bear were rescued by Noah's Ark Animal Sanctuary.

"We could have separated them," said the assistant director. "But since they came as a kind of family, we decided to keep them together." The trio had found comfort in each other during their time of mistreat-ment, and, despite their differences, they live peacefully together.

TODAY'S READING
Ephesians 4:1–6

Make every effort to keep the unity of the Spirit through the bond of peace. Ephesians 4:3

Unity is a beautiful thing. But the unity Paul wrote about in his letter to the believers in Ephesus is unique. Paul encouraged the Ephesians to live up to their calling as members of one body in Christ (EPH. 4:4–5). By the power of the Holy Spirit they would be able to live in unity as they developed humility, gentleness, and patience. These attitudes also allow us to lovingly bear "with one another in love" through the common ground we have in Christ Jesus (4:2).

Despite our differences, as members of the family of God we have been reconciled to Him through the death of our Savior and reconciled to each other through the ongoing work of the Holy Spirit in our lives. ❧ *MARVIN WILLIAMS*

Heavenly Father, help me to grow in gentleness and patience
toward others. Show me how to love others,
even when we may have differences.

We keep unity by being united in the Spirit.

Surround Sound

Walt Disney Studios was the first to introduce a new concept in listening to movies. It was called "stereo-phonic sound," or surround sound, and it was devel-oped because producers wanted the movie-going audience to hear the music in a new way.

But this wasn't the first use of "surround sound." Thousands of years earlier, Nehemiah introduced the idea at the dedication of the rebuilt wall of Jerusalem. "I had the leaders of Judah go up on top of the wall," he explained. "I also assigned two large choirs to give thanks" (NEH. 12:31). The two choirs began at the southern part of the wall, at the Dung Gate. One went to the left, one went to the right, and they surrounded the city of

TODAY'S READING
Nehemiah 12:27–43

The sound of rejoicing in Jerusalem could be heard far away.

Nehemiah 12:43

Jerusalem in praise as they marched toward the temple (VV. 31, 37–40).

The choirs led the people in rejoicing because "God had given them great joy" (V. 43). In fact, their rejoicing "could be heard far away" (V. 43).

Their praise resulted from God's help as the people over-came the opposition of enemies like Sanballat and rebuilt the wall. What has God given us that causes our joy to overflow into praise? God's clear direction in our lives? The comfort He alone can provide in times of trouble? Or our ultimate gift: salvation?

Perhaps we can't create "surround sound" with our praise, but we can rejoice in the joy God has given us. Then others can hear us praise God and see how He works. ❧   *DAVE BRANON*

We praise You, O Lord—with words, with song, and with our lives.
We offer You our hearts in response to Your great power,
loving provision, and constant care.

We can never praise Jesus too much!

The Gift of Encouragement

An old Merle Haggard song, "If We Make It Through December," tells the story of a man laid off from his factory job with no money to buy Christmas gifts for his little girl. Although December is supposed to be a happy time of year, his life seems dark and cold.

Discouragement is not unique to December, but it can be amplified then. Our expectations may be higher, our sadness deeper. A little encouragement can go a long way.

Joseph, a man from Cyprus, was among the early followers of Jesus. The apostles called him Barnabas, which means "son of encouragement." We meet him in Acts 4:36–37 when he sold a piece of property and donated the money to help other believers in need.

Later, we read that the disciples were afraid of Saul (ACTS 9:26). "But Barnabas took him and brought him to the apostles" (V. 27). Saul, later called Paul, had formerly been trying to kill the believers, but Barnabas defended him as a man transformed by Christ.

> **TODAY'S READING**
> **Acts 4:32–37; 9:26–27**
>
> **Joseph...whom the apostles called Barnabas (which means "son of encouragement"), sold a field he owned and brought the money and put it at the apostles' feet.** Acts 4:36–37

All around us are people longing to be encouraged. A timely word, a phone call, or a prayer can bolster their faith in Jesus.

The generosity and support of Barnabas demonstrate what it means to be a son or daughter of encouragement. That may be the greatest gift we can give to others this Christmas. ❧

DAVID MCCASLAND

Thank You, Lord, for the gift of encouragement. May we encourage others as they have encouraged us.

Encouragement may be the greatest gift we give this Christmas.

Wounds from a Friend

Charles Lowery complained to his friend about lower back pain. He was seeking a sympathetic ear, but what he got was an honest assessment. His friend told him, "I don't think your back pain is your problem; it's your stomach. Your stomach is so big it's pulling on your back."

In his column for *REV! Magazine*, Charles shared that he resisted the temptation to be offended. He lost the weight and his back problem went away. Charles recognized that "Better is open rebuke than hidden love. Wounds from a friend can be trusted" (PROV. 27:5–6).

TODAY'S READING
Proverbs 27:5–10

Wounds from a friend can be trusted. Proverbs 27:6

The trouble is that so often we would rather be ruined by praise than saved by criticism, for truth hurts. It bruises our ego, makes us uncomfortable, and calls for change.

True friends don't find pleasure in hurting us. Rather, they love us too much to deceive us. They are people who, with loving courage, point out what we may already know but find hard to truly accept and live by. They tell us not only what we like to hear but also what we need to hear.

Solomon honored such friendship in his proverbs. Jesus went further—He endured the wounds of our rejection not only to tell us the truth about ourselves but to show us how much we are loved. ❧

POH FANG CHIA

Think of a time when a friend said something honest
that caused you pain. Did it benefit you?
Is it wise to accept everything our friends tell us?

A friend is one who can tell you the truth in love.

Serving God with Our Prayers

God often chooses to move through our prayers to accomplish His work. We see this when God told the prophet Elijah, "I will send rain on the land," promising to end a drought in Israel that had lasted three and a half years (JAMES 5:17). Even though God had promised rain, a short time later "Elijah climbed to the top of Carmel, bent down to the ground and put his face between his knees"—praying intently for the rain to come (1 KINGS 18:42). Then, while he continued to pray, Elijah sent his servant to go and look out over the ocean "seven times," scanning the horizon for any sign of rain (V. 43).

TODAY'S READING
1 Kings 18:41–45

The earnest prayer of a righteous person has great power and produces wonderful results.
James 5:16 NLT

Elijah understood that God wants us to join in His work through humble, persistent prayer. Regardless of our human limitations, God may choose to move through our praying in amazing ways. That's why the letter of James tells us that "the earnest prayer of a righteous person has great power and produces wonderful results," all the while reminding us that "Elijah was as human as we are" (JAMES 5:16–17 NLT).

When we make it our aim to serve God through praying faithfully as Elijah did, we're taking part in a beautiful privilege—where at any moment we may be given a front-row seat to a miracle! 🌿

JAMES BANKS

How can I serve You through my prayers today, Father?

Great expectation on our part honors God.

The Money

Early in my career while doing work that I saw as more of a mission than a job, another company offered me a position that would give a significant increase in pay. Our family could surely have benefited financially from such a move. There was one problem. I hadn't been looking for another job because I loved my current role, which was growing into a calling.

But the *money* . . .

I called my father, then in his seventies, and explained the situation. Though his once-sharp mind had been slowed by strokes and the strain of years, his answer was crisp and clear: "Don't even think about the money. What would you do?"

> TODAY'S READING
> **Matthew 6:24–34**
>
> **You cannot serve both God and money.** Matthew 6:24

In an instant, my mind was made up. The money would have been my only reason for leaving the job I loved! Thanks, Dad.

Jesus devoted a substantial section of His Sermon on the Mount to money and our fondness for it. He taught us to pray not for an accumulation of riches but for "our daily bread" (MATT. 6:11). He warned against storing up treasures on earth and pointed to the birds and flowers as evidence that God cares deeply about His creation (VV. 19–31). "Seek first his kingdom and his righteousness," Jesus said, "and all these things will be given to you as well" (V. 33).

Money matters. But money shouldn't rule our decision-making process. Tough times and big decisions are opportunities to grow our faith in new ways. Our heavenly Father cares for us. 🌱

TIM GUSTAFSON

Never confuse temptation with opportunity.

Good News!

World news bombards us from the internet, television, radio, and mobile devices. The majority seems to describe what's wrong—crime, terrorism, war, and economic problems. Yet there are times when good news invades the darkest hours of sadness and despair—stories of unselfish acts, a medical breakthrough, or steps toward peace in war-scarred places.

The words of two men recorded in the Old Testament of the Bible brought great hope to people weary of conflict.

While describing God's coming judgment on a ruthless and powerful nation, Nahum said, "Look, there on the mountains, the feet of one who brings good news, who proclaims peace!" (NAH. 1:15). That news brought hope to all those oppressed by cruelty.

> TODAY'S READING
> **Nahum 1:7–15**
>
> **Look, there on the mountains, the feet of one who brings good news, who proclaims peace!** Nahum 1:15

A similar phrase occurs in the book of Isaiah: "How beautiful on the mountains are the feet of those who bring good news, who proclaim peace, who bring good tidings, who proclaim salvation" (ISA. 52:7).

Nahum and Isaiah's prophetic words of hope found their ultimate fulfillment at the first Christmas when the angel told the shepherds, "Do not be afraid. I bring you good news that will cause great joy for all the people. Today in the town of David a Savior has been born to you; he is the Messiah, the Lord" (LUKE 2:10–11).

The most important headline in our lives every day is the very best news ever spoken—Christ the Savior is born! ❧

DAVID MCCASLAND

The birth of Jesus is the best news the world has ever received!

Living in the Light

I t was a dark morning. Low, steel-colored clouds filled the sky, and the atmosphere was so dim that I needed to turn on the lights in order to read a book. I had just settled in when the room suddenly filled with light. I looked up and saw that the wind was pushing the clouds to the east, clearing the sky and revealing the sun.

As I went to the window to get a better look at the drama, a thought came to mind: "The darkness is passing and the true light is already shining" (1 JOHN 2:8). The apostle John wrote these words to believers as a message of encouragement. He went on to say, "Anyone who loves

TODAY'S READING
1 John 2:3–11

The darkness is passing and the true light is already shining. 1 John 2:8

their brother and sister lives in the light, and there is nothing in them to make them stumble" (V. 10). By contrast, he equated hating people with roaming around in darkness. Hatred is disorienting; it takes away our sense of moral direction.

Loving people is not always easy. Yet I was reminded as I looked out the window that frustration, forgiveness, and faithfulness are all part of maintaining a deep connection with the love and light of God. When we choose love instead of hate, we are showing our relationship with Him and reflecting His radiance to the world around us. "God is light; in him there is no darkness at all" (1 JOHN 1:5). 🌿

JENNIFER BENSON SCHULDT

Dear God, help me to experience Your love more fully
so that I can share it with others. I want to live in the light
of Your grace and mercy.

Choosing to love people well shows the world what God is like.

One Short Sleep

Henry Durbanville, a Scottish pastor from another era, tells the story of an elderly woman in his parish who lived in a remote part of Scotland. She longed to see the city of Edinburgh, but she was afraid to take the journey because of the long, dark tunnel through which the train had to pass to get there.

One day, however, circumstances compelled her to go to Edinburgh, and as the train sped toward the city, her agitation increased. But before the train reached the tunnel, the woman, worn out with worry, fell fast asleep. When she awoke she had already arrived in the city!

It's possible that some of us will not experience death. If we're alive when Jesus returns, we will "meet the Lord in the air" (1 THESS. 4:13–18). But many of us will pass into heaven through death and for some that thought causes great anxiety. We worry that the process of dying will be too difficult to bear.

> **TODAY'S READING**
> **1 Thess. 4:13–18**
>
> **We are confident, I say, and would prefer to be away from the body and at home with the Lord.** 2 Corinthians 5:8

With the assurance of Jesus as our Savior we can rest in the confidence that when we close our eyes on earth and pass through death, we will open our eyes in God's presence. "One short sleep past we wake eternally," John Donne said. 🌐

DAVID ROPER

I love the life You've given to me, Lord,
yet I wonder what it will be like to see You personally.
Help me to trust You with the future.
I look forward to that day when I meet You.

To see Jesus will be heaven's greatest joy.

Another Side of Comfort

The theme for our adult camp was "Comfort My People." Speaker after speaker spoke words of assurance. But the last speaker drastically changed the tone. He chose Jeremiah 7:1–11 and the topic "Wake Up from Slumber." Without mincing words and yet with love, he challenged us to wake up and turn away from our sins.

TODAY'S READING
Jeremiah 7:1–11

Hear the word of the LORD. Jeremiah 7:2

"Don't hide behind the grace of God and continue to live in secret sin," he exhorted, like the prophet Jeremiah. "We boast, 'I am a Christian; God loves me; I fear no evil,' yet we do all kinds of evil."

We knew he cared about us, yet we shifted uncomfortably in our seats and listened to our own Jeremiah declare, "God is loving, but He is also a consuming fire! (SEE HEB. 12:29). He will never condone sin!"

Jeremiah of old quizzed the people, "Will you steal and murder, commit adultery and perjury . . . follow other gods you have not known, and then come and stand before me in this house, which bears my Name, and say, 'We are safe'—safe to do all these detestable things?" (7:9–10).

This speaker's brand of "Comfort My People" was another side of God's comfort. Like a bitter herb that heals malaria, his words were spiritually curative. When we hear hard words, instead of walking away, may we respond to their healing effect. 🌿

LAWRENCE DARMANI

Heavenly Father, You love us too much to let us continue defying Your instructions. Your correction is never to harm us but only to heal us. You are the God of all comfort.

God's discipline is designed to make us like His Son.

Our Covering

When talking about faith in Jesus, we sometimes use words without understanding or explaining them. One of those words is *righteous*. We say that God has *righteousness* and that He makes people *righteous*, but this can be a tough concept to grasp.

The way the word *righteousness* is pictured in the Chinese language is helpful. It is a combination of two characters. The top word is *lamb*. The bottom word is *me*. The lamb covers or is above the person.

TODAY'S READING
Romans 3:21–26

Blessed is the one whose transgressions are forgiven, whose sins are covered.
Psalm 32:1

When Jesus came to this world, John the Baptist called Him "the Lamb of God, who takes away the sin of the world!" (JOHN 1:29). We need our sin taken care of because it separates us from God whose character and ways are always perfect and right. Because His love for us is great, God made His Son Jesus "who had no sin to be sin for us, so that in him we might become the righteousness of God" (2 COR. 5:21). Jesus, the Lamb, sacrificed Himself and shed His blood. He became our "cover." He makes us righteous, which places us in right relationship with God.

Being right with God is a gift from Him. Jesus, the Lamb, is God's way to cover us. ✝

ANNE CETAS

Dear Lord, thank You for dying on the cross for me and covering my sins so that I can have a relationship with You.

The only permanent covering for sin is the blood of Christ.

Who Do You Say He Is?

n a **1929** *Saturday Evening Post* interview, Albert Einstein said, "As a child I received instruction both in the Bible and in the Talmud. I am a Jew, but I am enthralled by the luminous figure of the Nazarene.... No one can read the Gospels without feeling the actual presence of Jesus. His personality pulsates in every word. No myth is filled with such life."

TODAY'S READING
Matthew 16:13–20

Who do you say I am? Matthew 16:15

The New Testament Scriptures give us other examples of Jesus's countrymen who sensed there was something special about Him. When Jesus asked His followers, "Who do people say the Son of Man is?" they replied that some said He was John the Baptist, others said He was Elijah, and others thought He was Jeremiah or one of the prophets (MATT. 16:14). To be named with the great prophets of Israel was certainly a compliment, but Jesus wasn't seeking compliments. He was searching their understanding and looking for faith. So He asked a second question: "But what about you? ... Who do you say I am?" (16:15).

Peter's declaration fully expressed the truth of Jesus's identity: "You are the Messiah, the Son of the living God" (V. 16).

Jesus longs for us to know Him and His rescuing love. This is why each of us must eventually answer the question, "Who do you say Jesus is?" ✎

BILL CROWDER

Lord, I long to know You better. Teach me more about Your beautiful character so that I might grow more in love with You and follow You with my whole heart.

The identity of Jesus is the central question of eternity.

Enemy Love

When war broke out in 1950, fifteen-year-old Kim Chin-Kyung joined the South Korean army to defend his homeland. He soon found, however, that he wasn't ready for the horrors of combat. As young friends died around him, he begged God for his life and promised that, if allowed to live, he would learn to love his enemies.

Sixty-five years later, Dr. Kim reflected on that answered prayer. Through decades of caring for orphans and assisting in the education of North Korean and Chinese young people, he has won many friends among those he once regarded as enemies. Today he shuns political labels. Instead he calls himself a *loveist* as an expression of his faith in Jesus.

> **TODAY'S READING**
> **Jonah 3:10–4:11**
>
> **If you love those who love you, what credit is that to you?** Luke 6:32

The prophet Jonah left a different kind of legacy. Even a dramatic rescue from the belly of a big fish didn't transform his heart. Although he eventually obeyed God, Jonah said he'd rather die than watch the Lord show mercy to his enemies (JONAH 4:1–2, 8).

We can only guess as to whether Jonah ever learned to care for the people of Nineveh. Instead we are left to wonder about ourselves. Will we settle for his attitude toward those we fear and hate? Or will we ask God for the ability to love our enemies as He has shown mercy to us? 🌐

MART DEHAAN

Father in heaven, like Your reluctant prophet,
we are inclined to love only those who love us.
Yet You loved us even when we cared only for ourselves.
Please give us the grace to be more like Jesus than Jonah.

Love conquers all.

Spreading Joy

When Janet went to teach English in a school overseas, she found the atmosphere gloomy and depressing. People did their jobs, but no one seemed happy. They didn't help or encourage one another. But Janet, grateful for all that God had done for her, expressed it in everything she did. She smiled. She was friendly. She went out of her way to help people. She hummed songs and hymns.

TODAY'S READING
John 16:16–24

> **The angel said to them, "Do not be afraid. I bring you good news that will cause great joy for all the people."**
>
> Luke 2:10

Little by little, as Janet shared her joy, the atmosphere at the school changed. One by one people began to smile and help each other. When a visiting administrator asked the principal why his school was so different, the principal, who was not a believer, responded, "Jesus brings joy." Janet was filled to overflowing with the joy of the Lord and it spilled over to those around her.

The gospel of Luke tells us that God sent an angel to ordinary shepherds to deliver an extraordinary birth announcement. The angel made the surprising proclamation that the newborn baby "will cause great joy for all the people" (LUKE 2:10), which indeed He did.

Since then this message has spread through the centuries to us, and now we are Christ's messengers of joy to the world. Through the indwelling of the Holy Spirit, we continue the practice of spreading the joy of Jesus as we follow His example and serve others. 🌱 *JULIE ACKERMAN LINK*

How might you spread the joy of Jesus to others today?

Take the joy of Christmas with you every day.

A Personal Story

A baby just hours old was left in a manger in a Christmas nativity outside a New York church. A young, desperate mother had wrapped him warmly and placed him where he would be discovered. If we are tempted to judge her, we can instead be thankful this baby will now have a chance in life.

This gets personal for me. As an adopted child myself, I have no idea about the circumstances surrounding my birth. But I have never felt abandoned. Of this much I am certain: I have two moms who wanted me to have a chance in life. One gave life *to* me; the other invested her life *in* me.

> **TODAY'S READING**
> **Exodus 1:22–2:10**
>
> **Even if my father and mother abandon me, the LORD will hold me close.** Psalm 27:10 NLT

In Exodus we read about a loving mother in a desperate situation. Pharaoh had ordered the murder of all baby boys born to the Jewish people (1:22). So Moses's mother hid him as long as she could. When Moses was three months old, she put him in a watertight basket and placed the basket in the Nile River. If the plan was to have the baby rescued by a princess, grow up in Pharaoh's palace, and eventually deliver his people out of slavery, it worked perfectly.

When a desperate mother gives her child a chance, God can take it from there. He has a habit of doing that—in the most creative ways imaginable. ✎

TIM GUSTAFSON

Father, today we pray for those facing desperate and lonely times.
We pray especially for poor and defenseless children everywhere.
Help us meet their needs as we are able.

Share the love of Christ.

The Best Gift Ever

At a winter retreat in northern New England, one of the men asked the question, "What was your favorite Christmas gift ever?"

One athletic man seemed eager to answer. "That's easy," he said, glancing at his friend next to him. "A few years back, I finished college thinking I was a sure bet to play professional football. When it didn't happen, I was angry. Bitterness ate at me, and I shared that bitterness with anyone who tried to help me."

"On the second Christmas—and second season without football—I went to a Christmas play at *this guy's* church," he said, gesturing toward his friend. "Not because I wanted Jesus, but just to see my niece in her Christmas pageant. It's hard to describe what happened because it sounds silly, but right in the middle of that kids' play, I felt like I needed to be with those shepherds and angels meeting Jesus. When that crowd finished singing 'Silent Night,' I just sat there weeping.

"I got *my* best Christmas present ever that very night," he said, again pointing to his friend, "when this guy sent his family home without him so he could tell me how to meet Jesus."

It was then that his friend piped up: "And that, guys, was *my* best Christmas present ever."

This Christmas, may the joyful simplicity of the story of Jesus's birth be the story we tell to others. ✸

RANDY KILGORE

> **TODAY'S READING**
> **1 Peter 3:8–16**
>
> **Always be prepared to give an answer to everyone who asks you to give the reason for the hope that you have.** 1 Peter 3:15

The best Christmas gift is Jesus bringing peace and forgiveness to others.

What Can I Give Him?

One year, those responsible for decorating their church for Christmas decided to use the theme of "Christmas lists." Instead of decorating with the usual shiny gold and silver ornaments, they gave each person a red or green tag. On one side they were to write down the gift they would like from Jesus, and on the other they were to list the gift they would give to the One whose birth they were celebrating.

TODAY'S READING
Psalm 103:1–18

Praise the LORD, my soul, and forget not all his benefits. Psalm 103:2

If you were to do this, what gift would you ask for and what would you offer? The Bible gives us lots of ideas. God promises to supply all our needs, so we might ask for a new job, help with financial problems, physical healing for ourselves or others, or a restored relationship. We might be wondering what our spiritual gift is that equips us for God's service. Many of these are listed in Romans 12 and 1 Corinthians 12. Or we might long to show more of the fruit of the Holy Spirit: to be more loving, joyful, peaceful, patient, kind and good, faithful, gentle and self-controlled (GAL. 5:22–23).

The most important gift we can ever receive is God's gift of His Son, our Savior, and with Him forgiveness, restoration, and the promise of spiritual life that begins now and lasts forever. And the most important gift we can ever give is to give Jesus our heart. 🌱

MARION STROUD

You overwhelm me with Your gifts, Lord.
In return, I want to give You the very best present that I can.
Please show me what You want most from me.

If I were a wise man, I would do my part.
Yet what can I give Him—give Him my heart. CHRISTINA G. ROSSETTI

Christmas in Captivity

Rev. Martin Niemoller, a prominent German pastor, spent nearly eight years in Nazi concentration camps because he openly opposed Hitler. On Christmas Eve 1944, Niemoller spoke these words of hope to his fellow prisoners in Dachau: "My dear friends, on this Christmas . . . let us seek, in the Babe of Bethlehem, the One who came to us in order to bear with us everything that weighs heavily upon us. . . . God Himself has built a bridge from Himself to us! A dawn from on high has visited us!"

TODAY'S READING
Isaiah 9:1–7

On those living in the land of deep darkness a light has dawned. Isaiah 9:2

At Christmas we embrace the good news that God, in Christ, has come to us wherever we are and has bridged the gap between us. He invades our prison of darkness with His light and lifts the load of sorrow, guilt, or loneliness that weighs us down.

On that bleak Christmas Eve in prison, Niemoller shared this good news: "Out of the brilliance that surrounded the shepherds a shining ray will fall into our darkness." His words remind us of the prophet Isaiah, who prophetically said, "The people walking in darkness have seen a great light; on those living in the land of deep darkness a light has dawned" (ISA. 9:2).

No matter where today finds us, Jesus has penetrated our dark world with His joy and light! ❧   *DAVID MCCASLAND*

Lord Jesus, we find hope and strength in knowing
that Your light shines in the darkness,
and the darkness has not overcome it.

The joy of Christmas is Jesus.

Joy for All

On the final day of a Christian publishing conference in Singapore, 280 participants from 50 countries gathered in the outdoor plaza of a hotel for a group photo. From the second-floor balcony, the photographer took many shots from different angles before finally saying, "We're through." A voice from the crowd shouted with relief, "Well, joy to the world!" Immediately, someone replied by singing, "The Lord is come." Others began to join in. Soon the entire group was singing the familiar carol in beautiful harmony. It was a moving display of unity and joy that I will never forget.

In Luke's account of the Christmas story, an angel announced the birth of Jesus to a group of shepherds saying, "Do not be afraid. I bring you good news that will cause great joy for all the people. Today in the town of David a Savior has been born to you; he is the Messiah, the Lord" (LUKE 2:10–11).

The joy was not for a few people, but for all. "For God so loved the world that He gave His one and only Son" (JOHN 3:16).

As we share the life-changing message of Jesus with others, we join the worldwide chorus in proclaiming "the glories of His righteousness and wonders of His love."

"Joy to the world, the Lord is come!" ✹

DAVID MCCASLAND

> **TODAY'S READING**
> **Luke 2:8–14**
>
> **Do not be afraid. I bring you good news that will cause great joy for all the people.**
>
> Luke 2:10

Father, give us eyes to see people of all nations
as recipients of Your grace and joy.

The good news of Jesus's birth is a source of joy for all people.

On Time

Sometimes I joke that I'm going to write a book titled *On Time*. Those who know me smile because they know I am often late. I rationalize that my lateness is due to optimism, not to lack of trying. I optimistically cling to the faulty belief that "this time" I will be able to get more done in less time than ever before. But I can't, and I don't, so I end up having to apologize yet again for my failure to show up on time.

TODAY'S READING
Luke 2:25–38

When the set time had fully come, God sent his Son.

Galatians 4:4

In contrast, God is always on time. We may think He's late, but He's not. Throughout Scripture we read about people becoming impatient with God's timing. The Israelites waited and waited for the promised Messiah. Some gave up hope. But Simeon and Anna did not. They were in the temple daily praying and waiting (LUKE 2:25–26, 37). And their faith was rewarded. They got to see the infant Jesus when Mary and Joseph brought Him to be dedicated (VV. 27–32, 38).

When we become discouraged because God doesn't respond according to our timetable, Christmas reminds us that "when the set time had fully come, God sent his Son . . . that we might receive adoption to sonship" (GAL. 4:4–5). God's timing is always perfect, and it is worth the wait. 🌱

JULIE ACKERMAN LINK

Heavenly Father, I confess that I become impatient and discouraged, wanting answers to prayer in my own time and on my schedule. Help me to wait patiently for Your timing in all things.

God's timing is always right—wait patiently for Him.

The Power of Simple Words

Raucous laughter marked the guests in my father's hospital room: Two old truck drivers, one former country/western singer, one craftsman, two women from neighboring farms, and me.

"*...and then he got up and busted the bottle over my head,*" the craftsman said, finishing his story about a bar fight.

The room bursts into laughter at this now-humorous memory. Dad, struggling for breath as his laughing fought with his cancer for the air in his lungs, puffs out a reminder to everybody that "Randy is a preacher" so they need to watch what they say. Everything got quiet for about two seconds, then the whole room exploded as this news makes them laugh harder and louder.

> **TODAY'S READING**
> 2 Peter 1:12–21
>
> We did not follow cleverly devised stories when we told you about the coming of our Lord Jesus Christ in power, but we were eyewitnesses of his majesty.
> 2 Peter 1:16

Suddenly, about forty minutes into this visit, the craftsman clears his throat, turns to my dad, and gets serious. "No more drinking and bar fights for me, Howard. Those days are behind me. Now I have a different reason to live. I want to tell you about my Savior."

He then proceeded to do just that, over my father's surprisingly mild protests. If there's a sweeter, gentler way to present the gospel message, I've never heard it. My dad listened and watched, and some years later believed in Jesus too.

It was a simple testimony from an old friend living a simple life, reminding me again that simple isn't naïve or stupid; it's direct and unpretentious.

Just like Jesus. And salvation. ✿

RANDY KILGORE

Go and make disciples of all nations. MATTHEW 28:19

Locked Into Love

I n June 2015, the city of Paris removed forty-five tons of padlocks from the railings of the Pont des Arts pedestrian bridge. As a romantic gesture, couples would etch their initials onto a lock, attach it to the railing, click it shut, and throw the key into the River Seine.

After this ritual was repeated thousands of times, the bridge could no longer bear the weight of so much "love." Eventually the city, fearing for the integrity of the bridge, removed the "love locks."

> TODAY'S READING
> **Romans 8:31–39**
>
> **Give thanks to the LORD, for he is good; his love endures forever.**
> Psalm 106:1

The locks were meant to symbolize everlasting love, but human love does not always last. The closest of friends may offend each other and never resolve their differences. Family members may argue and refuse to forgive. A husband and wife may drift so far apart that they can't remember why they once decided to marry. Human love can be fickle.

But there is one constant and enduring love—the love of God. "Give thanks to the LORD, for he is good; his love endures forever," proclaims Psalm 106:1. The promises of the unfailing and everlasting nature of God's love are found throughout Scripture. And the greatest proof of this love is the death of His Son so that those who put their faith in Him can live eternally. And nothing will ever separate us from His love (ROM. 8:38–39).

Fellow believers, we are locked into God's love forever. 🍂

CINDY HESS KASPER

I'm grateful for Your unending love, Father. I'm locked into Your love by
the Holy Spirit who is living in me.

Christ's death and resurrection are the measure of God's love for me.

Signet Ring

When I first made the acquaintance of a new friend from abroad, I noticed his posh English accent and that he wore a ring on his little finger. Later I learned that this wasn't just jewelry; it revealed his family's history through the family crest engraved on it.

It was a bit like a signet ring—perhaps like the one in Haggai. In this short Old Testament book, the prophet Haggai calls for the people of God to restart the rebuilding of the temple. They had been exiled and had now returned to their homeland and begun rebuilding, but enemy opposition to their project had stalled them. Haggai's message includes God's promise to Zerubbabel, Judah's leader, that he had been chosen and set apart as their leader, like a signet ring.

TODAY'S READING
Haggai 2:15–23

"I will make you like my signet ring, for I have chosen you," declares the LORD. Haggai 2:23

In ancient times, a signet ring was used as a means of identification. Instead of signing their name, people would press their ring into hot wax or soft clay to make their mark. As God's children, we too make a mark on the world as we spread the gospel, share His grace through loving our neighbors, and work to end oppression.

Each of us has our own unique stamp that reveals how we're created in God's image and expresses our particular mix of gifts, passions, and wisdom. It's our call and privilege to act as this signet ring in God's world. 🌳 *AMY BOUCHER PYE*

Father God, may I know my true identity as Your heir this day.
(See Luke 15.)

We are God's heirs and ambassadors, sharing His love in the world.

THE BIBLE in ONE YEAR
ZECHARIAH 13–14 and REVELATION 21

Time Alone With God

It was a busy morning in the church room where I was helping. Nearly a dozen little children were chattering and playing. There was so much activity that the room became warm and I propped the door open. One little boy saw this as his chance to escape so when he thought no one was looking, he tiptoed out the door. Hot on his trail, I wasn't surprised that he was headed straight for his daddy's arms.

TODAY'S READING
Matthew 14:13–23

[Jesus] went up on a mountainside by himself to pray.
Matthew 14:23

The little boy did what we need to do when life becomes busy and overwhelming—he slipped away to be with his father. Jesus looked for opportunities to spend time with His heavenly Father in prayer. Some might say this was how He coped with the demands that depleted His human energy. According to the gospel of Matthew, Jesus was headed to a solitary place when a crowd of people followed Him. Noticing their needs, Jesus miraculously healed and fed them. After that, however, He "went up on a mountainside by himself to pray" (V. 23).

Jesus repeatedly helped multitudes of people, yet He didn't allow Himself to become haggard and hurried. He nurtured His connection with God through prayer. How is it with you? Will you take time alone with God to experience His strength and fulfillment?

JENNIFER BENSON SCHULDT

Where are you finding greater fulfillment—in meeting the demands of life or in cultivating your relationship with your Creator?

When we draw near to God our minds are refreshed and our strength is renewed!

Now Is the Day

Our **preschool-age granddaughter** Maggie and her kindergarten-age sister Katie hauled several blankets to the backyard, where they proceeded to build a blanket tent in which to play. They had been outside a while when their mom heard Maggie call for her.

"Mom, come here quick!" Maggie yelled. "I want to ask Jesus into my heart, and I need your help!" Apparently at that moment her need for Jesus became clear to her, and she was ready to put her faith in Him.

> **TODAY'S READING**
> **2 Corinthians 5:18–6:2**
>
> **I tell you, now is the time of God's favor, now is the day of salvation.**
>
> 2 Corinthians 6:2

Maggie's urgent call for help in trusting Jesus brings to mind Paul's words in 2 Corinthians 6 about salvation. He was discussing the reality that Jesus Christ's coming—including His death and resurrection—instituted an era he called "the time of God's favor." We live in that time, and salvation is available to all right now. He said, "I tell you, now is the time of God's favor, now is the day of salvation" (v. 2). For all who have not yet trusted Jesus for forgiveness, the time to do so is now. It is urgent.

Perhaps the Holy Spirit has alerted you to your need to put your trust in Jesus. Like Maggie, don't put it off. Run to Jesus. Now is the day! ✿

DAVE BRANON

Heavenly Father, I now understand my need to have my sins forgiven.
I also realize that only Jesus—because of His sacrifice on the cross—
can forgive my sin. I put my faith and trust in Jesus today.
Please forgive me and become the Lord of my life.

There's no better day than today to enter into God's family.

About the Publisher

Our Daily Bread Ministries

Our Daily Bread Ministries is a nondenominational, nonprofit organization with more than 600 staff and 1,000 volunteers serving in 37 countries. Together we distribute more than 60 million resources every year in over 150 countries. Our mission is to make the life-changing wisdom of the Bible understandable and accessible to all.

Beginning in 1938 as a Bible class aired on a small radio station in Detroit, Michigan, USA, Our Daily Bread Ministries now offers radio programs; devotional, instructional, evangelistic, and apologetic print and digital resources. You can access our online resources at **ourdailybread.org**. Our signature publication, *Our Daily Bread,* is published in nearly 50 languages and is read by people in almost every country around the world.

Discovery House

Discovery House was founded in 1988 as an extension of Our Daily Bread Ministries. Our goal is to produce resources that feed the soul with the Word of God, and we do this through books, music, video, audio, software, greeting cards, and downloadable content. All our materials focus on the never-changing truths of Scripture, so everything we produce shows reverence for God and His Word, demonstrates the relevance of vibrant faith, and equips and encourages people in their everyday lives.

About the Authors

Dr. **James Banks** and his wife have two adult children and live in Durham, North Carolina, where he is the pastor of Peace Church. He is the author of *The Lost Art of Praying Together*, *Praying the Prayers of the Bible*, *Prayers for Prodigals*, and *Prayers for Your Children*.

If you've read articles by **Dave Branon** over the years, you know about his family and the lessons learned from father- (and now grandfather-) hood. After serving for 18 years as managing editor of *Sports Spectrum* magazine, Dave is now an editor for Discovery House. A freelance writer for many years, he has authored 15 books. Dave and his wife, Sue, love rollerblading and spending time with their children and grandchildren. Dave also enjoys traveling overseas with students on ministry trips.

Anne Cetas became a follower of Jesus in her late teens. At 19, she was given a copy of *Our Daily Bread* by a friend to help her read the Bible consistently. She also devoured Discovery Series topical study booklets. Several years later, she joined the editorial staff of *Our Daily Bread* as a proofreader. Anne began writing for the devotional booklet in September 2004 and is managing editor of the publication. Anne and her husband, Carl, enjoy walking and bicycling together, and working as mentors in an urban ministry.

Poh Fang Chia never dreamed of being in a language-related profession; chemistry was her first love. The turning point came when she received Jesus as her Savior as a 15-year-old and expressed to Jesus that she would like to create books that touch lives. She serves with Our Daily Bread Ministries at the Singapore office as an editor and is also a member of the Chinese editorial review committee. Poh Fang says: "I really enjoy exploring the Scriptures and finding passages that bring a fresh viewpoint, answer a question that is burning in my mind, or deal with a life issue I'm facing. My prayer is to write so that readers will see how presently alive the Bible is and will respond to the life-transforming power of the Word."

Bill Crowder joined the Our Daily Bread Ministries staff after more than 20 years in the pastorate. Bill serves as vice president of teaching content and spends much of his time in a Bible-teaching ministry for Christian leaders around the world. He has written many booklets for the Discovery Series, and he has published several books with Discovery House. Bill and his wife, Marlene, have five children as well as several grandchildren he'd be thrilled to tell you about.

Lawrence Darmani is a Ghanaian novelist and publisher. His first novel, *Grief Child*, won the Commonwealth Writers' Prize as best first book from Africa. He is editor of *Step* magazine and CEO of Step Publishers. He is married and lives in Accra with his family. Lawrence enjoys church life and volunteers at other Christian ministry activities. He says that he derives writing ideas "out of personal experiences, reading, testimonies, and observing the world around me."

Mart DeHaan, grandson of Our Daily Bread Ministries founder Dr. M. R. DeHaan and son of former president Richard W. DeHaan, has served with the ministry for more than 50 years. Mart is heard regularly on the *Discover the Word* radio program. He is also an author of many booklets for the Discovery Series. He and his wife, Diane, have two grown children. Mart enjoys spending time outdoors, especially with fishing pole in hand.

David C. Egner is retired from Our Daily Bread Ministries. During his years with the ministry, he was editor of *Discovery Digest* and *Campus Journal* (later changed to *Our Daily Journey*). He has written many Discovery Series booklets, and his work has appeared in a variety of other ministry publications. Dave was a college writing professor for many years and has enjoyed occasional guest-professor stints at Bible colleges in Russia. He and his wife, Shirley, live in Grand Rapids, Michigan.

Dennis Fisher received Jesus as his Savior at a church meeting in Southern California. He says, "I came under terrible conviction of sin. After receiving Christ, I felt like I had taken a shower on the inside." Dennis was a professor of evangelism and discipleship at Moody Bible Institute for eight years. In 1998, he joined Our Daily Bread Ministries, where he served as senior research editor. He is now retired but continues to assist the ministry through writing and reviewing. Dennis has two adult children and one grandson and lives with his wife, Janet, in Sacramento, California.

Dr. **Jaime Fernández Garrido** is director of the evangelical radio and television program *Born Again*, author of various books, and composer of more than 400 hymns and choruses.

Tim Gustafson writes for *Our Daily Bread* and serves as an editor for Discovery Series. As the adopted son of missionaries to Ghana, Tim has an unusual perspective on life in the West. He and his wife, Leisa, are the parents of one daughter and seven sons. Perhaps not surprisingly, his life verses say: "Father to the fatherless, defender of widows—this is God, whose dwelling is holy. God places the lonely in families; he sets the prisoners free and gives them joy" (Ps. 68:5–6 NLT).

Chek Phang (C. P.) Hia brings a distinctive flavor to *Our Daily Bread*. He and his wife, Lin Choo, reside in the island nation of Singapore. C. P. came to faith in Jesus Christ at the age of 13. During his early years as a believer, he was privileged to learn from excellent Bible teachers who instilled in him a love for God's Word. He currently serves in the Singapore office as special assistant to the Our Daily Bread Ministries president. He and his wife enjoy traveling and going for walks. They have a son, daughter-in-law, grandson, and granddaughter who also live in Singapore.

Cindy Hess Kasper served for more than 40 years at Our Daily Bread Ministries, where she was the associate editor for *Our Daily Journey*. An experienced writer, she has penned youth devotional articles for more than a decade. She is a daughter of longtime *Our Daily Bread* senior editor Clair Hess, from whom she learned a love for singing and working with words. Cindy and her husband, Tom, have three grown children and seven grandchildren, in whom they take great delight.

Randy Kilgore spent most of his 20-plus years in business as a senior human resource manager before returning to seminary. Since finishing his Masters in Divinity in 2000, he has served as a writer and workplace chaplain. He writes a weekly internet devotional, and a collection of those devotionals appears in the Discovery House book *Made to Matter: Devotions for Working Christians*. Randy and his wife, Cheryl, founded Desired Haven Ministries in 2007 and work together in Massachusetts, where they live with their two children.

Albert Lee, who lives in Singapore, was director of international ministries for Our Daily Bread Ministries for many years. Albert's passion, vision, and energy expanded the work of the ministry around the world. He continues to oversee a number of projects for the ministry. Albert grew up in Singapore and took a variety of courses from Singapore Bible College, served with Singapore Youth for Christ from 1971–1999, and taught a course on youth evangelism at Taylor University in Indiana. Albert appreciates art and collects paintings. He and his wife, Catherine, have two children.

After a lengthy battle with cancer, **Julie Ackerman Link** went to be with the Lord on April 10, 2015. Since 2000, Julie has written articles each month for *Our Daily Bread*. She is a popular author with *Our Daily Bread* readers, and her insightful and inspiring articles have touched millions of lives around the world. Julie also wrote the books *Above All, Love*; *A Heart for God*; *Hope for All Seasons*; and *100 Prayers Inspired by the Psalms*.

David McCasland began writing for *Our Daily Bread* in 1995. His books *Oswald Chambers: Abandoned to God* and *Eric Liddell: Pure Gold* are published by Discovery House. David and his wife, Luann, live in Colorado Springs, Colorado. They have four daughters and six grandchildren.

Keila Ochoa and her husband are very busy parents of two young children. She helps Media Associates International with their training ministry for writers around the world and has written several books in Spanish for children, teens, and women. She teaches in an international school. When she has time, she enjoys reading, talking to friends over a cup of hot chocolate, and watching a good movie.

Amy Boucher Pye is a writer and speaker who lives in North London. She's the author of the book *The Living Cross: Exploring God's Gift of Forgiveness and New Life* and the award-winning book *Finding Myself in Britain: Our Search for Faith, Home, and True Identity*. She runs the Woman Alive book club in the UK and enjoys life with her family in their

English vicarage. Find her at www.amyboucherpye.com or on Facebook or Twitter (@amyboucherpye).

David Roper was a pastor for more than 30 years and now directs Idaho Mountain Ministries, a retreat dedicated to the encouragement of pastoral couples. He enjoys fishing, hiking, and being streamside with his wife, Carolyn. His favorite fictional character is Reepicheep, the tough little mouse that is the soul of courage in C. S. Lewis's Chronicles of Narnia series. His favorite biblical character is Caleb—that rugged old saint who never retired, but who "died climbing."

Jennifer Benson Schuldt has been writing professionally since 1997 when she graduated from Cedarville University and began her career as a technical writer. Jennifer lives in the Chicago suburbs with her husband, Bob, and their two children. When she isn't writing or serving at home and church, she enjoys painting, reading poetry and fiction, and taking walks with her family. One of her favorite verses is Micah 6:8: "This is what He requires of you: to do what is right, to love mercy, and to walk humbly with your God" (NLT).

You may know **Joe Stowell** as the former president of Moody Bible Institute. Currently, he serves as president of Cornerstone University in Grand Rapids, Michigan. An internationally recognized speaker, Joe's first love is Jesus Christ and preaching His Word. He has also written numerous books, including *Strength for the Journey*, *The Upside of Down*, and *Jesus Nation*. He and his wife, Martie, have three children and 10 grandchildren.

After a battle with cancer, **Marion Stroud** went to be with her Savior on August 8, 2015. Since 2014 Marion has been writing devotional articles for *Our Daily Bread* that have touched the lives of readers around the world. Two of her popular books of prayers, *Dear God, It's Me and It's Urgent* and *It's Just You and Me, Lord,* were published by Discovery House. As an international author and writing mentor, Marion worked as a cross-cultural trainer for Media Associates International, helping writers produce books for their own culture.

Marvin Williams began writing for *Our Daily Bread* in 2007. Marvin is senior teaching pastor at Trinity Church in Lansing, Michigan. Educated at Bishop College in Dallas, Texas, and Trinity Evangelical Divinity School in Deerfield, Illinois, he has also served in several pastoral positions in Grand Rapids, Michigan. He and his wife, Tonia, have three children.

Topic Index

Topic Index

Topic Index

Enjoy this book?
Help us get the word out!

Share a link to the book or
mention it on social media

Write a review on your blog, on a retailer site,
or on our website (dhp.org)

Pick up another copy to share with someone

Recommend this book for your
church, book club, or small group

Follow Discovery House on
social media and join the discussion

Contact us to share your thoughts:

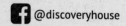 @discoveryhouse 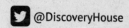 @DiscoveryHouse

Discovery House
P.O. Box 3566
Grand Rapids, MI 49501 USA

Phone: 1-800-653-8333
Email: books@dhp.org
Web: dhp.org